Praise for *Creating Outstanding Classrooms*

It does not take long to realise that *Creating Outstanding Classrooms* is based on a long and rich history of running schools, on two authors who know how to turn theory into practice, to learn from research and from others, and to focus on the important. With so many demands made of schools it is refreshing to see learning, knowing one's impact, and a sense of fun in creating outstanding classrooms. The many ideas and activities can be readily adopted but there is an underlying strength in their arguments while at the same time they confront some of the most difficult problems.
John Hattie, Director, Melbourne Education Research Institute, University of Melbourne

Drawing upon wide experience of teaching, senior leadership and curriculum development, Oliver Knight and David Benson have attempted the most comprehensive and practically grounded account yet of a disciplinary curriculum in action. With a winning and unusual integration of pedagogic, curricular and professional development concerns, they build their case that deep professional reflection on subject structure and subject knowledge leads to vibrant learning and shared, valid measures of the quality of that learning. Benson and Knight are trenchant in their critique of generic "thinking skills" approaches, arguing that different disciplines foster different ways of thinking and different forms of knowledge and that these distinctions enable rather than constrain, liberating both staff and students. They place these at the centre of whole-school professional development and professional debate, showing ways forward for the whole-school management of subject-driven learning that is knowledge-rich, demanding and lively.
Christine Counsell, Senior Lecturer, University of Cambridge Faculty of Education

Oli and David have proven they know how to run outstanding schools; this powerful manual captures how. It should be essential reading for every school leader and governor in the country. It is a practical and powerful end-to-end blueprint of how to run an outstanding secondary school.
Tom Shinner, Lead Proponent and Vice Chair of Governors, Greenwich Free School

Creating Outstanding Classrooms appears to be the 'missing link' in that it brings the best of practice in each discipline together and underpins them with good research and well thought out case studies... We will be purchasing copies for all our staff and using it to radically alter our approach to delivering the curriculum by adopting the concept of 'fertile questions' across all school subjects.
Sir Iain Hall, CEO, Great Schools for All Children

We know that effective schools are schools in which there are effective classrooms and this book provides a valuable set of resources to improve the quality of teaching in classrooms, with a clear focus on teaching for understanding...it is stimulating, thought-provoking, and eminently usable.
Professor Chris Husbands, Director, Institute of Education

Creating Outstanding Classrooms is a book that you need to read at least once. At times provocative and challenging it is always a practical handbook for those of us who are compelled to make our schools better.
Mark Keary, Principal, Bethnal Green Academy (Most Improved School in London 2011)

One of the greatest challenges facing school leaders is in-school variation. You just seem to solve a problem in one area when another one 'pops up' somewhere else. This book is a great resource for school leaders and teachers providing case studies and tools to crack inconsistency. It is a handbook that can be used every day to create outstanding practice.
John Baumber, CEO and Director of Education, The Learning Schools Trust

The quality of teaching and the vibrancy of learning is at the heart of school improvement. Sadly in all the discourse around structural change, curriculum and accountability such critical discussions are often lost. Fortunately, in their excellent new book, *Creating Outstanding Classrooms: A Whole-School Approach*, Oli Knight and David Benson have given us an insightful and strategic approach to enhancing teaching and learning.
David Hopkins, Professor Emeritus, Institute of Education, London and Director of Education, Bright Tribe Trust

This is a fascinating and important book, underpinned by deep, systematic thinking about the curriculum and pedagogy, and yet written with a light and wholly readable style that makes it practical, compelling and uplifting. All teachers will find ideas here to challenge as well as to reaffirm aspects of what they teach and how they teach it. Recommended.
Geoff Barton, Headteacher, King Edward VI School, Suffolk

Creating Outstanding Classrooms

This timely new book outlines a whole-school approach to embedding a sustainable model of teaching and learning that puts the learner at the heart of the system. It provides an entire framework for ensuring all students achieve above their expectations; incorporating school vision, teacher professional development, assessment models, school culture, leadership and management, and core classroom practices.

It takes what the current research suggests does – and does not – work and builds it into a practical approach that has been tried, tested and proven to work. Each section incorporates the research, a model of how this can be embedded across a school and then a training section that allows senior leaders in schools to teach the skill-set to others to ensure it can be embedded and reviewed.

Covering all aspects of teaching and learning including curriculum design, teacher practices, assessment and leadership, the book features:

- a clear planning framework that is easy to implement;
- subject based case studies to exemplify good practice;
- diagrams to clarify and consolidate information;
- training activities throughout each chapter, also available to download at www.routledge.com/9780415831178.

Designed to be used as a training tool for both new and established teachers, this book is essential reading for senior leaders that want to equip their teachers with the skills and knowledge to create a school of outstanding classrooms.

Oliver Knight is Director of Teaching and Learning for Bright Tribe Trust and was formerly Vice Principal with responsibility for Teaching and Learning at Ark Academy in Brent and a member of the Future Leaders programme.

David Benson is Principal of Kensington Aldridge Academy in North Kensington, and former Vice Principal at Ark Academy in Brent, with responsibility for Teaching and Learning, Assessment and Curriculum.

Creating Outstanding Classrooms

A whole-school approach

Oliver Knight and David Benson

Routledge
Taylor & Francis Group

LONDON AND NEW YORK

First published 2014
by Routledge
2 Park Square, Milton Park, Abingdon, Oxon OX14 4RN

and by Routledge
711 Third Avenue, New York, NY 10017

Routledge is an imprint of the Taylor & Francis Group, an informa business

© 2014 Oliver Knight and David Benson

British Library Cataloguing in Publication Data
A catalogue record for this book is available from the British Library

Library of Congress Cataloging in Publication Data
Knight, Oliver (Educator)
Creating outstanding classrooms : a whole-school approach / Oliver Knight, David Benson.
ISBN 978-0-415-83116-1 (hardback) – ISBN 978-0-415-83117-8 (paperback) – ISBN 978-1-315-88993-1 (ebook)
1. School improvement programs. 2. Student-centered learning. 3. Effective teaching. I. Benson, David (School principal) II. Title.
LB2822.8.K63 2013
371.2'07--dc23
2013009588

ISBN: 978-0-415-83116-1 (hbk)
ISBN: 978-0-415-83117-8 (pbk)
ISBN: 978-1-315-88993-1 (ebk)

Typeset in Celeste and Optima
by Saxon Graphics Ltd, Derby

Contents

Contents

List of training activities

List of additional resources

You can find the eResource for this book at www.routledge.com/ 9780415831178. Where you see this logo, you can download case studies and templates.

Acknowledgements

This book is very much written standing on the shoulders of giants. We are truly indebted to many people and organizations who have given us their time, ideas and experience.

The biggest thank you should go to Delia Smith and all of the inspirational teachers at Ark Academy in Wembley. This book is the product of opening Ark Academy and recruiting and training a dedicated set of teachers who all consistently taught according to the central pedagogical aims outlined in this book. Under Delia's guidance we were able to build on and develop the ideas and approaches we had encountered and designed throughout our careers. It is her leadership and unrelenting commitment to tackling underachievement that has led to this book, and the unwavering support of the teachers at Ark Academy that meant that 'outstanding' was our raison d'être.

We also doff our cap to the expertise and generosity of Fidelma Boyd, Deputy Head at St. Angela's Ursuline School in Newham. Under her mentorship Oli was able to experiment and try out many of the ideas and strategies we have refined for this book. Her commitment to our progression and her availability and constant support meant that we were never afraid to implement our ideas – both at St. Angela's and Ark Academy. Continuing along the St. Angela's thread we would also like to extend our thanks to Mark Johnson, Headteacher, for giving us permission to use the data we have in the leadership chapter.

Special mention must go to John Kirkman, English teacher extraordinaire and Aishling Ryan, Maths genius, for allowing us to use their work in this book. Also Tracey Keane, the brilliant Director of Science at Ark. Their support and willingness to adopt our approach and refine it for their disciplines, as well as creating outstanding progress, has ensured that we have evidence from across the curriculum that our approach works and is future-proof.

On a personal note, Oli would also like to thank Christine Counsell at Cambridge University and Nicolas Kinloch, formerly of Netherhall School. If it was not for Christine's patience and development of his 'extended' PGCE Oli would never have become a teacher and, without her advice, it is unlikely he would have got to where he is today. Nicolas has also played a particularly special role in Oli's career, supporting his PGCE as he tried to combine life as a full-time athlete with life as a trainee teacher. Needless to say Oli spent a lot of time in the Netherhall staff room eating and catching up on sleep in between training sessions but Nicolas kept the faith and helped him to scrape through.

Finally, a big thank you must go to the Institute of Education, in particular Adam Lefstein, Cathy Wallace and John Clegg. We are grateful to Adam for refining the thinking around inquiry or Fertile Questions and for many email exchanges about planning and trying to conceptualize learning. These had a very formative influence in helping make our approach concrete. Cathy and John allowed us to borrow their excellent thinking and work on language acquisition and progression. Without their work our approach to planning for language would not be as refined and robust as it is.

Grateful thanks must also go to Tracey Keane for her expert subject knowledge in Science and her ability to convert complex conceptual frameworks into accessible planning for students.

Thank you also to anyone else who has entered into conversation with us and showed belief in us. We are nothing more than the sum total of other people's support. A final point is that wherever we have borrowed from, adapted or modified the work of someone else, we have tried our best to fully reference it and acknowledge how it has helped us to build our argument and model. If we have failed to do this fully, then we apologize in advance and hope to be able to rectify this in future reprints.

About the authors

Oli Knight

Oli is director of teaching and learning for Bright Tribe; a new kind of multi-academy trust that puts the learner at the centre. Oli was previously Vice Principal with responsibility for teaching and learning at Ark Academy in London, part of one of the UK's leading academy chains, ARK Schools Group. He joined the academy a year before it opened and, with the Principal and senior team, led the school to its 'outstanding' Ofsted inspection in November 2010. The approach to teaching and learning that Oli implemented at Ark has subsequently been adopted as a best practice model in other ARK network schools and beyond. Ark Academy, although still a young school, is increasingly seen as a centre of excellence for teaching and teacher training.

David Benson

David is Principal of Kensington Aldridge Academy in North Kensington, and former Vice Principal at Ark Academy in Brent, with responsibility for Teaching and Learning, assessment and curriculum. He was also the ARK Network Lead for Assessment, supporting other schools in the ARK group in their use of assessment data. David and Oli worked together at Ark Academy from January 2010 where, with the Principal, they helped lead the set-up of an outstanding school. At Ark, David developed a whole-school approach to assessment that puts teachers and subject leaders in control of the assessment process and avoids data becoming a 'management exercise'. The approach is now being adopted in many other ARK schools.

Learning in the 21st century

A whole-school approach

> To instruct someone...is not a matter of getting him to commit results to mind. Rather, it is to teach him to participate in the process that makes possible the establishment of knowledge. We teach a subject not to produce little living libraries on that subject, but rather to get a student to think mathematically for himself, to consider matters as an historian does, to take part in the process of knowledge-getting. Knowing is a process not a product.[1]

This book has arisen from over 20 years of combined teaching experience, from being NQTs struggling to get to grips with the profession, through to being Senior Leaders in Outstanding schools. It is informed from experience in working in a variety of contexts and from having different 'education careers' of our own.

Our leadership journeys

Oli took a traditional PGCE path into teaching and had a diverse range of experiences: from being a Head of Department in one of the highest performing grammar schools in the country, to holding the same position at a school in Special Measures in Tower Hamlets. As an AST[2] at a Good school that was coasting, and a Senior Leader at an Outstanding school in Newham, Oli has witnessed first-hand different education contexts and varied approaches to school design and classroom consistency.

David joined teaching through the *Teach First* programme in 2004. He has worked in three different inner London comprehensives during his career – one judged by Ofsted[3] as Satisfactory, one as Good and one as Outstanding. He, like Oli, has seen both good and bad examples of school leadership. He has worked in transition schools where the priority has been to establish some degree of consistency and move practice from satisfactory to good, and in a brand new school where the challenge has been to fully exploit the unique opportunities of a start-up and raise the bar as high as possible.

We met in 2009 when we were appointed as the founding Vice Principals of Ark Academy, a new, all-through 3 to 18 academy in Brent, with Oli leading on teaching and learning and David on assessment and curriculum. This book draws heavily on our experience of setting up a new school, and describes how we used the opportunity of starting from scratch to think through the very best approaches and then embed a genuinely 'whole-school' model of teaching and learning.

Our model recognizes the sovereignty of the classroom in school life, and the simple fact that all areas of school culture flow from classroom teaching. Six great lessons a day, consistently across the school, and everything else will fall into place. Any decision about school management – whether it be about budget, uniform, or even corridors and playgrounds – needs to be considered in terms of how it affects the experiences of students as learners in the classroom.

Structure liberates

We have learnt from many inspirational teachers and school leaders during our careers. We have debated with those outside of schools: academics and professionals involved in teacher training and education policy. We feel indebted to everyone who has given us their time and their thoughts. Some of them we agree with, some we disagree with; but we recognize that all were working with the same goal in mind: to create outstanding schools, and an outstanding education system. This handbook is carved in that vein.

Through all of our experiences and all of the classrooms we have been in, both as teachers and observers, one thing was always apparent – it is teachers that make the biggest difference. This difference, however, is either helped or hindered by the culture and system in which the teachers operate. Many schools have pockets of expert teaching which fail to spread to other classrooms, because the management structures are not in place to effectively disseminate the good practice. At best the ideas are misappropriated or distorted and lose impact. At worst they are just ignored.

It is clear that there are many excellent teachers in the UK at present. It is also clear that there are few schools where we can say that the teaching is consistently excellent. Of the 20 per cent of schools rated Outstanding by Ofsted in 2010-11, only 6 per cent had outstanding teaching and learning. Reducing in-school variance in the standards of teaching, and supporting all teachers to get to the highest levels, is what this book hopes to achieve. If students in the same school are either inspired or disengaged by a subject, simply because of which teacher they are given, then many will continue to fall through the net. Furthermore we would argue that at best Ofsted only captures around 25 per cent of what an outstanding or expert teacher does and so the need for a more consistent approach is vital to enable more teachers to develop expertise.

The poverty of the generic 'thinking-skills' approach

Outstanding (or expert) teaching is not just about pedagogy – the strategies and techniques that the teacher uses. It is about what is being taught – the curriculum the school and department has chosen to follow. Over the past seven years, we have witnessed with regret the moves away from academic subjects towards genericism and competence-based frameworks in schools. This has proceeded hand in hand with the mistaken view that teaching academic subjects is merely about providing information, rather than about developing forms of disciplinary *thinking*. It is fashionable now to ask, 'if we have Google why do we need subjects? Pupils just need the *skills* to find the information'. Put another way, in the words of Counsell:

> The view that disciplines can neither engage nor serve most pupils often betrays two misapprehensions: first, an assumption that a subject equates to information, as opposed to knowledge; second, a lack of awareness that a school subject such as history has long involved the active and engaging exploration of the structure and form of that knowledge, using concepts and attendant processes.[4]

The thinking-skills argument ignores the distinctive purposes of academic disciplines. Disciplines are not sets of 'skills' so much as distinctive ways of building knowledge, weighing evidence and finding truth. In schools, subject specialists use their own disciplines to teach students how to think in particular, powerful ways. In our experience of working with teachers who are passionate about their subjects, the particular disciplinary context of a subject is central to that particular way of thinking, of researching, of judging evidence and of building knowledge about the world. Academic subjects in schools therefore provide disciplined forms of criticality; disciplined ways of reading, writing and speaking; and a disciplined understanding of how different types of knowledge are constructed. In our experience the best subject teachers are those that combine a flair for delivery and lesson design with a deep understanding of the foundational rules and principles of their subjects.

Sometimes the argument for genericism is linked to a changing economic climate. Its proponents make the case that we need to teach skills because the future is unknown, and flexibility not knowledge will be at a premium. The weakness of the skills approach is these 'learning skills' or 'thinking skills' cannot be taught in isolation. You cannot teach someone to solve a problem unless that problem is grounded in some context; unless it is a *mathematical* or *historical* or *scientific* problem. Or rather you can, but because the learning is not linked to an underlying concept in one of these subjects, it becomes superficial, and therefore cannot be transferred to new, unseen problems – which is exactly what the genericist skills approach is trying to achieve.

Those advocating genericism frequently argue that the curriculum should be designed through cross-curricular themes and projects that allow learners to see how all subject areas are connected. This might be a good intention, but the problem is that this is not normally achieved. As Howard Gardner points out so well, most of this type of activity is misleadingly labelled at best:

> Children may well benefit from carrying out evocative classroom projects or from pursuing a unit on generative topics like "patterns" or "water" or the "cradle of civilisation." But these endeavours do not involve disciplines in any legitimate sense of that term. In making a diorama or a dance, in thinking of water or cities in a variety of ways, students are drawing on common sense, common experiences, or common terminology and examples. If no single discipline is being applied, then clearly interdisciplinary thinking cannot be at work.[5]

We are all for cross-curricularity, but how about connecting subjects at a deeper conceptual level than that of surface content? If the skills most at premium in the twenty-first century are 'complex communication' and 'expert thinking' then generic curriculum approaches are no longer remotely suitable. What is needful, rather, is an ability to think about how the different disciplinary approaches are *distinctive*. Only then, might teachers, and students, be in a position to explore how they interrelate.[6]

Two routes through the curriculum

Let us look very briefly at what two different approaches might be to an enquiry incorporating the disciplines of History, Art and Geography. One framed within a competency curriculum, the other with a focus on teaching for conceptual understanding.

In the kind of cross-curricular approach that makes appeal to generic skills, and treats subject matter merely as information on which to practise generic skills, the typical pattern that we have observed is for teachers to come up with a generic theme (such as 'balance' or 'mountains') that claims to enshrine a cross-curricular project but is only connected at a surface level rather than a conceptual one. Sometimes teachers simply take a content area, such as 'the Romans' or 'India', and then weave students' work purely around the content but without any sense of disciplinary goal. Generic skills or competences are invariably invoked as the unifiers – e.g. finding or presenting information; research; team-work; reasoning; creativity – but, without any sense of purpose, the subject matter is reduced to 'information' rather than a disciplinary quest for a particular type of truth claim and a particular type of meaning. For example, a 'generic skills' approach to a cross-curricular project on the Romans might see pupils learning some surface detail and general information in the name of History, doing some map work and gathering/summarizing information on interrelationships and location in Geography and looking at Roman art or mosaics in Art, perhaps with students making their own mosaics. These elements might be linked by some general competencies, such as speaking and listening skills, research skills or reasoning skills, or creativity. Creativity might be expressed in all aspects of the work or in some final project. But how are pupils learning to think historically, geographically and aesthetically here? And how are these disciplines really being both taught well and linked together to become bigger than the sum of their parts?

Below is an alternative, and more powerful, version that leads to both deep and conceptual understandings.

Let us look at Year 7 and the Roman Empire. Firstly we need to decide on the disciplinary or conceptual focus – in this instance we could look at the concept of change; a focus on how far life changed and for what groups. We need to then connect the different subjects through the deeper understanding they can give to the concept students are developing an understanding of and also help students to see that the concept takes on different meanings as it crosses disciplinary thresholds. To do this we need to frame the learning as a 'Fertile Question': a problem to be solved. A way of achieving this could be to look at Leptis Magna in Libya as an expression of Roman thought and power – the way the Romans used art and the built environment as an expression of imperial greatness and higher culture as a way of controlling their empire.

The question might be something like *'Did the Roman Empire improve people's lives?'* In History we would look at the psychology of the art as an expression of power and an attempt at realizing hegemony, the changes that took place as the Romans entered (modern-day) Libya and the impact this had on different groups, interrogating the source material we find to say how people at the time might have experienced the change and reconstructing these experiences based on what the evidence does and does not tell us – a key difference from using 'research skills to access information'. In Art we would study how the Romans used art to express their wealth and power, their use of depth and perspective to create meaning and as a way of displaying their cultural superiority and attempting to transpose their cultural practices onto another people through their art; in Geography we would look at change – *how did different people experience the empire (directly or indirectly) and how did they communicate this experience? What has the nature, rate and extent of change been like? How might it be different in the future (prediction)?*

This would then culminate in a performance of understanding that would require students to use their deepening knowledge of the concept of change to either criticize or create something new that answers the Fertile Question.

It is clear to see that whilst both these examples nominally look at the same 'content area' one remains inert and simply provides surface information with little deep learning whilst the other seeks to induct students into an 'apprenticeship in thinking' through looking at the same event through different disciplinary lenses.

What does business want from education?

The Confederation of British Industry also recently rejoined the debate around UK education and where it has gone wrong. In their recent report 'First steps: A new approach for our schools' they have reclarified what businesses want from the education system; moving from a narrow focus on skills to a broader view of the whole person inculcated with a disciplinary perspective.

> In the past, the CBI has tended to discuss many of these areas in terms of 'employability skills.' This terminology was misleading, giving the impression that they {skills/behaviours} could be taught separately in the curriculum. That is not the case – the curriculum is the space in which we deliver core knowledge and enabling subjects.[7]

The inherent weakness of the genericist approach is further deepened by the fact that thinking skills are seen as tools to solve problems, without any reference to context. Apparently, you simply encounter a problem, choose the right skill, deploy it and the problem is solved and you move on. The thinking-skills approach is flawed, in that it sees the brain as a toolbox, and every problem as falling into a preconceived set of 'boxes' that map onto the tools provided. It has led to a cottage industry of suppliers publishing materials which will have little impact on students' understanding of proper academic subjects, and on their success in these subjects at GCSE and A-Level (particularly as these exams are strengthened over the coming years). We feel strongly that this misunderstanding has often polluted approaches to enabling students to engage with reading. Now all they do is access tiny de-contextualized snippets and teachers then wonder why students do not want to read.

Disciplines misunderstood

This book is written as a handbook to enable schools to get to grips with the idea of disciplinary thinking, outlining why it is so vital to students' success and therefore to the UK not being left behind by its international competitors. We detail how this approach can be embedded in every classroom and every space. If senior managers in schools do not have a firm grasp of how academic subjects develop thinking, and empower students to succeed far better than a thinking-skills approach, then 'how can they manage a curriculum in the first place?'[8]

Part of the blame for the predominance of thinking-skills in UK education at the moment must be apportioned to those on the other side of the debate, the 'saviours' of traditional teaching. By expounding the virtues of traditional subjects with their canons of knowledge (information) to be imparted and committed to memory, they have drawn an unhelpful dichotomy. In reality both camps are wrong, and a different approach is needed.

Students need to be active learners, who discuss, question and operate on the knowledge they are given in class; who connect it with other knowledge they have and use it to form new ideas. Those of us who advocate attention to the integrity of subjects as disciplines are not, contrary to the way we are often presented, arguing that students should be passive vessels, whose heads we fill up with facts and information that they can then recite back to us. A discipline-based approach is questioning, critical and active. It has to be, because to engage with a discipline is to engage with how knowledge is constructed in the first place.

An international perspective

There are many vocal opponents to this cause, and we do not expect to convince everyone, but this is a call to arms for all teachers and school Senior Leaders who know that disciplinary thinking and academic perspectives are vital if we are to create an education system in this country that can compete with the best in the world. We often hear about the impressive results of the Singapore education system, or why Chinese Maths students consistently outstrip their

UK and US counterparts. The differences are sometimes explained by the different ways these students' languages operate, or cultural factors to do with work-ethic and the values families place on education. Our answer is a simpler one: in all these education systems there is an emphasis placed on disciplinary thinking and the role of concepts in shaping and developing meaning. For example, in China Maths teachers have a very clear grasp of the fundamental concepts that underpin the subject of Maths, and their curriculum is built around these concepts. They are then in turn able to teach these conceptual understandings in a way that enables students to apply their learning to a range of unseen problems – proof that they have a deep understanding. We believe that a similar emphasis on subject concepts, and a move away from generic thinking skills, would benefit students here in the UK.

Disciplinary thinking and education policy

The proposed changes to the UK examination system, due to take effect in 2015, will make the above approach even more necessary. Harder GCSEs and A-Levels that test understanding of the key elements in each subject, and a move away from the excessive predictability of recent years, mean that results could dip. The students who are most at risk of missing out on a passable grade – those currently at the D/C borderline – often tend to be students from inner-city comprehensives with a higher proportion of students on Free School Meals.

Reform of the examination system is welcome – we must bring it in line with the rigour and challenge of our international competitors. But schools now need to make concurrent changes to the curriculum in order to best prepare students for the demands of these new exams. The only way to ensure all students have an equal chance of achieving good grades and getting into a good university is by teaching them to think in a disciplined way. And as we move through the twenty-first century the importance of a university education becomes ever greater:

> In 2008, a man with higher education could expect to earn 58% more than his counterpart with no more than an upper secondary education, on average across OECD countries. By 2010, this premium increased to 67%.[9]

In addition to increased earning potential, the unemployment figures from across OECD countries makes interesting reading.

> The OECD has found that throughout the economic downturn, education level has been a predictor of job security. Between 2008 and 2010, unemployment in OECD countries rose from 8.8% to 12.5% for people with

no upper secondary education, and from 4.9% to 7.8% for people with an upper secondary education. For those with tertiary education, unemployment increased from 3.3% to only 4.7%. Even in a time of economic crisis, OECD countries still need highly skilled employees.[10]

These statistics show the urgency of the situation. We need more inner-city schools that can deliver the very best outcomes for students, and deliver them against a backdrop of harder exams and increasing floor targets. The genericist approaches of the past will not deliver the change we need. Subjects matter, and disciplinary thinking is key to developing a more powerful education system which in turn will deliver more highly skilled employees. This handbook is built around that central premise. Academic subjects and their ways of thinking, talking, writing and knowing are not bodies of information to be found on a website; they are constructed and contested forms of knowledge that have come about through man's desire to understand the world around him. Our view, from our experience, is that if more teachers and school leaders can understand this, and adopt this approach with their students, then perhaps in 20 years' time countries around the world will be discussing how to emulate our education system, and not the other way around.

To sum up, it is estimated that we could add £8trn to the GDP of the UK over the lifetime of a child born today if we reached Finnish levels of achievement (outcomes) in education.[11] Our view is that disciplinary thinking is crucial to developing a more powerful education system and that genericist skills-based approaches are misinformed at best.

New technologies and the future of education

You will notice that nowhere in this manual do we talk about new technologies and the use of ICT in learning. The reason for this is twofold. First, the rate of change and development is so rapid in the technological world that to talk about a particular piece of software or programme would probably render the approach outdated within a year. Second, the evidence as it currently stands does little to support the use of technology as a lever on learning. We would argue that the reason for this is because technology is often used as a bolt-on, replicating and repeating teacher input of surface content with little progression in understanding (where understanding means thinking and acting flexibly, not reciting). There is huge value to the use of new technology and it is as follows.

Researchers are now fairly happy to acknowledge that there are three kinds of understanding: surface, deep and conceptual (Bereiter 2002). Hattie defines these as follows:

> The surface knowledge needed to understand the concepts; the deeper understandings of how ideas relate to each other and extend to other understandings; and the conceptual thinking that allows surface and deep knowledge to turn into conjectures and concepts upon which to build new surface and deep understandings. (Hattie 2008)

A more powerful way therefore of utilizing the benefits of new technologies is in using them to provide students with the surface knowledge they need. The role of the teacher is to help convert this surface understanding into deeper understanding and conceptual thinking. New technology, for all its merits, cannot fulfil this role but when used properly it plays a very significant part in helping to develop conceptual thinking in students. If most teaching currently focuses on surface understanding then building in technology to play that role frees up the teacher to focus on developing deeper and more sophisticated types of thinking.

To enable this to truly happen with little in-school variance, every teacher in the school must first understand how to plan for this progression in thinking and once that is embedded technology can be unleashed to secure even greater progress. This book is written to allow this process to happen.

Now that we have looked at the role of disciplines in delivering educational excellence at a national and international level, we will go on to look at how that fits with the unique challenges of the twenty-first century and the particular school systems and framework that we have developed to meet these challenges.

The challenge facing education

The core values of outstanding schools

This handbook outlines a whole-school approach to embedding a sustainable model of teaching and learning that puts the learner at the heart of the system. It provides an entire framework for ensuring all students achieve above national expectations. We cover school vision; teacher training and professional development; assessment models; culture and ethos; leadership and management; curriculum design; constructing schemes of work; and lesson planning and delivery. It is based on our combined experience in over seven different schools.

The single most important aspect of your school culture is establishing that *we are all learners* – students and staff alike.

Our experience has shown us that a key student misconception to challenge is that intelligence is fixed. Working with our staff teams, we have learnt that students need to see themselves as developing individuals, whose mistakes represent opportunities to review and better understand the work, not evidence that they are unable to do it. All students should be treated as intelligent and individual, capable of accessing complicated ideas and thinking in a disciplined manner. To secure this, we have prioritized some crucial planning principles:

i.   Lessons are not isolated events: all subjects are taught through enquiries that embody the structural features of the discipline.[12]

ii. All enquiries embed a 'Learner Profile' of the students.

Taken together, the disciplinary focus foregrounded in planning and the use of Learner Profiles, we have managed to avoid students thinking of themselves as 'high ability' or 'low ability', and, most crucially, allowing the latter to be forced down a non-academic, non-disciplinary pathway at a young age.

For staff, they must believe that teacher training and development is an ongoing process; that we never 'arrive' as teachers, but can always refine and improve our teaching, and better tailor our lessons to improve students' understanding and performance. Teaching is a craft, and a lifetime is not long enough to master it. In our experience, the best teachers reflect, evaluate, observe and are observed, seek and respond to feedback, engage with research, experiment, take risks and try new ideas. As soon as we stop seeing ourselves as learners we will be unable to model the learning behaviours we expect from our students, and unable to honestly develop the teachers we lead.

The challenge of twenty-first century education[13] – outcomes misunderstood

> A generation ago, teachers could expect that what they taught would last their students a lifetime. Today, because of rapid economic and social change, schools have to prepare students for jobs that have not yet been created, technologies that have not yet been invented and problems that we don't yet know will arise.
>
> (Andreas Schleicher, OECD Education Directorate.
> The case for 21st century learning)[14]

In this important study, the OECD considered the kind of education schools should provide in the twenty-first century. They proposed that students should be introduced to:

- **new ways of thinking**: including creativity, critical thinking, problem solving and decision-making;

- **new ways of working**: including new forms of collaboration and communication;

- **using new tools for working**: including the capacity to harness the potential of new technologies.

'Success will go to those individuals and countries that are swift to adapt, slow to resist and open to change. The task of educators and policymakers is to help countries rise to this challenge.' (Schleicher op. cit.)

It is in reaction to studies like this that generic frameworks of vaguely linked competencies were created. The problem is that teaching 'critical' or 'higher-order thinking skills' cannot be divorced from teaching academic subjects. Maths, Science, History, Geography – these are not dry information-gathering exercises that will not develop the creativity, critical thinking and problem solving the twenty-first century economy demands. They are fields of research and debate that have their own language, rules and modes of discourse, which, through studying, enable students to understand the world around them, and then develop that understanding in others.

To a certain extent it is true in that schools have, in the past, taught subjects in a dry way; viewing them as bodies of information to be consumed and committed to memory. If this was the only alternative then it might be sensible to discard Geography or English and teach a series of thematic projects instead. There is nothing engaging, motivating or real-world relevant about learning all the capital cities of the world off by heart – but this is not what we mean by teaching subjects. Instead we propose a disciplinary approach based on conceptual understandings; an approach which lifts academic subjects off the mundane plains of information-gathering and up into the ambitious heights of critical thinking and analysis – with all the complexities of thought that universities and employers want. This handbook maps out an approach to being future-proof as a school, and securing the best outcomes for all students.

Fit for purpose?

The current education system is not fit for the present, let alone the future. A 2012 study into what universities want from secondary education concluded:

Issues about...skills essential for undergraduate learning arose in interviews with universities. These included both specific academic skills, such as researching, finding sources, essay-writing and referencing, and the wider skills of problem solving, analysis and critical thinking.[15]

The kind of intellectual flexibility described here – the ability to make connections, think critically, be objective and original, work independently – can only be arrived at by studying discrete academic subjects from an early age, with a sustained focus on conceptual understanding. What universities want are students who have a deep academic understanding that allows them to self-direct their studies. To achieve this, students need to be taught to think in a disciplined manner. They must encounter and wrestle with powerful knowledge, and move from the everyday to the academic.

A paradigm shift[16]

Views on the role of schools and the purposes of education have shifted enormously over the past 20–30 years, as shown in Figure 0.1. The focus now is much more on processes and metacognition.

A new role for assessment[17]

Whatever our view is of the purposes of schools and education and the transformative and enlightening impact it can have, the test of any approach to teaching and learning has to be the measurable outcomes of students in national examinations. This is the currency the world uses and it is the currency we have to provide for all our students. In our experience, however creative or innovative a model sounds, if it cannot deliver the results it is of little use to students and teachers. It would be a mistake to think that the enquiry approach we outline here does not have a hard assessment edge to it. It does – it is just that we consider the best assessment results are not achieved by narrowly drilling students for the test. This approach will work to a point – it might get you more C grades or Level 4s – but it will not help you if the test changes, or if your ambition is for students to achieve the very top grades they will need for the best universities.

Assessment is covered in depth later in the handbook, but it is worth noting some key principles around assessment in schools here:[18]

i.   Assessment has a backwash effect on curriculum and teacher practice. It can undermine or support your philosophy of teaching, depending on how it is managed. This must be recognized so that teachers and schools focus on what we value.

Nineteenth/twentieth century assumptions	Twenty-first century assumptions
Intelligence is perceived as unitary, fixed and innate.	Intelligence is understood as multi-faceted, plastic and (to a certain extent) learnable.
Learning is the acquisition of subject content. Students are consumers of knowledge.	Students are producers, not just consumers of knowledge. The learning focus is on application of knowledge.
Curriculum focuses on content coverage and behavioural objectives.	Curriculum focuses on processes of learning to learn, metacognition and skill development.
The focus is on information and knowledge.	Information *literacy*, learning to handle information is the focus.
Education is limited to the school and for fixed periods.	Education is lifelong and unconstrained in time and place.
Teaching and learning roles are sharply defined and segregated. School is a place with clear rigid boundaries. School is like a factory.	The roles are blurred and overlapping. School is a network and part of a broader web.
Schools and teachers are autonomous.	Schools and teachers are embedded in complex interconnected relationships.
The focus is local, national and international.	The focus is local, national and *global*.
Schools prepare students for lifelong employment in one future occupation.	Students' identities and destinies are fluid and changing.

Figure 0.1 Hargreaves' synthesis of twenty-first century assumptions about education

ii. Curricula, with corresponding assessments, must be broad and balanced. Students must be assessed on the processes as well as the products of learning, and be able to demonstrate understanding and performance holistically in authentic contexts, as well as in examinations and tests. Fertile Questions help here.

iii. Good schools need to listen to the messages coming from universities about assessments, and avoid dumbing down tests or introducing excessive predictability. Work backwards from the assessment demands of the subject at undergraduate level; this way your students' long-term interests will be served, but they will still be suitably prepared for GCSE and A-Level.

iv. The central role of the teacher as a creative professional must be recognized and encouraged. In our schools, our teachers have eschewed shrink-wrapped, commercially produced tests. Such externally produced assessment packages, imposed on staff, will not lead to expert assessment. If subject leaders are writing their own schemes of work (which they must be if they are to have any ownership) then they can – and should – write their own assessments. Otherwise they will be in the peculiar situation where the end of term assessment does not link to the taught curriculum.

v. The feedback from summative assessments – including large exams – must be used as a planning tool and all teachers must be responsive to this. If (groups of) students perform badly in assessments this information must inform both what you teach those students next and how you teach that Fertile Question(s) differently next time to avoid the same issues.

The whole-school model

The paradigm shift articulated in Hargreaves' table above is of central importance to the approach outlined in this handbook. The approach and school model we have implemented is designed around these twenty-first century assumptions and what research suggests provides greatest traction for learning.

Where to go with school autonomy?

Current UK education policy is giving schools more freedom and autonomy. To make the most of these freedoms schools need to have not only a clear vision and sense of purpose but also a clear model for how to implement that vision.

The model outlined in this book fuses disciplinary approaches to subject teaching with what the science of learning currently does – and does not – tell us about how learning happens and meaning is made. It solves the challenges and complexities of the twenty-first century by focusing on developing deeper conceptual understandings and using assessment as a performance of understanding rather than a recital of pre-rehearsed skills. The model does not reject traditional subject divisions but neither is it a blinkered approach to teaching subjects and lessons as isolated events, divorced of connections and contradictions and focused on information absorption. It creates a *coherent curriculum* – coherent by being connected at the conceptual level rather than the surface content or thematic level – that revolves around application rather than acquisition of knowledge.

And it is a timely solution. The education system in the UK has changed dramatically under recent governments, partly in response to this paradigm shift. Although this book is not political it recognizes the likely direction of education policy over the next ten years and the emergence of the new GCSE examinations. The expansion of the academies programme; the introduction of free schools; the review of the National Curriculum – all these policies seek to devolve power and control to individual schools. And not just control over management and budgets; control over those areas of school leadership we concern ourselves with here: curriculum, teaching and learning, assessment.

Increased autonomy for schools in these areas is a positive thing. It is only by thinking through these defining questions – what subjects do I want to offer, what do these involve, how should I teach them, how will I assess students' understanding – that schools can achieve the highest standards. Teachers need to feel ownership of their classrooms, and that does not come from being told what to teach, and how to teach it. In school management you can 'prescribe adequacy', but you have to 'unleash greatness'.[19]

What are schools for?

Michael Young of the Institute of Education put it like this in a speech to Headteachers in 2012:

> I want to make an argument for a view of school leadership and a new way of thinking about leadership. It places the curriculum – the principles on which we decide what a school should teach – as shaping all the other responsibilities that face a Head teacher. It arises partly from my understanding of the new policy context that schools face...the new freedoms that the government claims to offer schools. ...It is a school's

curriculum priorities that convey to staff and students and to parents, (and ultimately, government) what a school's purposes are – what it can (and cannot) do. Schools are not social work agencies nor can they solve the problems of youth unemployment. So what can schools do that no other institutions in our society can do?

Schools can teach, and develop understanding of academic subjects to as wide a group as possible. This is the democratic promise of state education. We know that university is the biggest driver of social mobility, and in the twenty-first century this is more true than ever before. All students deserve a secondary school that will prepare them for entrance to university. All students *can think* in a disciplined manner, and developing 'powerful knowledge' in students is a social justice issue that is often overlooked.

Perhaps a terrifying report but a very relevant one is this:

> Four [independent] schools and one sixth-form college sent more pupils to Oxbridge between them over three years to 2011 than 2,000 [comprehensive] schools across the UK, according to a new study that analyses university admissions from individual schools. Westminster, Eton, St Paul's, St Paul's girls school and Hills Road sixth-form college, produced 946 Oxbridge entrants from 2007-09, the study by the Sutton Trust finds. In the same period, there were 2,000 schools and colleges which sent two or fewer pupils to Oxbridge, producing 927 in total. The difference in these schools' success rates is driven mainly by gaps in achievement at A-level. The Sutton Trust study underlines a familiar divide between the private and state sectors – finding that independent school pupils are twice as likely as comprehensive pupils to get into the 30 most selective universities and seven times as likely to get into Oxbridge. Even at the 30 highest achieving comprehensive schools, entry into competitive universities lags behind private and grammar schools. Just under 60% of pupils from the best state schools went to the most selective universities compared with just under 90% of pupils at the best private schools and 74% from the top grammars. Of a comprehensive and a private school in Cornwall, with near identical results, the former sent 17% to selective universities and the latter 66%. There are striking differences even between schools of the same type. At two comprehensives with similar results, almost 70% of 18-year-olds applied to go to university at one, but only 33% at the other.[20]

The disciplinary perspective

There are of course many factors that influence the proportion of student leavers a school sends to university each year. A school's careers programme, its historical experience, the local industry, the socio-economic background of the students – all of these things matter. But the ambition and challenge in the curriculum at Key Stage 3, 4 and 5, and the school's philosophy on teaching and its conception of the kind of learners it wants to develop its students into are the biggest factors.

We started out with the belief that all learners should encounter and wrestle with ways of constructing knowledge and ways of thinking that are above their everyday experiences, and see that academic concepts are different from everyday concepts and ways of explaining the world. For us this was the best way of preparing them to think like undergraduates before they even get close to deciding whether to apply to university. If instead students are taught only a skills and competencies approach, and denied the chance to view the world through more academic lenses, then it is likely their access to elite universities will be limited (or indeed their access to elite professions) and the two-tier society we currently inhabit will continue.

Exposure to subject disciplines connected at the conceptual level will teach students to:

- think critically
- solve problems and be analytical
- make connections
- communicate clearly and with passion
- argue and debate with clarity
- be creative
- be information literate
- be objective and original
- work independently.

These are exactly the characteristics that universities feel secondary schools often fail to develop in their students.

For this ambitious goal to be achieved all aspects of the school – teacher training, lesson observation, assessment, performance management, behaviour and ethos – need to pull in the same direction. There needs to be a strong, agreed version of what and how we teach, and this must be consistently applied across the school.

The whole-school approach to teaching and learning

Let us begin to move from theory to practice, and discuss how this approach could be implemented across a school. From our experience of teaching and of senior leadership, we have developed six guiding principles:

- **Learning is disciplined:** Different academic subjects stretch and develop different ways of thinking and talking. A scientist's questioning is not the same as a theologian's. Evidence in History is not the same as evidence in Mathematics. Each of the subjects that we teach has grown out of man's desire to understand the world around us and each subject has certain rules and ways of thinking that students need to understand if they are to engage fully with the world.

- **Teaching is exploratory:** All subjects are taught through substantial enquiries, or Fertile Questions. A Fertile Question is a planning device for knitting together a sequence of lessons around a problem posed, so that all of the learning activities – teacher exposition, reading, independent research, role-play, seminars – all move towards the resolution of a meaningful *historical/scientific/mathematical* problem by means of substantial, real and motivating activity at the end.

- **Learning is joined-up:** By being linked by a single, profound question, an enquiry-based approach engages pupils and helps them to see the links between concepts and knowledge. It also goes beyond traditional models, because the enquiry must enshrine a journey that helps pupils to *think* historically, *think* scientifically, *think* geographically, *think* mathematically and so prepare pupils, gradually, to see the differences and tensions, as well as interesting convergences, between these.

- **Teaching is public:** Through a constant programme of peer observation, review and feedback, joint planning and micro-teaching, teachers can enjoy building collective knowledge about their craft. In the schools that we have served, teachers plan together, teach together and review together, maintaining a constant reflective and collaborative dialogue.

- **Learning is meaningful:** People understand something when they can *think and act flexibly with what they know about it* – not just rehearse information and execute routine familiar skills. Students need to present knowledge, to operate on and with knowledge, and to criticize and create new knowledge if they are to really know.

- **Teaching is responsive:** Ongoing self-evaluation is a feature of any successful organization. Teachers should be constantly engaged in evaluating the impact of their strategies and changing or recasting them if they are not working. As learners progress through an enquiry, the teacher takes on different roles, moving from instructor, to facilitator, to mentor, to chair of a review.

Educating is more than teaching people to think – it is also teaching people things that are worth knowing. Good teaching involves constructing explanations, criticizing, drawing out inferences, finding applications, and there 'should never be a need for a teacher to think of ways to inject more thinking into the curriculum. That would be like trying to inject more aerobic exercise into the lives of Sherpa porters'. If the students are not doing enough thinking, something is seriously wrong with the instruction.[21]

How learning happens in our classrooms[22]

These principles form the framework for everything that follows. They are based on both the research into how learning happens as well as on two decades of teaching, observing and training in schools. These six principles form the bedrock of the approach and adherence to them is central to long-term success.

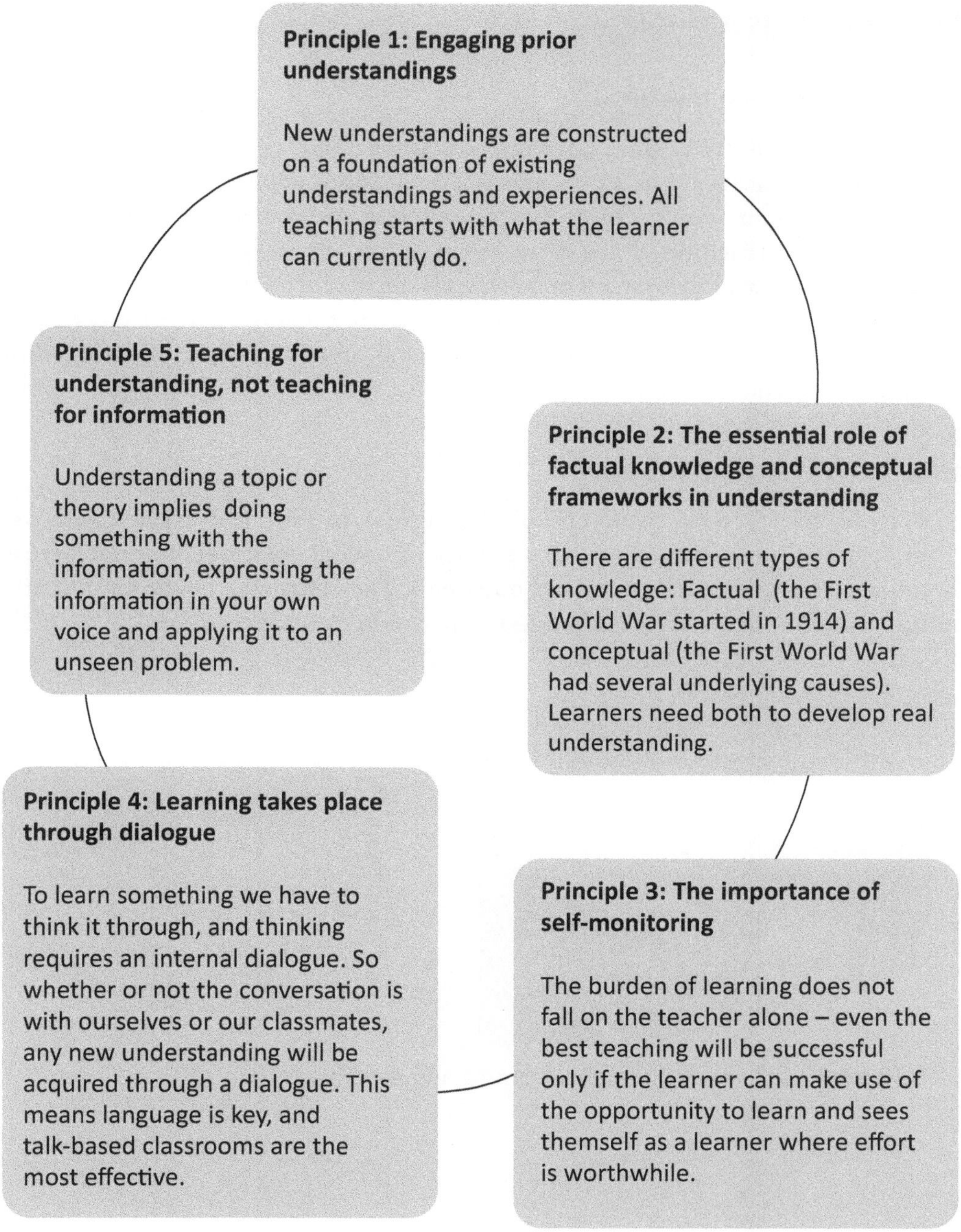

Principle 1: Engaging prior understandings

New understandings are constructed on a foundation of existing understandings and experiences. All teaching starts with what the learner can currently do.

Principle 5: Teaching for understanding, not teaching for information

Understanding a topic or theory implies doing something with the information, expressing the information in your own voice and applying it to an unseen problem.

Principle 2: The essential role of factual knowledge and conceptual frameworks in understanding

There are different types of knowledge: Factual (the First World War started in 1914) and conceptual (the First World War had several underlying causes). Learners need both to develop real understanding.

Principle 4: Learning takes place through dialogue

To learn something we have to think it through, and thinking requires an internal dialogue. So whether or not the conversation is with ourselves or our classmates, any new understanding will be acquired through a dialogue. This means language is key, and talk-based classrooms are the most effective.

Principle 3: The importance of self-monitoring

The burden of learning does not fall on the teacher alone – even the best teaching will be successful only if the learner can make use of the opportunity to learn and sees themself as a learner where effort is worthwhile.

Figure 0.2 How learning happens in our classrooms

How to use this book

'Teachers, teachers, teachers'

Teachers make the biggest difference in any school, as anyone who has ever worked in education knows. In many cases it is not what school you go to, but what classrooms you go to in that school, that dictates what your future life choices are. Teaching is the core business of any school, and as such the recruitment and development of teachers is the first priority of any Headteacher. We mean development in the broadest sense – not just five INSET days a year. Teaching using Fertile Questions, or focusing on disciplinary understanding, these are developmental tools.

Influences on student outcomes

The pie chart (see Figure 0.3) is based on Professor John Hattie's meta-analysis of over 800 international research studies into what does and does not have an impact on students' learning and outcomes. The chart clearly shows that after the students themselves, the biggest impact comes from teachers.

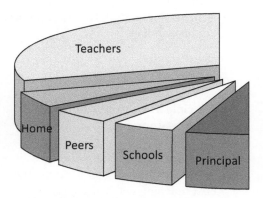 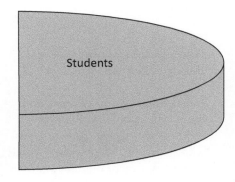

Figure 0.3 Influences on student learning and outcomes[23]

Eradicating in-school variance

> An effective school is [essentially] a school full of effective classrooms. It matters much less which school a child attends than which classrooms they are in at that school. In England there is a four-fold difference between the most effective and least effective classrooms. (Dylan Wiliam, Talk at the SSAT in May 2009)

So, limiting in-school variance, and ensuring consistently high standards of classroom teaching, is what this book aims to achieve. Six great lessons every day for every student will ripple out into all other areas of school life: attainment, progress, behaviour, culture and ethos, attendance and more. But to get that kind of consistency you need a model: a framework for teachers to follow and refer back to. This is not a prescriptive approach – we do not expect teachers' lessons to be formulaic or repetitive. Instead the ideas in the model provide a stimulus for teachers to plan their lessons. The structures in the book are liberating, not limiting.

Because, in our model, the classroom is sovereign, all areas of school management – training, lesson observation, performance management, curriculum design, assessment – need to cohere and support a school's aim of strong classroom teaching. It is our experience that if this approach is to become embedded then all other elements of school life should be aligned with it. If the behaviour policy does not reinforce the Learner Profile that the Senior Team is trying to develop in lessons, or if the performance management policy does not reinforce expectations on lesson planning, then the model will not take hold. Our advice is that everything the Senior Team initiates should be fully built in and integrated with the core provision, not bolted on as an afterthought. Ultimately, we will not raise attainment in Year 11 with intervention programmes. An 'intervention' implies that something has already gone wrong. To be fully transformative, we need to think beyond intervention. We have found that we can only raise attainment and sustain that rise with consistently strong teaching, across five years. And strong teaching does not come from a handful of training sessions or one snazzy questioning strategy. It comes from a carefully thought-through model of teaching and learning that is researched, written down, reinforced and trained at every opportunity.

A manual not a thesis

With that in mind we have designed this book to be a handbook and training manual to be drawn upon by every teacher, in daily practice. It is not something to read over the summer holidays and then to pick one or two nice activities from to try out in September. Nor is it something for the Senior Team to read and 'do' to the rest of the staff. It is a training manual to implement, evaluate and refine a whole-school approach to teaching and learning that will create an aspirational culture within school, and prepare students to play a meaningful role in society. It is intended to be read and reread, annotated, with key pages photocopied and stuck on your wall. Use it when you are writing a scheme of work, planning a lesson, designing a training session. Do not leave it on the shelf unused. It is a manual, not a thesis.

Each section outlines an aspect of the whole-school approach, what the research says about it and then how to embed it in every classroom. At the end of each section there is a training section or activity. These have been written to allow teachers to be trained on the ideas and practices contained within that section. They can either be used as they are or tweaked to fit with where the school is on its journey. The most effective method of creating a school of outstanding classrooms is to use each section as a series of training sessions. Then, as outlined in the leadership section, plan for a cyclical timetable of future training to revisit, revise and amend the initial training to ensure new teachers are inducted and existing staff continue to be developed. Throughout this book there are also in-depth case studies that help to demonstrate the thinking involved in putting the principles into practice. These case studies need to be shared and talked about, deconstructed, challenged and picked apart. They outline the approach that teachers have taken to engage with the five principles and make them come alive in their classrooms. Hold true to our five principles and the model will prove transformative.

Core practices that comprise the whole-school approach

The core practices of our model are broken into four strands. These strands encompass all areas of school life and provide a framework for creating a consistent approach across all areas. The book now goes on to describe each area in detail and looks at how to embed it in every classroom. Figure 0.4 is a model of how our approach operates.

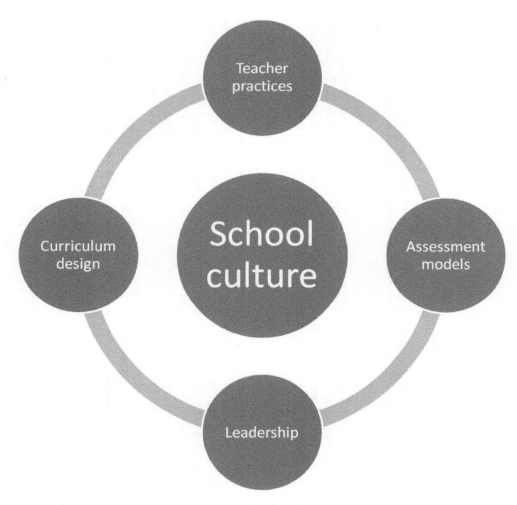

Figure 0.4   How the whole-school model operates

How could you seek to implement the approach outlined in this book?

This table shows the different levels of implementation and how you could move through them.

Functioning	Embedding	Innovating
<ul><li>understands the five principles;</li><li>can design a sequence of learning experiences that revolve around a Fertile Question;</li><li>each Fertile Question planned around a core concept;</li><li>the curriculum design allows for progression in thinking to be seen as a ladder with conceptual thinking escalated over time and earlier concepts revisited and expanded;</li><li>following the letter of the approach:</li></ul>i. students receive feedback – mainly about task completion – and set strategies – mainly around procedures to complete the task; ii. precise planning by the teacher through a Fertile Question; iii. feedback focused on performance and the successful completion of the task in hand; iv. an intention to teach or assess the next pre-determined thing in a linear progression through the curriculum plan/ map; v. opportunities for language development built in to the Fertile Question but not planned for over a 3-5 year plan;	<ul><li>uses the five principles to shape the planning;</li><li>the curriculum model is mapped out from undergraduate level to Year 7 through a spiralling set of Fertile Questions;</li><li>Fertile Questions over time revisit and strengthen core conceptual understandings over a 3-5 year plan;</li><li>the curriculum design sees the curriculum as a spider's web, with students constantly revisiting prior thinking as a way of strengthening their understanding;</li><li>following the spirit of the approach – growing out from a fixed path through the curriculum to:</li></ul>i. flexible planning which incorporates alternative resolutions to a Fertile Question and multiple ways of explaining the resolution; ii. primarily open tasks with questioning by teachers and learners directed at 'helping' rather than testing; iii. a focus on miscues – aspects of learners' work which yield insights into their current understanding – and on prompting metacognition;	<ul><li>innovates with the five principles;</li><li>uses core conceptual understandings as the starting point for planning and designing Fertile Questions;</li><li>transcending the approach – the curriculum shifts from a fixed map to a kaleidoscope with different journeys to the same destination by:</li></ul>i. complex planning which constantly amends itself to learner achievement; ii. formative assessment focused on a holistic view of criteria, the learners' understandings of them and how they fit into wider notions of knowledge and competence; iii. involvement of the learners as initiators of assessments as well as recipients and students as devising their own Fertile Questions; iv. an analysis of the interaction of learners and the curriculum from the point of view of both learners and the curriculum; v. a view of assessment as a collaboration between and amongst teachers and students; vi. language being seen as an integral part of learning;

vi. staff trained on all aspects of the approach and lessons observed to ensure uptake.

iv. exploratory, provisional or provocative feedback aimed at prompting further engagement from the learner and challenging assumptions;
v. discussion prompting reflection on the task and its context with a view to constructing understanding of future situations in which new knowledge might be applied;
vi. language development planned over the duration of the curriculum map;
vii. cyclical staff training with time planned for co-teaching and peer observation as part of normal duties;
viii. students involvement in target-setting and review.

vii. staff designing their own training programmes and creating bespoke observation timetables;
viii. staff regularly working in small groups and following the process of 'micro-teaching';
ix. students regularly predicting their performance and being involved in setting goals and the short or medium-term targets that they believe will help them reach these goals.

Notes

1   Bruner, J. (1966) *Toward a theory of instruction*: Harvard University Press.

2   The term AST stands for Advanced Skills Teacher; which was a quality standard used by successive governments to inspire the best teachers to stay in the classroom.

3   Up to 2012 Ofsted used these terms to categorize the quality of school provision.

4   Christine Counsell (2011) 'Disciplinary knowledge for all, the secondary history curriculum and history teachers' achievement', *Curriculum Journal*, 22:2, 201-225.

5   Gardner, H. (2006) '5 minds for the future', Harvard Business School Press.

6   See for example, Monaghan, M. (2010) 'Having "Great Expectations" of Year 9. Inter-disciplinary work between English and History to improve pupils' historical thinking', *Teaching History, 138*, March 2010.

7   CBI (2012), 'First steps: A new approach for our schools', November 2012.

8   Christine Counsell (2011) 'Disciplinary knowledge for all, the secondary history curriculum and history teachers' achievement', *Curriculum Journal*, 22:2, 201-225.

9   Schleicher, A. (2012), http://www.theworkfoundation.com/blog/895/Investing-in-the-future 2012.

10 Dody, J. (2013) 'Building the knowledge economy', *OECD Education Today*, 2 January 2013. For a deeper analysis of this look at 'Education at a Glance 2012: OECD Indicators', www.oecd.org/edu/eag2012.htm

11 CBI (2012) 'First steps: A new approach for our schools', November 2012.

12 Enquiries (or Fertile Questions) are explained later in the handbook.

13 Stobie, T. (2012) 'The Educational Challenge': CERPP.

14 Andreas Schleicher, OECD Education Directorate, 'The case for 21st century learning', http://www.oecd.org/general/thecasefor21st-centurylearning.htm

15 Ofqual (2012) 'Fit for purpose? The view of the higher education sector, teachers and employers on the suitability of A levels – March 2012, http://www.ofqual.gov.uk/files/2012-04-03-fit-for-purpose-a-levels.pdf

16 Hargreaves 'Helping students to become better learners', presentation made in Delhi, March 2006 cited in Stobie, T. (2012) 'The Educational Challenge': CERPP.

17 Stobie, T. (2012) 'The Educational Challenge': CERPP.

18 We developed our own approach independent of reading Stobie's report that mirrors his principles directly. Stobie summarizes them so effectively we have chosen to use his framework here but have amended them to reflect our experience.

19 Mona Mourshed, Chinezi Chijioke and Michael Barber (2010) 'How the world's most improved school systems keep getting better', report 29 November 2010: McKinsey & Co.

20 From an article on a study by The Sutton Trust published in *The Guardian*. Jeevan Vasagar (2011) 'University admissions study reveals extent of Oxbridge divide', *The Guardian*, 8 July 2011.

21 Bereiter, C. (2002) *Education and mind in the knowledge age*: Lawrence Erlbaum Associates.

22 Adapted from Donovan, M.S. and Bransford, J.D. (2005) *How Students Learn. History, Mathematics and Science in the classroom*: The National Academies Press.

23 Diagram taken from Lefstein, A. (2008) Talk at the SSAT National Conference 2008.

1

Curriculum planning

1

Curriculum planning

The design and implementation of the curriculum is at the heart of school life. It creates the atmosphere for learning and sets the tone and philosophy for teachers. An inconsistent or incoherent approach to curriculum design and roll-out leads to a messy and disjointed learning experience.

This part of the handbook deals with the theoretical aspects of this approach. It outlines what the research currently says works best and what this research looks like in practice. The curriculum design section culminates in pulling together all of the constituent parts and providing a living example by taking the reader through the construction and implementation of a Fertile Question. The design of the curriculum is shaped by the five principles of expert teaching and learning outlined on page 21.

This chapter of the book is broken down into stages to help make progress in understanding more fluid. There are training activities built in throughout the stages that can either be used as they are or adapted to better suit the needs of the audience.

Woven into this chapter are two case studies. These are articles that have been published externally but that help to bring clarity to the process by outlining the thinking that individual teachers grappled with in constructing their teaching around the core principles of our approach.

What forces shape our curriculum model?

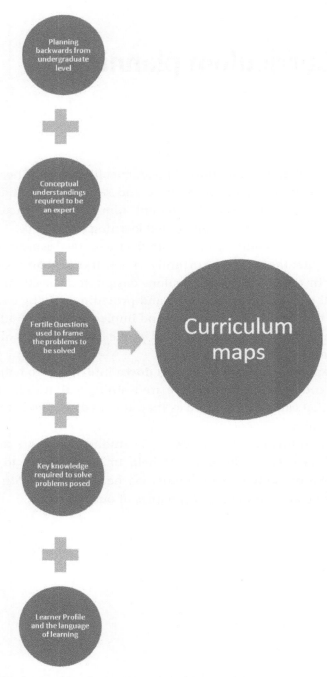

Figure 1.1   The forces that shape our curriculum model

Why do we consider this approach to be effective?

A high-level review of the National Curriculum carried out by Tim Oates in 2010 emphasized the importance of a focus on concepts and knowledge in developing students' understanding. Moreover, it also looked at where the UK's current curriculum focus had gone wrong and what needed to be done to fix this. The extract below from Oates' paper adds justification to our case for the approach outlined in this book.[1]

There is strong empirical and theoretical evidence for a very strong focus on concepts and principles. Transnational comparisons make clear that high-performing systems indeed focus on concepts and principles. 'Concepts and principles' include 'conservation of mass', 'elasticity', 'metaphor'; within 'concepts' we can include understanding of 'key operations' such as 'working with vectors' in mathematics. But this focus on concepts is justified not only by the fact that high-performing systems include such a focus, it is also strongly endorsed by theory. The crucial nature of 'organising concepts' has been highlighted in psychological research since the 1960s (Ausubel DP 1960). The more recent work on organising concepts (or 'schemata') has been used to develop highly effective medical training (Newble D & Clarke RM 1986). The research in this area is compelling. 'Organising concepts' are needed to facilitate retention in memory, develop economic mental processing, and support analytic reasoning. Concepts and principles are critical. The specific information embedded in contexts can decay into mere 'noise' unless individuals have concepts and principles to organise and interpret the content of those contexts. The critical role of concepts is reinforced by work on 'surface' and 'deep learning' (Black P & Wiliam D 1998).

Work by Michael Shayer (King's College, London) (Shayer M & Ginsburg D 2009) suggests that, in England, 11 year olds' understanding of fundamental 'conservations' (of volume, of mass, etc) have decayed over the last two decades. The precise cause of this decay has not been established (change in children's play, increased focus on context rather than concepts in teaching and assessment have been postulated) but whatever the cause, this work highlights the importance of clear focus on development of these fundamentals.

The later population of young people studied by Shayer were educated through the National Curriculum – the entitlement function appears to have decayed for these children. Knowledge is, of course, fundamental – as is retention of information in memory (Wyer RS (ed) 1995). Pupils should emerge from schooling with large bodies of knowledge (Young M 1971;

Young M 2010) – but the critical issue is this: organizing concepts and principles are crucial to the acquisition and retention of this knowledge (Bernstein B 1971) – bodies of specific knowledge can be tied to the progressive development of these fundamental concepts and principles.

So what does the approach look like?

It is all very well saying we need to foreground academic concepts in our lessons, but how do we actually go about this?

Stage 1: Introduction to medium-term planning – the Teaching and Learning cycle

What is the Teaching and Learning cycle?

The Teaching and Learning cycle is a way of ensuring medium-term planning has an impact on progress and attainment. The cycle forms the overarching scaffold for every lesson and enquiry (Fertile Question). The cycle works by posing seven key questions that enshrine the construction of an enquiry (medium-term plan). It is the simplest and most effective way of enshrining the medium-term planning process into a manageable and accountable model for all teachers.

This is the first step in planning for progression in disciplinary thinking. Once the cycle is understood it is possible to move into more complex ways of planning using Fertile Questions.

Central to all medium-term planning when designing enquiries are these questions:

i.   *What can my students currently do?*

ii.   *What do my students need to understand next?*

iii. *What will they do to generate those understandings?*

iv.   *How will we all know they have been successful?*

v.   *What will their feedback be at the different stages?*

vi.   *What performances will there be – both intermediary and final?*

vii. *What does this enquiry prepare students for next and how does it build on what they have already done (link to the BIG picture of your five or seven year plan)?*

These questions provide the rigidity of ensuring that the needs of the curriculum are met whilst being loose enough to allow for creativity and freedom in the planning and delivery from both teacher and learner.

What does the Teaching and Learning cycle look like?

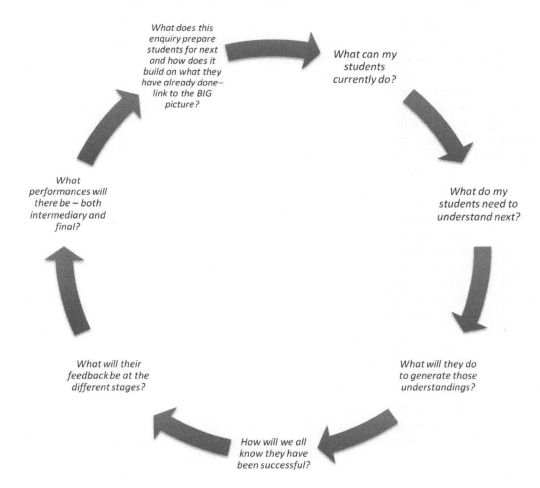

Figure 1.2 The Teaching and Learning cycle

TRAINING ACTIVITY

Planning using a set of guiding questions

The purpose of this activity is to enable you to think about planning using a set of guiding questions. It is the first stage in developing a disciplinary approach to expertise and so is deliberately simplistic. Think about a unit of work you have recently taught and complete the planning grid below as a way of designing an enquiry around that unit using the cycle. Try to fill in the chart shown in Figure 1.3.

Enquiry focus (content)	
Stage of the cycle	Notes and ideas
i. What can my students currently do?	
ii. What do my students need to understand?	
iii. What will they do to generate those understandings?	
iv. How will we all know they have been successful?	
v. What will their feedback be at the different stages?	
vi. What performances will there be – both intermediary and final?	
vii. What does this enquiry prepare students for next and how does it build on what they have already done (link to the BIG picture)?	

Figure 1.3 Planning grid for the Teaching and Learning cycle

Now we have looked at a simple planning tool, we are going to weave in deeper layers of thinking and see how that can be built into the planning framework.

Stage 2: Getting more complex – surface, deep and conceptual understanding

A central theme running through this handbook is the idea of disciplinary and academic thinking and their importance in giving every student the opportunity to achieve the highest grades in their subjects and therefore access a university education.

A fundamental principle of disciplinary thinking is the role of knowledge and this has often been misunderstood by many educators – dividing the debate into two opposing camps. The traditional *facts, facts, facts* brigade versus the *knowledge is everywhere, what matters is skills* army. Some then seem to occupy the middle ground (or no-man's land) of talking about dispositions and linking them to some kind of competency framework that mistakes knowledge for information.

It is our belief that this is a distracting dichotomy[2] at best and in fact what is needed is an approach based on *teaching for understanding*. This approach believes that there is a symbiotic relationship between knowledge and concepts and that without the one you cannot have a deep understanding of the other.

However, these concepts are not universal, as different disciplines handle matters of description, explanation, justification and causal relationship differently.

- **Evidence in Maths** consists of formal deductive proof.

- **Evidence in Science** consists of theories tested against the way the world behaves.

- **Evidence in History** can be used successfully only if it is understood in its historical context.

If learners are not aware of the distinctions between these concepts and how experts in the different academic fields make sense of the information they use, then they are doomed to be left bobbing around amongst the surface debris of the world and unable to make sense of it or see deeper patterns and currents at play within it.

Therefore, teaching for understanding requires learners (and teachers) to have a firm grasp of the core conceptual understandings within their subject, to understand how experts use those concepts to make sense of their research and how those concepts take on a different role as they cross between disciplinary thresholds.

What do we mean by powerful knowledge?[3]

Whilst it is beyond the scope and relevance of this book to go into depth about the tensions and arguments in defining *what knowledge is and what schools are for*, it is nonetheless useful to (briefly) explain how we define knowledge and the role of the school in helping learners to develop this. It is here that we draw upon the timely and important work by Michael Young.

According to Young, schooling is about providing access to the specialized knowledge that is embodied in different domains. The key curriculum questions will be concerned with:

i.   the differences between different forms of specialist knowledge and the relations between them;

ii.   how this specialist knowledge differs from the knowledge people acquire in everyday life;

iii. how specialist and everyday knowledge relate to each other; and

iv.   how specialist knowledge is pedagogized (turned into teaching activities).

In other words, how we select, pace and sequence knowledge for different groups of learners.

Young argues that differentiation, therefore, in the sense used here, means:

●   the differences between school and everyday knowledge;

●   the differences between and relations between knowledge domains;

●   the differences between specialist knowledge (e.g. Physics or History) and pedagogized knowledge (school Physics or school History for different groups of learners).

Underlying these differences is a more basic difference between two types of knowledge. One is the *context-dependent* knowledge that is developed in the course of solving specific problems in everyday life. It can be *practical* – like knowing how to repair a mechanical or electrical fault or how to find a route on a map. It can also be *procedural*, like a handbook or set of regulations for health and safety. Context-dependent knowledge tells the individual how to do specific things. It does not explain or generalize; it deals with particulars.

The second type of knowledge is *context-independent* or *theoretical knowledge*. This is knowledge that is developed to provide generalizations and makes claims to universality; it provides a basis for making judgements and is usually, but not solely, associated with the sciences. It is context-independent knowledge that is at least potentially acquired in school, and is what we refer to as *powerful knowledge.*

Schools should help learners develop powerful knowledge and the ways of thinking that this knowledge enshrines.

What does the research say about this?

It is helpful at this point to return to the review by Oates we looked at earlier. The excerpt below supports the approach of the handbook in that Oates argues that schools and their curriculum need to be concept-led.

> It was not a trivial problem that, prior to the National Curriculum in England, pupils could be involved in studying topics such as 'The Vikings' four times in the course of 5–14 education (Graham D & Tytler D op cit; Johnson M et al op cit). The National Curriculum sought, quite rightly, to prevent this. However, 'contexts' have become dominant in revisions of the National Curriculum, displacing vital knowledge and concepts.
>
> Contexts – such as the environment, specific industrial processes, atomic power – can provide motivation to study and show the relevance of conceptual material. Used carefully, they can be the **curriculum vehicle** for concept-based and knowledge-based National Curriculum content. However, unless managed carefully in learning programmes, contextual material can be systematically misleading and distracting, preventing the effective acquisition of underlying concepts.
>
> Black's and Wiliam's work on Assessment for Learning highlights the acute dangers in attending only to superficial aspects of pupils' work rather than underlying conceptual development. The work on iteration of theory and practice in pedagogy in high performing Asian nations (Stigler and Stevenson op cit) suggests that different contexts constantly should be woven into lessons, and the contexts adapted to each child, in order to find the particular key to opening their understanding of a crucial concept. Spending more time on larger 'blocks' of cognate material allowed deeper, more secure learning to be achieved. In addition, teachers in these Asian settings are free to use different contexts as they see fit, in order to unlock understanding (Stigler and Stevenson op cit; Stigler J & Hiebert J 1999). The central specification of contexts through a national curriculum undermines this essential flexibility.
>
> The National Curriculum should be concept-led and knowledge-led, not context-led.[4]

TRAINING ACTIVITY

Exploring the tensions involved when talking about knowledge

i. *What is the difference between context-dependent and context-independent knowledge?*

ii. *Is this an important point for schools to be aware of?*

iii. *What does powerful knowledge look like in your subject area?*

iv. *How does this knowledge differ from the everyday knowledge people acquire?*

v. *Why is powerful knowledge important?*

vi. *How does the specialist knowledge of experts in the field differ from the pedagogized knowledge of your school subject?*

vii. *Does the way your students develop powerful knowledge differ from the way experts in the field do?*

viii. *Is this important?*

ix. *Do you think your students currently develop powerful knowledge in your subject or are they more likely to receive context-dependent procedural knowledge that enables them to complete pre-determined tasks?*

x. *What might need to change to help move your students from procedural knowledge to powerful knowledge?*

TRAINING ACTIVITY

Using conceptual understandings to shape the curriculum (Part 1)

A famous research study[5] that highlighted the core relationship between knowledge and concepts is outlined below and is an invaluable training aid to beginning to get teachers to look at how the core concepts of their subject area influence ways of thinking and ways of talking.

Stage 1: Five seconds – how much can you remember?

Pop up the chess board with its pieces below on a screen for five seconds.

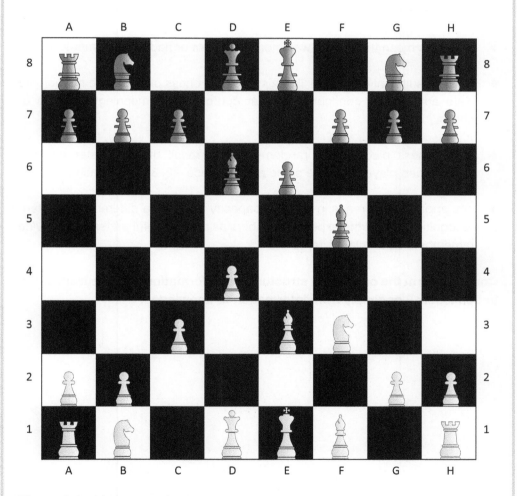

Figure 1.4 Memory and concepts

Stage 2: Take it off the screen and, on a blank chess board (photocopied on paper!) in front of them, give them 60 seconds to map out the pieces they saw on the screen onto the board.

Stage 3: Put the original screen of the chess board back up and compare. Ask how many got 1, 2, 3, 5, etc. pieces right.

Stage 4: Share the research with them.

- Study conducted with master, novice and experienced chess players.

- The master continually placed more correct pieces than the experienced player who in turn placed more correct pieces than the novice.

- Does this mean the master was more intelligent or had a better memory?

- These results only occurred like this when the chess pieces to be memorized were arranged in configurations that conformed to meaningful games of chess.

- When chess pieces were randomized, the recall of the master and the experienced player were the same as the novice – 2–3 pieces each time.

- The apparent difference in memory capacity is due to a difference in pattern recognition – what the expert remembers as a meaningful pattern, the novice remembers as unrelated items.

Concepts form the organizing structures for information to move from 'inert' to applicable – or simply from information to knowledge.

Differences between content, skill and concept

The generic 'thinking-skills' argument ignores the distinctive purposes of academic disciplines. These need to be understood as interplay between content, subject-specific skills and larger disciplinary concepts that structure the kinds of question each discipline asks. Each discipline is a distinctive way of building knowledge, weighing evidence and finding truth. In schools, therefore, subject specialists use disciplines to teach students how to *think* in particular, powerful ways. A discipline shapes the way one learns to read, to question and to research in a subject.

Thus subject-specific skills and disciplinary concepts can work together with substantive content to build powerful knowledge – a rich, useable knowledge base that is more than just facts and information. Disciplinary structure gives information meaning. It makes it possible for students to assimilate and retain that information as knowledge. *Knowledge,* unlike *information,* has memorable structures. As Senior Leaders, we have realized more and more that the finest subject teachers spend much time helping pupils to think about those very structures. Thus pupils can acquire useable frameworks, and increasingly discern them for themselves.

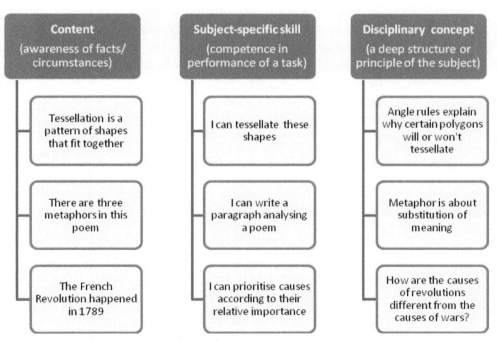

Figure 1.5   Content, subject-specific skill and disciplinary concept

A sign that pupils are gaining more powerful ways of thinking and more powerful knowledge is when they start to use those concepts to think in the way the discipline demands, to ask the typical questions of the discipline, to solve problems and construct accounts with structure and direction. Figure 1.5 shows what we mean by content, by subject-specific skill and by disciplinary concept.

Consider the middle row – the metaphor example from English. The concept of metaphor is fundamental to the study of English Literature. Writers use metaphor to compare one thing to another in a way that conveys meaning more powerfully than a straightforward description. Martin Luther King famously used metaphors in his 'I have a dream' speech on civil rights. When he promised that 'every hill and mountain shall be made low' he was not literally talking about flattening the landscape. For him the 'mountains' symbolized the racism, discrimination and lack of equality black people faced at the time. These obstacles had qualities in common with a mountain: they were large, loomed over you, were difficult to overcome, seemingly permanent and so on. So the concept of metaphor is about substitution – the idea that one thing can be usefully substituted for another to achieve a poetic or rhetorical effect.

When teaching a poem an English teacher has a choice. They could drill their class with the three key metaphors from the text, going over and over the same quotes and spoon feeding students with the analysis they need to remember for their exam. This approach may enable the students to pass. But, if the same teacher instead focused on the underlying concept of metaphor, the idea that metaphor is about substitution, then students would be able to analyse not just these metaphors from the set poem, but other, unseen metaphors in different poems. They would be able to identify and analyse metaphors independently. They will be able to write their own metaphors. This approach will enable students to excel.

TRAINING ACTIVITY

Using conceptual understandings to shape the curriculum (Part 2):

i.   *What are the core disciplinary concepts of your subject area? The key concepts that, once understood, bring learners to a deeper and broader sense of a discipline.*

ii. *Are learners in your lessons aware of the specific disciplinary game they are playing? Do they understand the key concepts and big ideas of the subject?*

iii. *Are learners aware of how the disciplinary rules change as they move from one lesson to another, from one topic to the next?*

iv. *How do you currently use concepts to organize information?*

Curriculum leadership belongs to curriculum leaders

Once subject leaders understand that an effective curriculum emphasizes *concepts* alongside facts and subject-specific skills they can then set about designing their schemes of work. This process of thinking through the curriculum is absolutely vital if the lessons are going to be well delivered. In our experience, only if teachers feel personal ownership of the Fertile Questions that they are teaching, will they be able to energize and inspire their students. A teacher needs a clear understanding of where each lesson and series of lessons is heading and they need to be able to communicate this in crystal-clear fashion to every student. All students need to know in every lesson where they are going, where they currently are on that journey and what they need to do next to keep moving forward. This means ensuring that the central, Fertile Question is alive, driving the cumulative curiosity, lesson by lesson, as pupils discover the deepening complexity of the puzzle, and the facets of the discipline it reveals. This foresight and sense of direction cannot be achieved by copying and pasting a curriculum from an external source.

This is partly why the recent National Strategies for Numeracy and Literacy failed to deliver the improvements that were hoped for. They were well thought through programmes of study, grounded in solid research, but because the teachers being told to deliver them were not conversant with the thinking behind them they could not get the best from the materials. What they had was essentially a recipe mix to follow, and as soon as something went wrong they could not reshape the lessons to fit the original objectives.

Figure 1.6 shows the steps a subject leader should go through when designing their curriculum in their school.

The case study below looks at designing a unit of work around conceptual understandings. As noted at the beginning of the book, the role of the case studies is to provide examples of how the approach has been embedded at classroom level and the challenges and solutions teachers encountered in making this happen. You will notice that in several of the case studies the approach differs from the letter of the book – that is OK as all the case studies remain true to the underlying principles.

In summary

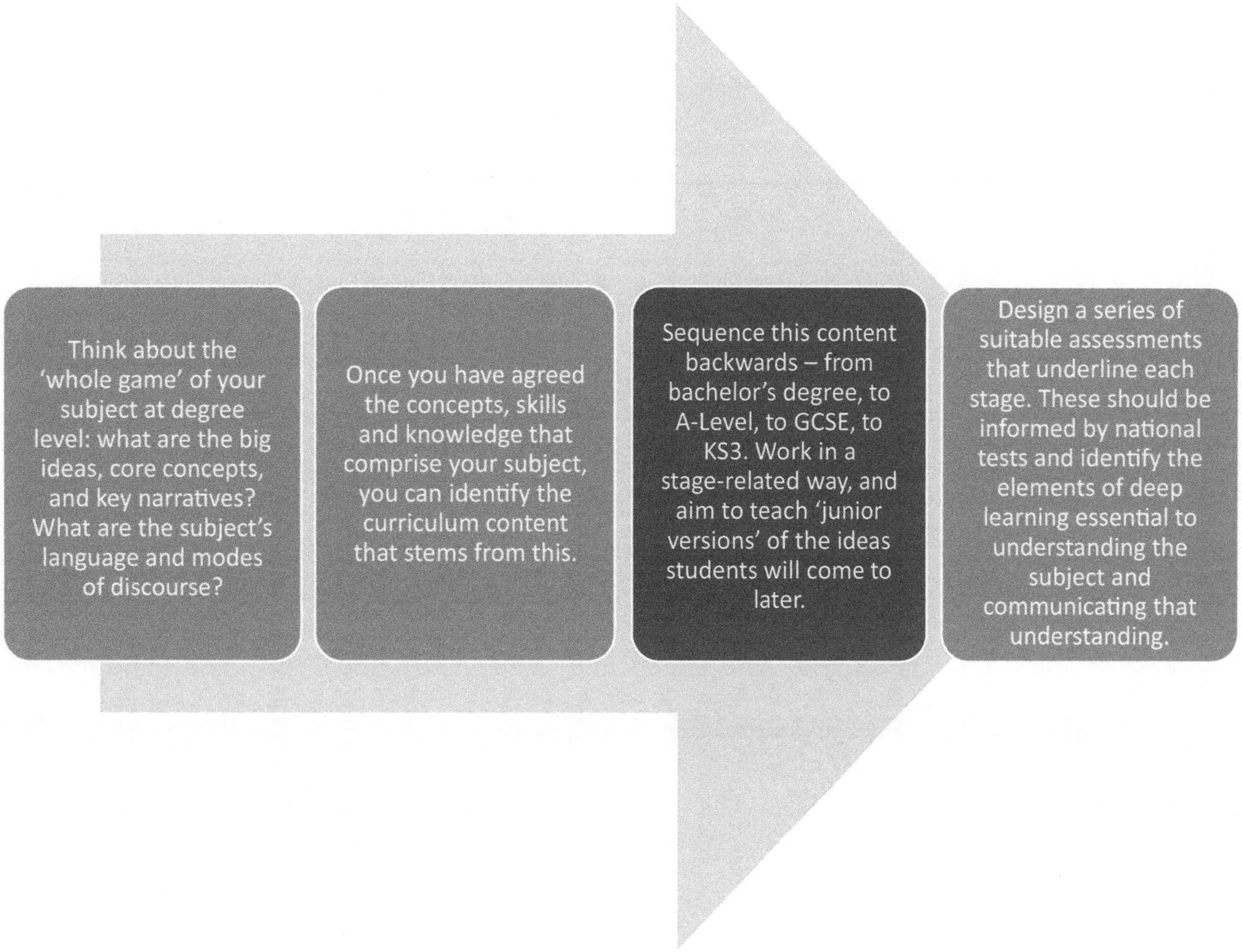

Think about the 'whole game' of your subject at degree level: what are the big ideas, core concepts, and key narratives? What are the subject's language and modes of discourse?

Once you have agreed the concepts, skills and knowledge that comprise your subject, you can identify the curriculum content that stems from this.

Sequence this content backwards – from bachelor's degree, to A-level, to GCSE, to KS3. Work in a stage-related way, and aim to teach 'junior versions' of the ideas students will come to later.

Design a series of suitable assessments that underline each stage. These should be informed by national tests and identify the elements of deep learning essential to understanding the subject and communicating that understanding.

Figure 1.6 Design pathway for the curriculum

Case study 1 – Building a curriculum module around conceptual understanding – a planning odyssey

This article first appeared in *Teaching History* 132, September 2008, published by The Historical Association. It was written by Oli Knight and edited by Tony McConnell.

It is included here as an example of grappling with the ideas outlined in this book and how they can be applied. It is not the perfect approach and is included as much for analysis as modelling.

A hankering for the blank spaces: enabling the very able to explore the limits of GCSE History

My Year 10s had just sat their end of year exam, the previous year's OCR Paper 1. Of the 47 girls that I taught in Year 10, almost all of them got over 80 per cent, many gaining over 90 per cent and some even 100 per cent. I had tried to mark as harshly as possible, but there was only so much I could do to keep the marks down to try to prevent them from taking their foot off the accelerator.

Whilst this was rather pleasing (and after some initial gloating about what an amazing teacher I must be) I started to feel that I was failing my pupils.

Was a focus on results enough? At the end of the day I had simply drilled them effectively in structuring their responses to the repetitive style of exam questions. They knew how to answer the questions, had the language to access the top levels of the mark scheme, had a writing-frame for every style of question and had learnt the detail needed. This was what Torrance and Pryor would label convergent formative assessment, whereby I assess if the learners know what I want them to in order to complete pre-determined tasks.[1] I had created classes of robots, chained to the exam system.

I was starting to grapple with my own conception of what I thought learning was. So far I had only ever really thought of it as attaining objectives, a linear progression where I was in control and dominated proceedings and the kids came out the other end of the production line with a nice exam result. Could I change this relationship, move from teacher- to pupil-centred learning and thus help my pupils to see learning as constructing knowledge rather than simply consuming an already constructed body of knowledge?[2]

*Beyond the syllabus, beyond the A**

I had five weeks of the summer term left. The course was finished and I thought that perhaps I should allow myself the luxury of a little experimentation before moving to my new and very different school.

By some small miracle I had managed to persuade the students to have total faith and trust in me and I felt that now it was time to see just how far I could take them. This was going to be a big test, especially as none of the initial surface content I wanted to teach had anything to do with their exam, and these girls are *all* about the exam. They would happily sit there in silence, lesson after lesson, copying out the textbook if they knew there was an A* waiting for them at the end. Year 10 parents' evening was coming up. What would the parents say if they discovered I was teaching their children content which was not on the exam syllabus? I knew it would help them. I knew it would engage them. I knew it would allow them to see the wider focus and relevance of history. But would the parents see this? Would the Head?

So, what was I hoping to achieve? For me this was going to be about enabling the pupils to develop some kind of historical consciousness, focusing on both their metahistorical understanding and their conceptualizations of the past.[3] Put another way, I wanted

> to allow them to see the past as though looking through a kaleidoscope: the patterns are ordered and determinate but do not yield a single, stable picture. Individual pupils may express personal preferences for patterns or narratives for whatever reason, but the view and understanding of the whole would be impoverished were all other possibilities to be disregarded.[4]

I felt that this consciousness would allow for more powerful understandings of their course and perhaps see the beginnings of some kind of orientation within a larger narrative framework. It is also my feeling that too many GCSE textbooks and exam syllabuses remove the questioning and hedgings that are central to the creation of an account of the past and reduce the past to, in the words of Barton, a kind of trivia game where all of the interpretation and inference is missing.[5] Thus the past becomes a story and the GCSE course in particular paints a past that offers one view, a predetermined narrative that is agreed upon and accepted. I had been teaching my Year 10 pupils using the excellent textbook by Ben Walsh.[6] Whilst the textbook is moulded perfectly to the exam syllabus and provides an excellent base, it is, as with most instructional resources, guilty of the 'referential illusion'. That is, it fosters centrally-held and politically-supported cultural and national assumptions about a 'shared' past. I wanted my students to move beyond this.

Textbooks and the truth

The danger of this presentation of the past as offered by Walsh is particularly clear in his chapter on Russia 1905–1941, in that there is a story running through the chapter that reinforces contemporary political and cultural narratives. The textbook offers, in the words of Griffin and Marciano, an obvious means of realizing hegemony in education in that within the textbook the omission of crucial facts and viewpoints limits profoundly the ways in which students come to view historical events and in turn shapes their understanding of how the past is constructed.[7]

It is this notion of aggregative progression and simple knowledge acquisition that I wanted to move beyond and challenge. But was this really Dionysian in that I was liberating my pupils from the procedurally-based educational outcome of creating *homo Sovieticus* and creating a new pupil, a *homo novus* for the twenty-first century or was this merely hot air, a mirage produced by too much time in the Portakabin marking exam scripts? How was I going to go about constructing a rigorous, academically-based enquiry that enabled my pupils to grapple with this idea?

I was reading an article on the Khmer Rouge (and I have to confess to being a total novice on the subject) and their seizure of power in 1975. Hmm, I thought, there are a few parallels with the Bolsheviks' seizure of power. I wanted to get the girls to explore this notion. I was aware that I was taking a slight gamble as my subject knowledge was rather shaky but I justified this by telling myself that the focus was also on letting the students come on this learning journey with me. I did not have answers and knowledge; I was going to construct this as I went along, reshaping and restructuring as I went. I wanted my pupils also to experience this. I wanted this to be a way of getting them to reflect on the contested nature of the past and work with some of the ideas and understandings of professional historians.

Substantive History as an academic discipline

This would reinforce everything the students had been studying on Russia. It would get them to grapple with historical concepts far beyond the remit of the GCSE and hopefully reinvigorate the course after the climax of the exam. It was here that I really started to grapple with ideas about History as an academic subject and reflect upon how I conceptualized it, and what I wanted to provide my pupils with in terms of a History education. History is really shaped by two symbiotic frameworks – the substantive and the conceptual.

Substantive History is the content of History, the knowledge that we want the pupils to possess, and is made up of particular events, individuals and concepts. 'Concepts', in this instance, means ideas such as peasant, feudal system, rather than second-order or structural concepts. Therefore progression in Substantive History means pupils developing a deeper knowledge of the past. In my own understanding of my planning for substantive progression within this experiment I drew on the work of Christine Counsell. One of her key ideas from *Historical knowledge and historical skills: a distracting dichotomy* is the idea of resonance, making sure that each unit builds upon the themes and knowledge of previous enquiries, thus marking out substantive progression as being like a spider's web, whereby students scuttle back and forth, revisiting, strengthening and shedding new light on prior knowledge and weaving in new strands of understanding – the idea of fingertip and residual knowledge.[8] It was with this in mind that I planned the 'knowledge route' through the enquiry.

My planning then expanded this idea by linking it into the work of Shemilt and Lee on frameworks, big pictures and historical consciousness.[9] Thus the substantive element is also woven into the framework of the past that the students situate themselves within. This therefore allows for greater historical clarity and rigour. Conceptual progression in this case means students being able to develop more powerful ideas about the past – that is, about History as a discipline where the past is constructed.

This therefore helps them to see that the ideas of historians are just that, ideas and stances. I wanted to move away from the traditional 'overview' style that I had been using and focus more on historical consciousness. I had often thought of overviews as helping pupils to place their depth studies into some kind of context, but I did not feel that this was terribly successful, mainly because this 'overview' style of teaching failed to secure progression. My pupils had just filled up event space, rather than developing and referring to a useable framework of knowledge.

I had been teaching my pupils to see the past as a series of isolated events that might somehow be connected through an arbitrarily chosen idea without enabling them to see that this framework was speculative and open to change itself.

Concepts: patterns in the past

When we had touched on Marxism during the Russia lessons the girls had seemed fascinated by Marx and his beliefs. This would also be the ideal opportunity to look at his political theory and his influence on the twentieth century. How would I go about this? How would I teach this effectively? How would I draw out the two key issues of metahistorical progression and the question of the cyclical, or unique, nature of history? Do the same patterns within history keep repeating themselves, just in a slightly different guise? In particular, in this case:

- *Did the Khmer Rouge set out to replicate the Bolshevik revolution, wittingly or unwittingly, and was it, by this fact, set to repeat the same developmental pattern (and the same ensuing human cost)?*

- *What impact has Karl Marx had on the twentieth century?*

- *Is Marxist political theory fundamentally flawed or is it attainable for humans?*

- *Is Marxism dead?*

This was not to be the Citizenship approach of using snippets from a pre-determined past to teach about present political needs. I was not looking at teaching the Cambodian Genocide as a provider of moral sermons whereby, after a series of inspiring lessons, my pupils were suddenly better citizens. Nor would it be simple fact-finding about some horrific past event or series of events. The motivation for the lessons lay in helping my students to become better historians, lifting them above the mundane plains of the GCSE and all its rigid structures and looking at history as immensely difficult, politically charged, interwoven and multilayered.

Making progress on progression

I was also starting to reflect more fully on what I thought progression in History was all about. My notion of progression was informed partly by the work of Phillips, who measures progress in the way in which a pupil responds to, and poses, questions.[10] The changing nature of the questions would seem to fit with Bloom's taxonomy and appear to be moving up the scale towards higher-order thinking-skills, a reflection of the idea that progression is linear and accumulative. This is an important step for pupils to make and he is right to highlight this but we can extend Phillips' ideas to take account of the disciplinary nature of History, with its substantive, colligatory and second-order conceptual understandings. I wanted to distinguish between them, and set out what progress might look like within them. So I required a tighter definition within which to frame my enquiry.

Lee and Dickinson define progression as follows:

- in the case of ideas – the acquisition of more powerful concepts and the increasing scope of those concepts in organizing and explaining a wider range of subject matter;

- in the case of abilities – the increasing size of the domain in which the abilities can be employed, and the difficulty upon which the ability is to operate.[11]

Progression in History may be measured by pupils' ideas within and about structural concepts of History. Within each structural concept it is possible to find sets of ideas, tacit or explicit, that allow or inhibit certain cognitive moves. Levels are higher or lower because they create or solve more or fewer problems, because the ideas with which children work can have greater or less explanatory power.[12] Progression is measured through the substantive gains pupils make and how they use this knowledge to express their conceptual understandings. What this means is that teachers need to shift their views of what a History education is and when learning History is thought of as coming to grips with a discipline, with its own procedures and standards for evaluating claims, it becomes easier to envisage progression in History, rather than just the aggregation of factual knowledge, whether the latter is construed as deepening or expanding.[13]

Thus for Lee and Ashby, as well as acquiring knowledge of the past, students develop more powerful understandings of the nature of the discipline, which in turn legitimate the claim that what they acquire is indeed knowledge.

Objectives and enquiry

I wanted my students to:

- have a developed awareness of the significance of Marxist theory;

- start to question why, in the West, Marxism, Communism and Socialism have seemed to be dirty words;

- grapple with the wider issues of the creative forces of the past and their impact on present day belief, taking my inspiration from Overy's *The Dictators*, which is a thematic comparison of Hitler and Stalin which addresses the similarities and differences between Hitler and Stalin's dictatorships across themes such as control of culture and the economy, seizure of power, architecture and the politics of extermination.[14]

The first thing I needed then was an enquiry question, something that would encompass all of the above and at the same time engage the students, make them want to find out about it and give them something difficult to get their teeth into. I wanted them to grapple with the same issues I had been in deciding if I could teach this. I always find developing good enquiry questions really hard. After much wrestling, mainly with my own ineptitude, I decided that theft was the only solution. I thought that I could go for the simple theft of a question such as:

How could the Holocaust have happened?

and simply change it to:

How could the Cambodian Genocide have happened?

and use this as an avenue to explore the concepts. But this was lacking the precision I wanted, I was looking at a comparative analysis of historical events and their reliance on political theory as justification and needed a question that reflected this. In the end I opted for:

Dysfunctional Socialism: Does the desire to make all men equal have to lead to murder?

I felt that this incorporated both Russia and Cambodia but left enough to the imagination. It did not give away the whole process straight away, retaining an element of surprise. I hoped it illuminated the initial broad focus but left the journey a mystery, something to be discovered. Although there is of course scope to argue that the question does hint at a pre-determined outcome and is just as guilty as others in maintaining a 'Western' view of socialism, I also hoped it would enable the girls to run with the enquiry more and almost structure their own path, with me offering guidance and key questions where needed but leaving the outcome up to them. I did not need an enquiry question here that gave the whole picture, just one that got them thinking with no set conclusion. I wanted them to make the connections, to explore new lines of enquiry and really to get grips with the difficulties of political theory and the role of ideas in shaping historical events. I did not want to spoon-feed them knowledge in the hope that they could demonstrate some kind of short-term knowledge gain. This was about them making real progress as historians.

Next, I needed to think about the overview of the lessons. What would the lesson questions be, how many lessons would I need and how was I going to tie it all together at the end?

The path through the enquiry was designed with a series of smaller questions helping to answer the overarching enquiry question. Each lesson can use a variety of activities to reach a conclusion or judgement on the question being answered. The key point to the lessons is that throughout the enquiry layers of knowledge are added and these layers help pupils to change or amend their view on the enquiry question and to help challenge their preconceptions. This process then needs to be drawn out with whole class and small group reflection to meet the aims expressed earlier.

Assessment for learning

With engaged pupils a lot of progress can be created through effective use of questioning and structured discussion. It is important to let pupils run with the enquiry, to leave it fluid and to allow their questions and responses to shape the direction of the lessons and, especially, of their homework. This is where the initial intrigue created at the beginning of the lesson will bear most fruit, encouraging pupils to research and question individually, allowing them the freedom to explore the enquiry question, to discover for themselves the pitfalls and joys of History as an academic subject. This takes a lot of courage, departing from the comfort blanket of a lesson plan that maps out exactly what pupils will be able to do at the end of the lesson is difficult. We give students the questions, but the methods of answering them can be as individual as the students are. As their knowledge develops, so their lines of enquiry will change and, here, the comparative nature of the enquiry must be kept sharply in focus.

Whilst the lesson may change as it progresses, with knowledge gaps having to be plugged and new information shared, the end point must always be kept in the back of the mind. One of the purposes of the enquiry is to enable the kids to develop as historians, to recreate the processes, decisions and dead-ends of a professional historian. If by the end of the enquiry they are not actually able to answer the enquiry question, is this such a bad thing? A well-run feedback session on why this happened and what this tells us about the study of the past is surely just as valuable as a nicely written essay or ripple diagram, especially if we are looking at metahistorical progression.

GCSE success – at AS Level

The important thing is not the choice of activity for activity's sake but that each activity focuses on the question and the comparative nature of the enquiry. The point is not to fill our students' heads with knowledge but to equip them with the understandings and problem-solving techniques of an academic historian, to answer such questions as:

- how historians draw comparisons between periods/actors in the historical process;

- how the public views the past;

- how Hollywood creates its own version of events – to entertain or enforce the current political viewpoint.

Very able pupils tend to soak up facts like sponges, arriving in our classroom with a head full of stories and richness and interest in human beings. Learning 'one damn thing after another' is not the way to engage them and help them see the importance and fun of the subject. Whilst we have an obligation to give them the best possible preparation for their exams we also have an obligation to our subject and to their intellectual development.

For me, however, the most obvious measure of success was that 20 out of 23 pupils in one class selected History at AS Level.

References

1. Pryor, J. and Crossouard, B. (2007) 'A socio-cultural theorization of formative assessment', *Oxford Review of Education*, 33(5).
2. Hargreaves, E. (2005) 'Assessment for learning? Thinking outside the (black) box', *Cambridge Journal of Education*, Vol. 35, No. 2.
3. Lee, P. (2004) '"Walking backwards into tomorrow". Historical consciousness and understanding history', *International Journal of History Learning, Teaching and Research*, Vol. 4, No. 1.
4. Shemilt, D. (2000) 'The Caliph's coin', in Stearns, P., Seixas, P. and Wineburg, S. (2000) *Knowing, Teaching and Learning History*: New York University Press.
5. Barton, K. and Levstik, L. (2004) *Teaching History for the common good*: LEA.
6. Walsh, B. (2001) *GCSE Modern World History (History in Focus)*: John Murray; 2nd edition.
7. Foster, S. and Crawford, K. (2006) *What shall we tell the children? International perspectives on History textbooks*: Information Age Publishing.
8. Counsell, C. (2000) 'Historical knowledge and historical skills: a distracting dichotomy' in Arthur, J. and Phillips, R. (eds) *Issues in History teaching*: Routledge.
9. For a full explanation of narrative frameworks see Shemilt, D. (2006) *The future of the past: How adolescents make sense of past, present and future*: Trinity and All Saints College.
10. Phillips, R. (2002) *Reflective teaching of History 11-18*: Continuum.
11. Dickinson A., Lee, P. and Rogers, P. (eds) (1984) *Learning History*: Heinemann.
12. Dickinson A., Lee, P. and Rogers, P. (eds) (1984) *Learning History*: Heinemann.
13. Ashby, R. and Lee, P. (2000) 'Progression in historical understanding among students ages 7-14' in Stearns, P., Seixas, P. and Wineburg, S. (2000) *Knowing, teaching and learning History*: New York University Press.
14. Overy, R. (2004) *The dictators: Hitler's Germany and Stalin's Russia*: Allen Lane.

TRAINING ACTIVITY

Reflecting on what the key disciplinary concepts are in your subject

Oli has a very clear view about what progress in History looks like and how school History should mirror the History undertaken by professionals in the 'field'. Use this case study as a tool for reflecting on what the key disciplinary concepts are in your subject and how you can plan for progression within them through your curriculum map. The research suggests that students need to constantly revisit prior exposure to concepts and that new learning must be placed within their existing conceptual frameworks.

i.   *What does Oli see as the main differences between conceptual understanding and knowledge acquisition?*

ii.   *Is this a concept-led or content-led Fertile Question?*

iii.   *How do you know?*

iv.   *What role do concepts play in the teaching of this Fertile Question?*

v.   *How is progress in these different types of thinking 'measured'?*

vi.   *What similarities are there between this approach in History and your own subject?*

vii.   *What can you take away from this case study to help you in your own thinking about disciplinary thinking and the role of conceptual understandings in framing a curriculum map?*

Stage 3: Going deeper still – Performances of Understanding and evidence of thinking

Medium-term plans need outcomes – concrete end-points where the students demonstrate what they have learnt. We call these 'Performances of Understanding'. We have seen that understanding something is being able to think and act flexibly with it, so we need to design approaches to assessment that allow for this to happen. This is where the notion of Performances of Understanding: constructing something to show what you have learnt (from a talk given at a conference in 2011 by Y. Harpaz) comes in.

The table below by Harpaz outlines a clear planning tool for getting learners to carry out different Performances of Understanding for different stages of a Fertile Question, and for different stages across a year or Key Stage. You will see how some sections of the table carry more cognitive challenge (and therefore deep learning) than others. However it is not written as a hierarchical taxonomy – a cycle of assessments will blend the different areas and allow for escalation over time.

To present knowledge	To operate on and with knowledge	To criticize and create knowledge
To express knowledge in your own words (examples needed)	To analyse knowledge	To give reasons to knowledge
To explain knowledge	To synthesize knowledge	To find contradictions or tensions in knowledge
To interpret knowledge	To imply knowledge	To question knowledge
To construct a model	To bring example, to invent metaphor, to make comparison, etc.	To expose the basic assumptions of knowledge
To present knowledge in various ways	To generalize	To formulate counter-knowledge
To present knowledge from different perspectives	To predict on the basis of knowledge	To generate new knowledge

TRAINING ACTIVITY

Thinking flexibly – an example[6]

This is an example from a training activity we have used successfully with teachers. It illustrates neatly the difference between being able to recall something and truly understanding it.

Imagine your overall outcome is for students to demonstrate an understanding of Newton's three laws of motion:

i. **First law**: If an object experiences no net force, then its *velocity* is constant: the object is either at rest (if its velocity is zero), or it moves in a straight line with constant speed (if its velocity is nonzero).

ii. **Second law**: The *acceleration* of a body is *parallel* and directly proportional to the net *force* acting on the body, is in the direction of the net force, and is inversely proportional to the *mass* of the body.

iii. **Third law**: When a first body exerts a force F_1 on a second body, the second body simultaneously exerts a force $F_2 = -F_1$ on the first body. This means that F_1 and F_2 are equal in magnitude and opposite in direction.

So, what does understanding look like?

Common activities teachers use to gauge understanding:

● The student reciting the laws (making a mind map);

● The student writing some correct equations solved using the laws;

● The student succeeding with three or four end of textbook problems – some of which might be similar to problems encountered in the teaching phase but worded differently.

All these activities could be taken as evidence of understanding. But none of them require the students to reason with the knowledge they have been given. Understanding means performance. A better test of students understanding would be:

Puzzle

- Imagine a snowball fight in space. Twelve astronauts are arranged in roughly a circle with some snowballs in their pockets.

- A signal sounds and the astronauts begin the snowball fight.

What will happen as they attempt to continue their snowball fight?

What would actually happen?

i.   As they start the fight they will begin to move away from one another.

ii. Throwing the snowball will also place the astronaut into a spin.

iii. To avoid this, the astronaut will have to throw from their mid-section – so the action occurs on a vector directly outward from their centre of gravity.

This is an example of thinking with Newtonian laws of motion: the game of prediction and explanation. If you understand these laws, you should be able to reason with them. If you do not, simply working from everyday thinking is unlikely to solve the problem.

   The point about assessment is simple – the same student who can successfully complete a mind map or answer a few formulaic equations may urge, when presented with the snowballs in space problem, that the astronauts could hit one another if they were not too far away and had a good aim.

So, understanding means performance

- People understand something when they can *think and act flexibly with what they know about it* – not just rehearse information and execute routine skills.

- If you cannot think with Newton's laws, you do not really understand them.

TRAINING ACTIVITY

Understanding

Think of a topic of unit of work you have just taught:

- *How did you assess student understanding?*

- *Had the students been prepared for the assessment beforehand?*

- *Was the assessment the resolution of an unseen problem or a recital of learnt information – even if the wording was different?*

- *Do you think your students could apply the knowledge they have gained to solve a new problem they have not seen before?*

- *What could you do differently to really test out their understanding?*

Performances of Understanding: Key questions

i. *How do you currently know if your students understand something?*

ii. *How could we design teaching to allow students to demonstrate understanding? Look at the table above from Harpaz. Do you currently mainly get your students to present knowledge?*

iii. *How can you get them to move from presenting knowledge to operating on or criticizing knowledge? What might a performance look like?*

iv. *How might you plan to move students from presenting to criticizing through a Fertile Question?*

v. *How do we use this to inform the next steps in our planning?*

vi. *How do we use this to allow students to know where they are and decide on what their next steps should be?*

Playing the whole game

'Playing the whole game' is a term used by David Perkins to describe the process of learning within a disciplinary framework. In its simplest form it means understanding what the subject looks like when performed in full and how experts in that field perform with the subject. Having a clear conception of the 'whole game' of your subject, and using it as the foundation of all your planning, is an important part of the approach in this book. If students are to become experts in the subject they need to have the whole game presented to them – or rather 'junior versions' of the whole game, which explain the same core concepts and ideas in a form that is comprehensible to them. A Fertile Question should enshrine an aspect of the whole game (or a 'junior version' of it).

Perhaps the easiest way to explain this is to use two examples from sport:

Example 1: Learning to row (a personal reflection from Oli)

Learning to row is probably my most prominent learning experience. I went from novice to elite in six months – not through some natural talent but through learning the whole game (and training six hours every day).

From the very first day I was rowing a full stroke, not fast, not in a race, but in a boat rowing straight away. I could see how everything fitted together, I knew where the parts of the stroke were, I could not do it and did not know what they were called but I had a vague picture of what the whole stroke looked like. I had watched videos of people rowing and knew exactly what I was aiming for.

If I had spent the first four weeks sitting on a rowing machine learning small sections of the stroke or spending hours on technique, I would have got bored very quickly, but by doing the whole thing I could spend a bit of time working on a small aspect and I could see how that fitted into the rest of the stroke. At the end of each session I felt I had achieved something as I had been *somewhere* and felt like I was an oarsman – albeit a very bad one!

To make rapid progress though I had to be able to deconstruct the stroke and work out what parts were hard for me to do. I had to seek out feedback from coaches and peers, ask them to watch me and watch videos of myself. I could then devote time to practicing them, developing strategies and then placing that back into the whole stroke – talking to myself and monitoring myself as I performed the actions. I could then revise my strategies as I could instantly see if they were solving the problem or not because I knew what the picture of a perfect stroke looked like from the beginning. Telling me I was 70 per cent there was not enough feedback, I needed to know the millimetre precision body movements I needed to make to connect better with the water. I also had to learn to copy, watching experts do it and then copying their body position and movements; listening to them talking about the stroke and then getting them to explain it to me. I had to watch videos of experts and then sit in front of the mirror copying their positions and even their breathing patterns.

But if I was to become an expert it was not enough just to row on the same stretch of water or with the same people, I had to learn to row in different settings, on different types of water, in different types of boat and transfer my learning from setting to setting – how would I adapt my positions to allow for a headwind, a crosswind? To get good quickly I had to learn about the physics of the rowing blade, to understand drag factors and levers, I had to understand biomechanics and psychology – the hidden aspects of a sport. From my first day I was rowing with Olympic and world championship gold medallists. I could watch them, speak to them, row with them and copy their body movements. Every day I would watch videos of people rowing, listen to sound recordings of coaching and race commentary so that I could maximize my learning in a short space of time.

Finally I had to learn how to learn the rowing stroke by myself. I had to diagnose the hard parts for myself – what was I struggling with, what felt wrong; devise the strategies, find the videos and talk to other athletes and review myself as I went through the motions. Every day I had evidence of improvement through the scores on the rowing machine and every day I could evaluate my own performance and draw up targets for the next session – because I always knew what the end goal was and what expertise would look like.

TRAINING ACTIVITY

Playing the whole game (Part 1)

Example 2: Learning to swim

Think back to when you learnt to swim:

- *How did you go about it? What was the process?*

- *Was this a small elements/sections first approach or a whole game approach?*

- *Was it effective?*

Trainer input – playing the whole game[7]

- Anyone who learns to swim already has a mental model of what swimming looks like – seeing other people swim. As soon as you walk into the swimming pool on day one you can see people swimming the whole stroke, and you know why you are there and what you are aiming for – what success looks like.

- Compare this with pupils studying Maths, who very often will begin with limited understanding of what Maths is really for, or how experts in the field demonstrate mathematical understanding or apply it to solving problems.

- So what students need is to be able to have a picture of the whole game of their subject and then be able to play 'junior versions' within it. This is not dumbing down or removing the challenge, but is very much in the spirit of Bruner – 'We begin with the hypothesis that any subject can be taught effectively in some intellectually honest form to any child at any stage of development.'[8]

- Practising kicking and breathing is a junior version – you are coordinating movements to replicate the whole game. You are fitting in smaller pieces to the bigger picture – you know why you are kicking or breathing and you regularly practice them within the whole game of swimming. You do not just do some kicking, get assessed on how well you kick whilst holding onto the side and then move on and never kick again!

- From the very beginning you are putting the pieces together in a junior version that stops you from drowning but that still involves the whole game.

TRAINING ACTIVITY

Playing the whole game (Part 2)

i.   *What does playing the whole game mean within your subject area?*

ii.   *How do academics/experts play the whole game in your subject area?*

iii. *What junior versions of these games exist in your area?*

The theory of transfer: Does learning currently travel with our students between classrooms?

One of the major problems faced by schools is how to ensure that what a student learns in one lesson helps them to learn in another. Unfortunately, too often this 'transfer' does not take place. Indeed, one of the major problems with 'Learning to Learn' programmes and other such schemes is that students learn to use thinking-skills in a Learning to Learn lesson, but very rarely does this skill transfer to other areas. To expand: [9]

> Both the meaning and the challenge of "transfer of learning" are well-expressed in a story told to one of us by a disappointed professor of physics at a nearby college. Amongst the stock problems explored in the physics course was one like this: "A ball weighing three kilograms is dropped from the top of a hundred meter tower. How many seconds does it take to reach the ground?" (Aficionados of physics will recognize that the weight of the ball has nothing to do with the problem; it is a distraction. The answer depends only on the acceleration of gravity.)
>
> On the final exam, the professor included a problem like this: "There is a one-hundred-meter hole in the ground. A ball weighing three kilograms is rolled off the side into the hole. How long does it take to reach the bottom?" Some students did not recognize the connection between the "tower" problem and the "hole" problem. One student even came up after the exam and accosted the professor with a complaint. "I think that this exam was unfair," the student wailed. "We never had any *hole* problems!"
>
> Two points become plain from this anecdote. First of all, it tells us what transfer means. The term "transfer" applies when something learned in one situation gets carried over to another – in this case, from the context of "tower" problems to the context of "hole" problems. Second, the anecdote warns us that all is not well with transfer. Very often, in instructional settings (and in everyday life) we do not get the transfer we want. Learners acquire skills and knowledge in one situation and fail to make connections to other situations where those skills and knowledge would prove valuable.

The best way for students to make connections and transfer knowledge from one classroom to another is for them to have a deep understanding of the knowledge in the first place, and then to be accustomed to applying that knowledge to new, unforeseen problems. The students in Perkins' example above are used to being given the answer and then repeating it, not to operating on the knowledge they are given and creating new ideas. So, knowledge transfer links to the Harpaz diagram above, and to our concept of teaching for understanding.

An everyday example of transfer from life in Oli's house

> The other day I was preparing my daughter's bottle before she went to bed. I was scooping the powder into the water when I noticed that the scoop had two very small holes in the bottom of it. My initial thought was 'how stupid, surely the powder falls out of those'. A brief second later however my knowledge of vacuums kicked in and I thought 'well, maybe those holes are there to prevent a small vacuum being created and stopping the powder falling out of the scoop and into the bottle'. I have no idea why the holes are there and I may well be way off the mark, but I was able to reach a fairly sound hypothesis by applying learning from physics to my everyday question.

This is the transfer of learning the whole-school approach seeks to create.

A recent research paper by the Task Group on Learning Processes for the US Department of Education, focusing on cognition in Maths again highlighted the central role that conceptual understanding plays in long-term progression and understanding. The excerpt below summarizes their findings.

> **Conceptual understanding promotes transfer of learning to new problems and better long-term retention.** Research has demonstrated that factors that enhance initial acquisition are not necessarily the same as those that maximize long-term retention (i.e., that minimize forgetting). For example, material that is too easy to understand can promote initial acquisition or learning, but it leads to lower retention than material that is harder to understand initially (e.g., Bjork, 1994). Challenging material causes the learner to exert more attentional effort and to actively process information, leading to superior retention. Similarly, transfer of learning is promoted by deeper conceptual understanding of learned material. Although this phenomenon was demonstrated in the early work of Gestalt psychologists (e.g., Wertheimer, 1959), it has since been verified repeatedly (for illustrative empirical studies on transfer and reviews of such studies, see Bassok & Holyoak, 1989; Reed, 1993; Wolfe, Reyna, & Brainerd, 2005). Transfer of learning refers to the ability to correctly apply one's learning beyond the exact examples studied to superficially similar problems (near transfer) or to superficially dissimilar problems (far transfer). Surprisingly, instruction using more abstract representations has been shown in some instances to benefit learning and transfer more than concrete examples (e.g., physical

representations, such as manipulatives) (e.g., Sloutsky, Kaminski, & Heckler, 2005; Uttal, 2003). Thus, the cognitive processes that facilitate rote retention (e.g., of over-learned arithmetic facts), such as repeated practice, can differ from the processes that facilitate transfer and long-term retention, such as conceptual understanding....Research has shown that there is much room for improvement in students' metacognitive judgments because they rely on misleading assumptions about their learning (e.g., using misleading cues such as retrieval fluency and familiarity, which are not perfectly correlated with strength of learning; see Benjamin, Bjork, & Schwartz, 1998).[10]

Stage 4: Disciplinary thinking

Now that we have looked at planning for progression and understanding we need to add in another piece of the jigsaw. This is the idea of disciplinary thinking and how to build it into to our classrooms.

What is disciplinary thinking?[11]

- The sad truth is that most students probably see themselves as only studying subject information and see their main task as committing to memory what the teacher tells them they need to 'know' and regurgitating it in the exam hall.

- Disciplinary thinking is the exact opposite – a discipline constitutes a way of thinking about the world and an understanding of the distinctive, disciplinary concepts that turn subject information into useable knowledge. This is the idea of application rather than acquisition.

- Whilst a student needs subject information to study Science, History, Maths, etc. – divorced of their connections to one another, or to underlying questions, or to a disciplined way of construing this pile of information, facts are simply 'inert knowledge'. A fact only becomes 'useful' when it can be applied to a problem that has relevance to the way experts solve problems in the real world.

- So, students and teachers must see information not as an end in itself but as a vital piece of the jigsaw in enabling thinking in a disciplined manner.

- The role of the teacher is to act in part as coach – providing feedback on their students' ability to pick up the distinctive habits of mind and behaviour of the professional; and part as co-explorer, delighting in the journey one step at a time.

- In disciplinary thinking there is a primacy placed on concepts – the developed and accepted structural ideas that form the underlying principles of a domain or subject. These are the same concepts that are used by experts within that field.

Thus the progressive character of modern sciences and disciplines is also characteristic of knowledge building pedagogy. This does not mean that students are expected to produce an original theory of gravitation to stand alongside Newton's. Rather, what they produce would likely be consistent with Newton but enriched by insights that made gravitational theory come alive for them and made it something they could apply to new problems of understanding. Considerable original scientific thought on the part of the students will have gone into such a product. (Centuries elapsed between Newton and Einstein, yet creative scientific work was being done throughout that period; so we should not expect students to do better than that in a school term.)[12]

In the words of Gardner:

In contrast to the naïve student or information-crammed but still ignorant adult, an expert is a person who really does think differently about his or her specialty….Expertise generally arises as a result of several years of sustained work within a domain, discipline or craft, often courtesy of a traditional apprenticeship. Part of that training involves the elimination of habits and concepts that, however attractive to the naïve person, are actually inimical to the skilled practice of a discipline or craft. And the remaining part of that training involves the construction of habits and concepts that reflect the best contemporary thinking and practices of the domain. (Gardner 2000)

So, put simply, thinking in a disciplined manner means adopting the ways of thinking, talking and 'being' that experts within that field use to make sense of their subject or area of expertise. This approach is supported by our use of Fertile Questions as a planning tool. Fertile Questions provide the framework for students to immerse themselves in problems that experts in that field are working on. These questions help students to develop the conceptual understandings that make thinking like a scientist different from thinking like a historian.

What does this look like in the 'real world'? An analogy on teaching for understanding through concepts

I was watching master chef last night and it got me thinking – their (top chefs) model of learning is an interesting one. They put absolute importance on classical knowledge – flavours, textures, combinations, history behind the recipes, etc. but then expect the chef to use this knowledge to invent new methods and dishes through synthesizing, combining and inventing. This is an example of disciplinary thinking and thinking flexibly with it. This is a bit like in medicine where doctors have to know the 'facts' but then recognize that each patient presents in a different way and you have to be able to think flexibly with your core medical 'facts' to make a diagnosis. Thus they use structural concepts to help frame knowledge.

This is probably where I see the role of academic subjects in the twenty-first century. They equip you with rules and ways of thinking but you need to be flexible with this so you are not only aware of how you are thinking in a given context, but also aware of its limitations and the need for alternative rules or strategies. (Oli in conversation with his [slightly bored] wife, 2012.)

Jerome Bruner sums it up perfectly:

The curriculum of a subject should be determined by the most fundamental understanding that can be achieved of the underlying principles that give structure to a subject. Teaching specific topics or skills without making clear their context in the broader fundamental structure of a field of knowledge is uneconomical. ... An understanding of fundamental principles and ideas appears to be the main road to adequate transfer of training. **To understand something as a specific instance of a more general case— which is what understanding a more fundamental structure means—is to have learned not only a specific thing but also a model for understanding other things like it that one may encounter.**[13]

How to embed disciplinary thinking

i. The approaches outlined in this handbook are the best way to enable disciplinary thinking to take place – by considering the whole game of your subject, by teaching for understanding not recitation, and by using Fertile Questions as a way of enabling 'an apprenticeship in thinking' to happen.

ii. At the end of a Fertile Question, set up Performances of Understanding and give students ample opportunities to perform their understandings under a variety of conditions – the only reliable way to determine whether understanding has truly been achieved is to pose a *new* question or puzzle – one on which students could not have been coached – and to see how they fare.

iii. Research (Willingham, 2007) also suggests that special thinking-skills programmes are not worth it: despite their widespread availability, the evidence that thinking programmes succeed in teaching students to think critically, especially in novel situations, is very limited. Indeed, thinking critically should be taught in the context of subject matter. This does not mean that teachers should not teach students to think critically – it means that critical thinking should not be taught on its own. People do not spontaneously examine assumptions that underlie their thinking, try to consider all sides of an issue, question what they know, etc. These things must be modelled for students, and students must be given opportunities to practice – preferably in the context of normal classroom activity. For example, an important part of thinking like a historian is considering the source of a document – *who wrote it, when, and why*. But teaching students to ask those questions, independent of subject matter knowledge, will not do much good. Knowing that a letter was written by a Confederate private to his wife in New Orleans just after the Battle of Vicksburg will not help the student interpret the letter unless he knows something of US Civil War history.[14]

It should be clear now why a 'fact-based' approach will make even less sense in the future. One can never attain a disciplined mind simply by mastering facts – one must immerse oneself deeply in the specifics of cases and develop one's disciplinary muscles from such immersion. Moreover, in the future, desired facts, definitions, lists, and details will literally be at one's fingertips: Either one will be able to type out a brief command on a hand-held computer or one may even be able simply to blurt aloud, 'What is the capital of Estonia?' Sheer memorization will be anachronistic; it will be necessary only to show students their way around the current version of Encarta. Increasingly, the art of teaching will inhere in aiding students to acquire the moves and the insights of major disciplinary fields.[15]

What does the new economic landscape suggest?[16]

The trends in this diagram are clear. As the demand in the job market for routine cognitive tasks decline and complex communication and expert thinking rises, disciplinary thinking will be more and more important. If

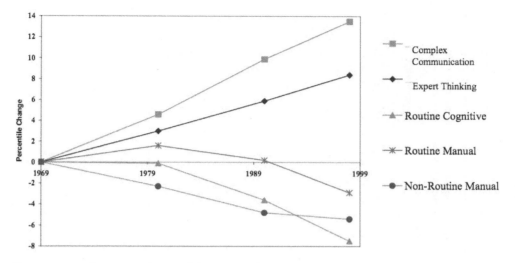

Figure 1.7   Change in demand for types of job

education is to be future-proof and we are to realize its democratic promise, schools will need to maintain a focus on teaching students to think in a disciplined manner rather than to either learn lots of facts and regurgitate them, or 'learn to learn' but never be able to fit what they are learning into a structural framework so it actually makes sense and has explanatory power or provides them with the ability to transfer those skills to new or novel situations. Learning how to balance your cheque book but being unable to explain why history never repeats itself, or the place of God in our universe, is not going to have a transformative effect on your life (or indeed your finances).

Planning for progression in disciplinary thinking

The planning grid on the next page is taken from Peter Lee, probably one of the leading experts in the world on developing conceptual understandings in education. The grid forms part of the planning process for each Fertile Question and ensures that a disciplinary perspective is built in.

Once this type of thinking has become a 'no brainer' it is possible to stop completing the grid and to streamline the planning process. However, it is advisable to maintain use of the grid until this is the case as the thinking involved is complex at first and the structure of the grid is a helpful tool.

Disciplinary planning grid[17]

Fertile Question (based around a conceptual understanding)	Core content and target generalizations to be taught	Target ideas to be taught about core conceptual understanding	Preconceptions to be checked out	Key conceptual understandings to be taught	Metacognitive questions we want pupils to develop/grapple with
For example, if it is a 'how do we know' type question then the teaching will need to focus on the concept of evidence relevant to that subject domain.	*Residual knowledge – in six months' time what things do we want pupils to remember/feel about the topic? What knowledge do they need in order to be able to apply it to new settings later on in the curriculum?*	*What are we aiming for in terms of conceptual progression? For example, an evidence focused enquiry might have a target of enabling pupils to see that explanations of why people do things are not always the same as explanations of why things happen.*	*What likely preconceptions might we encounter about the conceptual understanding that will need to be addressed before we can continue with our target focus? For example, many pupils believe that we can only know what happened if we were there or if we read the eyewitness account of someone else.*	*What is the core concept? What will mastery look like?*	*What questions do pupils need to ask themselves to monitor their own progress through the Fertile Question?*

Example disciplinary planning grid for Fertile Question 'What made Cromwell tick?'

Fertile Question (based around a conceptual understanding)	Core content and target generalizations to be taught	Target ideas to be taught about core conceptual understanding	Preconceptions to be checked out	Key conceptual understandings to be taught	Metacognitive questions we want pupils to develop/grapple with
For example, if it is a 'how do we know' type question then the teaching will need to focus on the concept of evidence relevant to that subject domain.	*Residual knowledge – in six months' time what things do we want pupils to remember/feel about the topic? What knowledge do they need in order to be able to apply it to new settings later on in the curriculum?*	*What are we aiming for in terms of conceptual progression? For example, an evidence focused enquiry might have a target of enabling pupils to see that explanations of why people do things are not always the same as explanations of why things happen.*	*What likely preconceptions might we encounter about the conceptual understanding that will need to be addressed before we can continue with our target focus? For example, many pupils believe that we can only know what happened if we were there or if we read the eyewitness account of someone else.*	*What is the core concept? What will mastery look like?*	*What questions do pupils need to ask themselves to monitor their own progress through the Fertile Question?*
What made Cromwell tick? (Was there a continuity of aspiration in Cromwell's vision for England?) *Concept = change and continuity.*	*i. Cromwell's reign and his relationship with Parliament.* *ii. The relationship between Cromwell and his religion.* *iii. The status of religion in England at this time.*	*To enable pupils to see that change does not always lead to progress.* *To enable pupils to see that continuity for one group in society can mean change for another.*	*Change means progress and as we progress through time things change for the better.* *Change is the intentional outcome of human actions.*	*Change and continuity – the change lurking within the continuity.* *Mastery = analysing the extent and nature of change for different groups and the locomotive for that change.*	*Are change and/or continuity constant?* *Is change happening for all groups or just a few?* *Is the change/continuity determined by agents or accidental?*

So, there are a number of underlying principles that must be embedded at the curriculum planning and design stage to allow for deep learning and conceptual understanding to occur. Now that we have seen what these principles are we can go on to look at the best way of implanting them within the school and ensuring that all teachers use the same planning framework.

Stage 5: Fertile Questions – planning for progression in understanding

Now that we have looked at a complex model of learning and understanding, we are going to look at a simple but flexible way of embedding this approach to understanding across all classrooms and subjects.

The Fertile Question – what is it?

> Most people teach Biology by starting with the molecule! This is exactly the wrong way to go. No one cares about the molecule. I don't care about the molecule. Unless I have a reason to care – that is, a problem that I am working on that requires understanding molecules to address it. (E.O. Wilson, Professor of Biology, Harvard University.)

We would argue that planning a curriculum around Fertile Questions is the best way to train students to think in a disciplined manner.

- A Fertile Question is a planning device for knitting together a sequence of lessons, so that all of the learning activities – teacher exposition, narrative, source-work, role-play, plenary – all move towards the resolution of an interesting and meaningful *historical/scientific/mathematical/RE* problem by means of a substantial motivating activity at the end.

- Planning using Fertile Questions prevents the curriculum from becoming a series of isolated 'bore holes' or bits of information taught but not connected. It allows for a thread to be created across all areas of the curriculum – the thread of enquiry learning, and thinking in a disciplined manner – and allows for students to develop a meaningful and useable framework for each subject.

- Fertile Questions allow students to replicate the thoughts and actions of experts within that field. They create opportunities for students to see how knowledge has been created and how it is often contested whilst enabling them to apply knowledge to solving meaningful problems.

- Fertile Questions are naturally engaging – questions demand answers and problems, solutions. They do not focus on 'learning' snippets of information but on turning information into knowledge through applying it to a problem and testing how far it resolves that problem or tension.

- An approach based around a Fertile Question engages pupils and helps them to see the links between concepts and knowledge. It also goes beyond traditional models and instead promotes the idea that the enquiry is a journey that helps pupils to *think* historically, *think* scientifically, *think* geographically, *think* mathematically.

In other words, the approach addresses the importance of balancing students' knowledge of facts against their understanding of concepts. In History they are learning about change and cause not just dates and events. It helps teachers transform straightforward science experiments into a true understanding of scientific principles in the way that a scientist at CERN might apply them. In Maths it balances the quest for absolutes with the need for multiple approaches.

Fertile Questions are helpful because they put the teacher and the student on the same intellectual plane. 'OK class, I genuinely don't know the answer to this question, but over the next six weeks we are going to puzzle it out together; maybe we should look at this, maybe that, but I'm going to need your help and your ideas to do it' (or something like that). They are an equalizing force – this makes it much easier to model the kind of thinking and intellectual habits we want from the students, and much safer for them to ask questions and take risks.

Designing a Fertile Question

The key to designing a good Fertile Question is to ensure that it is connected to both the students' current thinking *and* the desired kind of thinking – that of expert practitioners. Just as with a good lesson plan, it starts with what the students can currently do and explores what they need to be able to do next – framed as a problem to be solved. Scardamalia is clear why it is much more powerful to use a problem as the focus of a Fertile Question.

Although problems are often expressed as questions, we have found that pursuing solutions to problems rather than answers to questions best encourages knowledge building. Answers have a certain finality to them, whereas problem solutions are generally continually improvable. Whereas comparing answers to questions puts students into the belief mode, solutions to problems, including solutions to knowledge problems, can be carried out in design mode—judging what different solutions do and do not accomplish, what new problems a solution raises and what problems need to be solved in order to progress in solving the main problem. Knowledge Building pedagogy differs from Problem-Based Learning in that the preferred problems are ones of considerable generality.[18]

Summary of design principles[19]

i. Start with a BIG, essential question that is debated in the world and is used by practitioners of the discipline. In other words a question that a professional mathematician or historian might ask before venturing into the unknown for answers.

ii. It is essential that the question is framed within the concept it is focused on. For example a Fertile Question about evidence will revolve around a *How do we know* type question or a Fertile Question about perspective will revolve around *developing multiple perspectives on the problem presented.*

iii. Identify a concluding activity that requires a constructed response to the question (a *performance of understanding*) that will create a tangible product that solves the problem posed by the question.

iv. Plan backwards from the end product by deciding what activities will develop the conceptual understandings and abilities essential to address the question and create a meaningful response to it. What needs to happen in each phase to allow for resolution of the problem?

The eight stages of the Fertile Question[20]

One of the reasons why Fertile Questions provide such leverage is because they emphasize the aspects of learning that make the most difference to student progress. The main focus is on developing student metacognition by constantly providing opportunities for reflection and discussion about *how* as well as *what*, and on providing opportunities for a constant feedback cycle to be built in to the process. The focus of this feedback is always against the criteria outlined at the beginning of the enquiry, and focuses on the three key factors: *Where am I going, how am I doing, where to next?*

Once you have created your Fertile Question, you need to follow the eight stages below:

i.   Introduce the new Fertile Question – engage and motivate pupils, discover what they already know and check out their existing preconceptions. Outline and focus on the concept that frames the question and plan to build on their current thinking. Make this known to the pupils and set clear outcomes and challenging goals; acceleration happens when expectations are high. You can activate undergraduate level thinking in Year 8 students by creating a Fertile Question that creates a junior version of an expert problem.

ii. Allow pupils to decide what research question(s) they might like to formulate that answers the Fertile Question. This does not always have to be co-constructed and can be teacher set. This stage enables metacognition by allowing students to work out where they are and what they need to do next. This stage needs to be carefully planned for to allow for a reduction in scaffolding over time. This stage also consists of direct instruction – giving students the fingertip knowledge they need to solve the problem; moving from acquisition to application.

iii. Start the process of enquiry with a focus on dialogue not monologue – *what small questions do we need to answer to formulate a response to the BIG question; can we divide the BIG question up; what happens if we disagree; where might we go for information; what will we do if we get stuck; how will we know if we are on the right track; how much information do we need; how do we turn the information into knowledge; what language is essential to answering the question; how are we going to display our thinking; what are the success criteria; who is the intended audience; what is the purpose of this piece of learning?* Use strategies like reciprocal teaching and Home and Expert groups to enable meaningful dialogue to occur.

iv. Come back as a whole class to discuss findings so far and any problems that have arisen. Use teacher and peer review to critique current thinking and plan where to go next to ensure the problem posed by the question is solved.

v.   Create an initial (draft) response to the question in groups or individually – using tentative answers and provocative feedback to encourage deeper reflection (Oral rehearsal). Use this stage to model and deconstruct the language required to replicate 'expertise'.

vi. Follow this with peer review and redrafting of the first draft in light of feedback, moving from everyday to more formal language.

vii. Ask groups/individuals to give a concluding performance of the solution to the problem. Use a real (peer, teacher) or virtual (ICT) audience to give the response meaning and purpose.

viii. The final stage should be a class concluding performance and feedback/ review – *can we settle on one final answer, what does this prepare us to do next?*

What does a good performance of understanding look like?

As outlined earlier, the work of both Perkins and Harpaz suggests that knowing is when you can think and act flexibly with the knowledge you have acquired – applying it to an unseen problem or case. The key word then is *performance;* it must require the students to do something – preferably something new. So, the performance of understanding must be more than recital or rewording. It must require students to be able to demonstrate that they can use and apply, not replicate. It should require them to (amongst other things and not all at the same time):

● synthesize

● predict

● critique

● construct/create something new

● question

● interpret.

It is important that the culminating piece of work is something you can *see, hear or read.* It is equally crucial that not all Humanities questions finish with an essay and all Maths questions finish with some questions to answer! How can we assess understanding and thinking if it is a representation of the work and thinking of the teacher? Instead the role of the teacher throughout the different stages of a Fertile Question is a changing one – see the diagram on page 84.

The six principles of a good Fertile Question:[21]

i. **An open question.** A question that in principle has no one definitive answer; rather, it has several different and competing possible answers.

ii. **An undermining question.** A question that undermines the learners' basic assumptions, casts doubt on the self-evident or commonsensical, uncovers basic conflicts lacking a simple solution, and requires the critical consideration of origins.

iii. **A rich question.** A question that necessitates grappling with rich content that is indispensable to understanding humanity and the world around us. Students cannot answer this question without careful and lengthy research; such research tends to break the question into sub-questions.

iv. **A connected question.** A question relevant to the learners, the society in which they live, and the discipline and field they are studying.

v. **A charged question.** A question with an ethical dimension. Such questions are charged with emotional, social, and political implications that potentially motivate inquiry and learning.

vi. **A practical question.** A question that can be researched in the context of the learners, facilitators, and school facilities and from which research questions may be derived.

Why Fertile Questions?

The graph on the next page is a model of the Ebbinghaus Forgetting Curve. The graph displays what happens to information we have received over a period of 31 days. As you can see most of the information is lost unless it is revisited and used in multiple contexts. This idea will be revisited later on in the reading section of the handbook.

Fertile Questions are a way of overcoming this curve by forcing students to constantly revisit prior learning and use what they have learnt previously to help them answer other smaller lesson questions, which are building towards the resolution of the BIG Fertile Question.

Or, to look at it another way, what might a five-stage sequence look like?

Figure 1.9 is designed to be an antidote to the familiar but misplaced cries that 'I have to get through the content, so I do not have time for all this fancy stuff'. By following this pathway you will find that your students not only learn more 'content' but that they can use it to solve unseen problems – the true test of understanding.

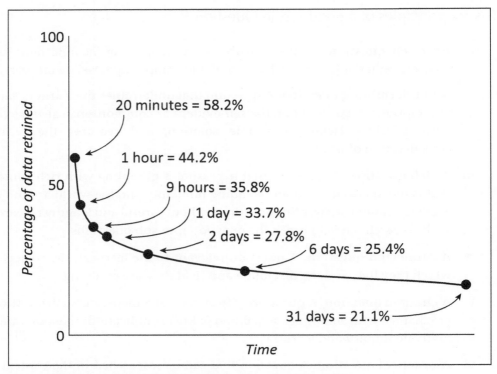

Figure 1.8 A model of the Ebbinghaus Forgetting Curve[22]

Introduce the Fertile Question and the scope of the enquiry. Use the Fertile Question as a hook - to engage and intrigue. Make links back to previous learning and forward to future learning.

Check out pre-conceptions - what pupils currently think about the core concepts and what the disciplinary rules are - and give the BIG picture and purpose of this piece of learning.

Develop the research questions - the small questions that answer the BIG question - led either by pupils or the teacher. Use this stage to further clarify learning intentions. Each small question becomes a lesson.

Start the enquiry process - using talk-based activities to elicit evidence of learning. Use talk as a process to discuss current understandings. Co-construct success criteria. The role of teacher is to focus on pupil miscues and provide constant feedback as pupils start to devise answers.

Use learners as a resource for each other - pupils decide how they can best display learning: what will be their concluding performance, where will they go for information/help/feedback?

Come back as a whole class to discuss findings and review learning so far - using talk as performance before moving into writing at a later stage.
Have we answered the question? What else do we need to do?

Use peer review of talk as performance and redraft in light of feedback.
Does it solve the problem?
Why have they said what they said? Does their evidence support their judgement?
Start joint construction of text - oral or written. Use provocative feedback to deepen thinking and challenge.

Organize a group or individual concluding performance - either using a real (teacher or peers) or virtual (ICT) audience to give the task meaning.

Judge performances against success criteria. Feedback and review.
How might this new knowledge be applied in different situations?

Figure 1.9 The journey through the Fertile Question

Stage 1
- Introduce the new problem or question and the scope of the enquiry. Use the Fertile Question as a hook - to engage and intrigue. Make links back to previous learning and forward to future learning.
- Check out pre-conceptions - what pupils currently think about the core concepts and give the BIG picture and purpose of this piece of learning: what are we learning to do and how will we assess competence?
- Start the enquiry process - using talk-based activities to elicit evidence of prior learning. Use talk as process to discuss current understandings of the concept and content. Co-construct success criteria.
- Pupils decide how they can best generate understanding: where will they go for information/help/feedback? What is the process going to be for them?

Stage 2
- Equip learners with the fingertip knowledge they need to solve the problem.
- Ensure learners are aware of the conceptual framework and understand the role the new learning will play in exploring this framework.
- Equip learners with the language to explore the topic.
- Ensure the factual knowledge required is framed as a problem to be solved.
- Teach by asking - create puzzles and model ways of solving them. Think with, not for, the students

Stage 3
- Are there opportunities for students to practice working with and on the knowledge they have been processing?
- Can learners self-monitor? Are there opportunities for them to reflect on their work and improve it?
- Are you using a variety of performance opportunities to allow learners to demonstrate understanding, or is it just more writing?
- Students create initial responses to the assessment.

Stage 4
- Peer review draft responses using talk as performance and subsequently redraft in light of feedback.
- Can learners reflect on where they currently are and what they need to do next?
- Does their response solve the problem?
- Why have they said what they said?
- Does their evidence support their judgement?
- This leads into joint construction of text - oral or written. Use provocative teacher feedback to deepen thinking and challenge before final assessment.

Stage 5
- Organize a group or individual concluding performance - either using a real (teacher or peers) or virtual (ICT) audience to give the task meaning.
- Judge performances against success criteria. Feedback and review.
- How might this new knowledge be applied in different situations?
- How does the performance demonstrated link back to the previous learning and prepare learners for the next stage? End with a question mark not a full stop.
- Is feedback from the learners being used as a planning tool for the next episode?

Figure 1.10 A five-stage sequence for using a Fertile Question

Another way to conceive of the journey through a Fertile Question is described here:

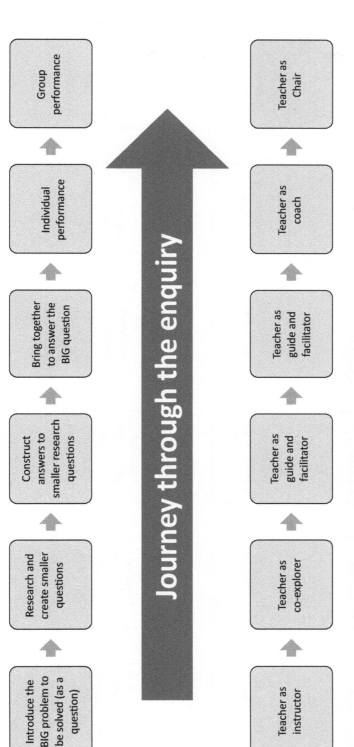

Figure 1.11 An alternative diagram of the journey through a Fertile Question

And here with an example from a GCSE English enquiry on *Macbeth*:

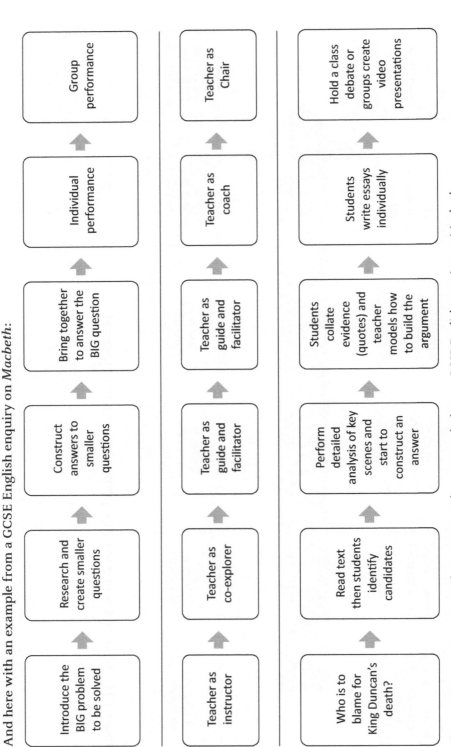

| Introduce the BIG problem to be solved | → | Research and create smaller questions | → | Construct answers to smaller questions | → | Bring together to answer the BIG question | → | Individual performance | → | Group performance |

| Teacher as instructor | → | Teacher as co-explorer | → | Teacher as guide and facilitator | → | Teacher as guide and facilitator | → | Teacher as coach | → | Teacher as Chair |

| Who is to blame for King Duncan's death? | → | Read text then students identify candidates | → | Perform detailed analysis of key scenes and start to construct an answer | → | Students collate evidence (quotes) and teacher models how to build the argument | → | Students write essays individually | → | Hold a class debate or groups create video presentations |

Figure 1.12 Demonstrating the journey with an example from a GCSE English enquiry on *Macbeth*.

And here is a final table that can help with planning Fertile Questions. This one is designed to promote high-cognitive pathways through the enquiry.

Designing high-cognitive pathways[23]

Types of cognition (thinking)	Apply	Analyse	Evaluate	Create	Present
Types of teaching activities (doing)	• Sketch • Manipulate • Experiment • Report • Record • Classify • Draw comparison • Simulate	• Classify • Categorize • Compare • Contrast • Diagram • Identify characteristics	• Judge • Discuss • Debate • Editorial • Rank • Consider	• Combine • Invent • Estimate • Predict • Design • Imagine • Speculate	• Observe • Identify • Listen • Sort/sequence • Match • Discuss • Restate
Types of knowledge outcome (applying)	• To construct a model • To generalize • To give reasons to knowledge	• To analyse knowledge • To bring example, to invent metaphor, to make comparison • To explain knowledge • To find contradictions or tensions in knowledge	• To imply knowledge • To question knowledge • To expose the basic assumptions of knowledge	• To synthesize knowledge • To formulate counter-knowledge • To generate new knowledge • To predict on the basis of knowledge	• To express knowledge in your own words • To present knowledge in various ways • To present knowledge from different perspectives
Types of end product/ assessment (creating)	• Model • Map/mind map • Board game • Diagram • Graphic organizer	• Graph • Report • Chart • Essay	• Report • Review • Advise • Recommendation	• Poem • Pantomime • News story • Cartoon • Song	• Radio broadcast/podcast • Diagram • Model • Storyboard • Role-play

Planning a Fertile Question – a detailed example

The grid below is the lesson sequence described in Case study 1 earlier in the book. Each lesson is framed by a small research question that helps students develop the thinking required to resolve the problem posed by the Fertile Question. These smaller lesson or research questions were devised by the teacher in advance.

Fertile Question:

Dysfunctional Socialism: Does the desire to make all men equal have to lead to murder?

Lesson question (sequence of ten lessons)	Main themes and outcomes
i. *Who was Karl Marx and why was he so important to the development of the twentieth century?*	• Was Marxist political theory a pipe dream or an effective programme? • Use a song by the Manic Street Preachers – deconstruct it and ask why they are singing about Marxist theory. What can we learn about Marx's theories from this? • Explore Marx the man and his writings. Get them to draw a picture of what they think he looks like, compare it to the real man. Get them intrigued by him as a person. • Students are equipped with the knowledge of Marxism, and its perception, which they will need to grapple with the issues thrown up by the next five lessons.

ii. *What role has Marx played in the twentieth century?*	• Having looked at the background theory of Marx, pupils now need a familiar hook on which to hang their new knowledge. The Bolsheviks' seizure of power seemed ideal and would also form a great bridge into the Khmer Rouge next lesson.
	 • Who were the Bolsheviks and what did they believe in?
	 • Who were the Khmer Rouge and what did they believe in?
	 • Introduction of the comparative nature of the enquiry. Also use this to look at the Russian versus the Chinese models of Communism. The Khmer Rouge were influenced by the Chinese model.
	     ○ Students begin to consider questions such as: Is Marxism flawed?
	     ○ Beginnings of the similarities between the two processes.
	     ○ Why has the work of Marx been interpreted differently?

iii.	*Is socialism installed by force really socialism?*	• Card sort on the Khmer Rouge seizure of power and its similarities to the Bolshevik seizure of power. • Make their own cards on the Bolshevik revolution and colour-code them to show the similarities to and differences from Pol Pot's seizure of power. • Link back to last lesson to answer the lesson question. Was the Bolshevik or Khmer Rouge seizure of power Marxism in action or the destruction of his life's work? • Students reflect on the role of external forces – especially foreign powers – in the path to dictatorship, and on whether Marxism is just a front.
iv.	*The devil incarnate?*	• How similar were the journeys to power of Stalin and Pol Pot? • What influenced them? • Did these two personalities make it inevitable that mass murder would ensue?
v.	*The enemy within: how did Stalin and Pol Pot secure their positions?*	• Students consider the human cost of the two dictatorships and the similarities between the two regimes. • Did they both use purges and state murder to secure political and cultural hegemony? • Students then revisit the Marxist theory they both used – how was it applied? • Is Marxism a byword for violence and death – or did these leaders use it as an excuse?
vi.	*An inevitable tragedy?*	• Why did both dictatorships lead to mass murder? Can Marxist society ever be just? Does Marx have blood on his hands?
vii.	*Cambodia and the West: how does Hollywood remember the past?*	• How does Hollywood present controversial and emotionally charged subjects? • The role of the West as portrayed through Western film. Orientalism and the creation of opposites and of right and wrong from a Western perspective. Does Hollywood choose to ignore America's role in the Cambodian Genocide?
viii.	*How should we view the writings of Karl Marx?*	Why does Marx have the reputation he has and how just is it?

TRAINING ACTIVITY

Planning a Fertile Question:

i. *Is there a clear sequence to the lesson questions?*

ii. *Can you see a link between lessons?*

iii. *Is it obvious how the lessons guide the students to a resolution?*

iv. *The last two lessons have been deliberately left off. How would you plan to assess understanding of the Fertile Question at the end of the lesson sequence?*

In our second case study, we look at how a subject leader in Ark Academy set about using the Fertile Questions approach to design a Key Stage 3 Mathematics curriculum. It looks in depth at the thinking, problems and solutions involved in teaching through Fertile Questions to move beyond surface understanding to a model that enables conceptual understandings to develop.

Case study 2: Fertility in the Maths Department – structuring a curriculum around Fertile Questions

(First published in *Ark Academy case studies 2012*)
Aishling Ryan | Director of Maths | Ark Academy

Context

This case study aims to explore whether teaching through Fertile Questions can enhance student progress in Mathematics. It is divided into four main sections:

- The vision: what we mean by 'Fertile Questions' and what we hoped they would achieve;

- 'Fertility' in the Maths department: the process of developing a Mathematics curriculum centred on Fertile Questions;

- Teaching the big 'why?': our experience of developing an enquiry classroom;

- The results: students' reactions, and the discernible impact on their attainment and progress.

Fertile Questions and the vision of our school

A new school offers the opportunity to do something truly special. All the obstacles to change and innovation are blown away. As a senior team, we talked about the kind of students we wanted to develop at Ark Academy. Together, we looked at the work of Professor Guy Claxton, and his idea of a 'Learner Profile'. Claxton talks about eight habits of mind[24] successful learners need to develop: they should be curious, courageous, exploratory, experimental, imaginative, reasoned and disciplined, and sociable and reflective.

To achieve this we knew that a fully integrated approach was necessary. All aspects of the system – teaching and learning, assessment, staff training, behaviour and rewards, etc. – needed to pull in the same direction. This case study is concerned with just one aspect – that of using 'Fertile Questions' as a framework for planning lessons. I will describe what I mean by Fertile Questions, and then how we implemented them within the Maths department.

A Fertile Question is:

> A planning device for knitting together a sequence of lessons, so that all of the learning activities – teacher exposition, narrative, source-work, role-play, plenary – all move towards the resolution of an interesting historical/scientific/mathematical/RE problem by means of substantial motivating activity at the end.[25]

It is a rich, open, engaging question which takes students on a journey of enquiry, and away from the idea of rote learning.

Studying a Fertile Question over a period of weeks helps students see the link between the knowledge they are learning and the key concepts of the subject. Enquiries help students to *think* mathematically, *think* historically, *think* scientifically, *think* geographically, and so on. They engage and motivate students *(what is a healthy life?)*, and help them to see the big ideas of the subject *(whose story does history tell?)*.

When I heard about Fertile Questions as an approach to lesson planning it immediately resonated with me. Like all great ideas, I did not know how I had not thought of it before. Intuitively it made sense – give students the big picture, teach them to explore the key questions, and then construct authentic answers. And it was not a total departure from how I had done things previously. Questioning is at the heart of effective teaching – this was hardly a revolution. On page one of *The Republic* Socrates encourages his students to debate, *'Is it always better to be just than unjust?'* That is a Fertile Question if ever there was one.

From theory to practice

I was excited by the ideas and the possibilities for our students. In many ways, this was the kind of teaching I had always dreamed of doing. With the other Core Directors and members of the Senior Team we thrashed out what enquiry learning would look like in practice – how you explain Fertile Questions to students, how you deliver them over a series of lessons and how you help students formulate their answers. Important to us at this stage was the work of Adam Lefstein, an Institute of Education researcher whose book about enquiry learning, *Communities of Thinking*, had been taken up by twelve schools in Israel. We attended a Lefstein training session in the summer term. He said: 'The ability to pose questions to understand ourselves and our world is at the heart of what it means to be human...{however} questioning has some paradoxical characteristics that suggest its potentially powerful, yet problematic, role in pedagogy'.[26]

Problematic was an understatement. Creating the right Fertile Questions was extremely challenging. My first concern was that there was no research on or examples of using an enquiry approach specifically when teaching *Mathematics*. The sole reference to Maths I had come across during our training was the charged and controversial question: 'Is beauty mathematical?' It is a great question, and I could see how it would help develop students' mathematical creativity – combining their understanding of transformational geometry and proportional relationships – but how to extrapolate a whole curriculum map from just that one example was not obvious.

For a while I thought maybe the KS3 and KS4 curricula were just too varied, and the assessment foci too distinct to be drawn together using enquiries. But then I questioned myself. This resistance to Fertile Questions, to overhauling everything that we had done before as teachers in order to create something new, was felt by every curriculum leader at Ark Academy at some point. We all hit the Fertile Questions wall, so to speak. But the process of thinking your way around this wall was actually the most valuable thing we could have done. The intellectual challenge of reshaping KS3 into a series of enquiries led to a thorough understanding of what we wanted to teach and how we wanted to teach it. It made a big difference to the quality of our planning and teaching in that first year.

In Maths, for example, I had to deconstruct all the content of the curriculum – the mathematical concepts I wanted to cover, the knowledge and skills I wanted students to have – and then build it back up again, organized around these guiding questions that would filter the content down and present it in a more memorable, relevant, engaging form. It was a big task, stimulating and challenging in equal measure, and it took a lot of time. In a sense I was limited by what I had learnt during teacher training, or by my previous experience of teaching Maths, or even by my own memories of being a pupil in Maths lessons. But even at the very beginning, when I could not see the specifics of how Fertile Questions would work in my subject, I had an intuitive sense that they would increase students' engagement and deepen their conceptual understanding. So we began planning in earnest…

'Fertility' in the Maths Department: Structuring our curriculum around Fertile Questions

The best planning starts with thinking about the endgame. For us, that was the GCSE Maths examination. We needed a Year 7 curriculum that would maximize the chances of Year 11 success. I quickly discovered that there is a tension in planning with Fertile Questions. If you are not careful you can let a great enquiry lead you down a particular curriculum path and away from the breadth of coverage you need. Fertile Questions can be seductive – you find one that is so rich, so engaging, so likely to yield high-level conceptual debate and discussion, that you end up missing out basic topics which are less readily attached to an enquiry.

To ensure that this did not happen, I began my planning with a GCSE Maths inventory – detailing the knowledge, skills and conceptual development students needed in order to succeed in KS4:

Number and algebra

a. real numbers, their properties and their different representations
b. rules of arithmetic applied to calculations and manipulations with real numbers, including standard index form and surds
c. proportional reasoning, direct and inverse proportion, proportional change and exponential growth
d. upper and lower bounds
e. linear, quadratic and other expressions and equations
f. graphs of exponential and trigonometric functions
g. transformation of functions
h. graphs of simple loci.

Geometry and measures

a. properties and mensuration of 2D and 3D shapes
b. circle theorems
c. trigonometrical relationships
d. properties and combinations of transformations
e. 3D coordinate systems
f. vectors in two dimensions
g. conversions between measures and compound measures.

Statistics

a. the handling data cycle
b. presentation and analysis of large sets of grouped and ungrouped data, including box plots and histograms, lines of best fit and their interpretation
c. measures of central tendency and spread
d. experimental and theoretical probabilities of single and combined events.

Although the KS4 topics were grouped into three conventional areas, they needed to be sequenced so there was a logical progression between each subtopic and across the three areas. Logical both in terms of gradually increasing the level of complexity and making the learning age related. In Maths, many new topics require a body of pre-existing knowledge: you cannot tackle transformations of functions until you understand both the properties of transformations and graphs of linear, quadratic, exponential and trigonometric functions. Another example might be probability – students need to be able to manipulate, order and convert between fractions and decimals before they learn how to calculate the probability of different events. Breaking down the curriculum like this and then sequencing it backwards gave us a solid platform on which to build our Fertile Questions.

An important consideration was to allow students to have a taste of all areas of the Mathematics curriculum over the course of the year. To get a bit technical for a second, at the heart of Mathematics are certain core concepts: equivalence, proportional thinking, algebraic structure, relationships, axiomatic systems, symbolic representation, proof, operations and their inverses. Exposure to every concept would help our students understand the bigger picture (or 'whole game' of the subject, as we call it) and aid recall and understanding of new topics in Year 8 and beyond.

Identifying the curriculum inventory and then mapping it backwards was easy compared to the next part – developing the Fertile Questions which would guide students' learning. I wanted questions which would elucidate the key concepts in each topic, as opposed to just the skills or knowledge they encompassed; questions that introduced the language of the subject, the forms of thinking and discussion that mathematicians use; questions that allowed students to see things from multiple perspectives, and to approach mathematical problems with flexibility and confidence.

Using the topics I had roughly structured in the first draft of my curriculum map, I brainstormed idea after idea – and hit brick wall after brick wall. I looked for inspiration in smaller enquiries and investigations, for example those found on the Nrich website or the Nuffield Foundation's Application of Mathematical Processes. One example is the Nrich task *'Can they be equal?'* where students consider the relationship between area and perimeter and are challenged to engage in some sophisticated mathematical thinking. We adjusted the question and added some depth, centring a Year 7 unit of work on the Fertile Question *'Can the perimeter and area of a shape ever be the same?'* Throughout this planning period, I was reminded of the challenge of ensuring all exciting activities and questions *served my learning objectives and outcomes*, not the other way around.

Each time I came up with a question, I asked myself four more questions:

- *What is different about this question?*

- *What kind of a response will it provoke in students?*

- *What might happen in the first lesson?*

- *How might the enquiry develop, and what does the outcome look like?*

I began to think more creatively. I realized that I should be open to questions which required making connections unusual to the Maths classroom. A good example is the question Lefstein had used in his training: 'Is beauty mathematical?' As a starting point for the unit, I planned for students to investigate physical beauty using the golden ratio (also known as the divine proportion, golden mean, or golden section). It is a number often encountered when taking the ratios of distances in simple geometric figures such as the *pentagon, pentagram, decagon* and *dodecahedron*.

The investigation progressed to dissecting Islamic geometry patterns, allowing students to learn about the transformations used to create beautiful patterns, and angle rules to develop their understanding of how and why tessellations work. It is unusual for students to make connections between 'number' topics and 'geometry and measures' topics (and even sub-topics within these areas like tessellations and angles) because students are normally taught one 'conventional' subject area at a time. Furthermore, curriculum planning is often focused on the teaching of a skill (like tessellating) and not on the mathematical concepts behind the skill (how angle rules can explain why certain regular polygons will/will not tessellate). This emphasis on teaching concepts is indicative of our approach to all subjects at Ark Academy, as detailed in the figure below. The third column is where you want to be.

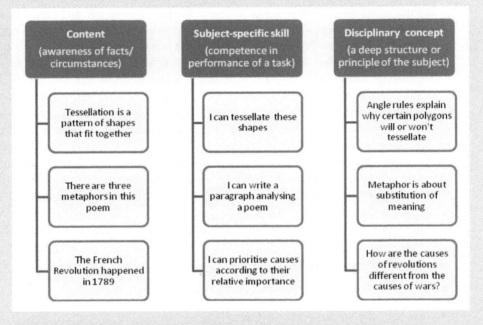

Figure 1.13   Content, subject-specific skill and disciplinary concept

To assess the 'fertility' of a draft question I used the criteria for a successful Fertile Question detailed in our Teaching and Learning handbook (Ark Academy 2010). I have listed these below, with an example of a Fertile Question from Maths alongside each one:

- **Open** questions have several competing answers:
  Does speaking a different language mean that we count differently?

- **Undermining** questions challenge an orthodox view:
  Can the area and perimeter of a shape ever be equal?

- **Rich** questions embody key conceptual knowledge:
  Are there equations with no solutions?

- **Connected** questions are relevant to learners:
  How can you create a fair game?

- **Charged** questions get you intellectually fired up!
  What is the price of money?

- **Practical** questions are linked to learners' context:
  Is life fairer because of Maths?

We were beginning to make progress. Once we had an established approach to formulating questions things sped up – below is the full plan for Fertile Questions across Years 7 and 8.

Year 7 Fertile Questions		Year 8 Fertile Questions
Does speaking a different language mean that we count differently?	Autumn 1	*Is your guess as good as mine?*
Can the perimeter and area of a shape ever be equal?		*Does enlargement affect length, area and volume in the same way?*
Is life fairer because of Maths?	Autumn 2	*What is the price of money?*
Could a world without algebra survive?		*Can you always predict the next term in a sequence?*
Is beauty mathematical?	Spring 1	*What is so special about congruent shapes?*
What is in your bowl: can Maths help you figure out your food choices?		*Does jail work?*
Are there different ways to represent the same number?	Spring 2	*What does simple mean in Maths?*
How do we use 2D shapes to understand 3D shapes?		*How do you decide where to put a fire escape?*

Year 7 Fertile Questions		Year 8 Fertile Questions
Are there numbers big enough and small enough to measure everything? How can you create a fair game?	Summer 1	Is it possible to draw a journey? What are the chances of winning at 21?
Are there equations with no solutions? How is a geometry problem constructed?	Summer 2	How many ways are there to solve an equation? Is there always a connection between the side lengths of a shape and the angles inside?

Teaching the big 'why?': Our experience of developing an enquiry-led classroom

The next stage was to think about how we would enhance our students' learning through the enquiries. How would we design lesson activities that would break down the question for students and allow them to start to build their answers? How would we generate the necessary independence and enthusiasm students would need to be able to puzzle their way through the enquiries?

In this regard we were helped massively by being a start-up school – our first Year 7 intake arrived with no fixed idea of how secondary learning will be structured, and no older cohort of students to influence their attitudes. They were open, inquisitive and enthusiastic about what lay ahead of them, and we were able to leverage that enthusiasm to great effect.

We decided to induct Year 7 into an enquiry-based Mathematics classroom through a 'Welcome to Mathematics' assembly and a separate induction lesson during their first week. Our objectives were to ensure learners understood:

* what being a mathematician is all about – and the link between this and enquiry learning and Fertile Questions;

* how important 'talk in Maths' is;

* the structure of a Fertile Question.

We highlighted what mathematicians do when they become interested in a problem:

* play with the problem and collect and organize data about it;

- discuss and record notes and diagrams;

- seek and see patterns or connections in the organized data;

- make and test hypotheses based on the patterns or connections;

- look in their strategy toolbox for mathematical skills which could help;

- check their answer and think about what they can learn from it;

- publish their results.

We taught students specific strategies for discussion in the classroom, focusing on developing 'exploratory talk'. This can be defined as 'consisting of critical and constructive exchanges, where challenges are justified and alternative ideas are offered'.[27] Students discussed the Improving Standards Unit 'Discussion in Mathematics' guidance, a copy of which was later added to each student's Maths book for easy reference during lessons. We also designed 'Discussion in Mathematics' displays in each classroom.

We developed a set of questions that groups of students would use in the first lesson of each Fertile Question, to help them to see the challenges and possibilities that lay ahead.

- Identify the most important words in this question.

- Do you already know anything that will help you answer this question?

- What do you need to find to be able to answer this question?

- Suggest some maths you think you might use or learn about during this investigation.

In the final lesson of each Fertile Question, we deliberately returned to these questions as part of the students' reflection on their learning during the enquiry.

The results: Student reactions, attainment and progress data

From the first lesson, students' reactions were exceptionally positive. Our level of student engagement was high in those first weeks and this was maintained throughout the year. Students' passion for Maths was evident early on from their participation in discussions on our Fronter page (Virtual Learning Platform). Their enthusiasm was further evidenced by the uptake of Mathematics enrichment activities, participation in the House Mathematics competitions and the participation in online Mathematics gaming, such as 'Matheltics'.

Students made exceptional progress in Mathematics in the first year of Ark Academy. On average, students made 2.63 sub-levels of progress, well above the national average of 1.3 sub-levels.[28] Furthermore, 53 per cent of the year group made three sub-levels of progress. In terms of attainment, at the end of Year 7, 67 per cent of students were working at a level 5 or above (only 26 per cent had been at this level on entry to secondary school).

Perhaps the most insightful data comes from the surveys completed at the end of the first year. Ninety eight per cent of students' surveyed enjoyed learning Maths through Fertile Questions. A significant number cited the reason that learning Maths in this way was simply 'fun' and the second most popular reason was that Fertile Questions 'made me think more'.

Throughout the year, we had many visitors, including Ofsted and ARK schools, who observed our lessons and fed back very positively about teaching and learning in our Maths classrooms. We have shared good practice outside of the academy, including at network events and during a course run with the Prince's Teaching Institute. Of the Mathematics lessons formally observed during the first year, *65 per cent were graded Outstanding*.

As a department, we felt a real sense of achievement at the end of last year. It is clear to us now that organizing curriculum content around enquiries is at the heart of effective Mathematics teaching. As well as facilitating high levels of engagement and effectively developing students' conceptual understanding, teaching through Fertile Questions also succeeds in making teacher and student partners in learning. As students develop an intellectual flexibility and a questioning, logical mind, an unknown and demanding problem (including in an exam situation) becomes a familiar and welcome challenge – to be embraced, not avoided.

We believe that teaching through Fertile Questions has developed confidence and a love of Maths in every student, and that this will support them in mastering GCSE Mathematics and beyond. I will leave you with a quote from one student who entered Ark Academy on a level 3A and finished the year on a level 5C:

My name is Ronnie and yes I do love maths because when I am really sad all I have to do is think of maths and then I am joyful and spectacular

TRAINING ACTIVITY

Designing Fertile Questions – lessons from an Outstanding Maths Department (Part 1)

Thinking about Aishling's approach:

- *What problems did Aishling encounter in her initial planning stages?*

- *How did she overcome these?*

- *What did Aishling do differently that enabled her to design the curriculum the way she wanted?*

- *What lessons and ideas can you take from this case study to help you in your own planning?*

TRAINING ACTIVITY

Designing Fertile Questions – lessons from an Outstanding Maths Department (Part 2)

Reflecting on Fertile Questions

Discuss the questions below as a 'student' and a 'teacher':

i.   *Does change mean progress?* (History)

Student hat: Discuss the Fertile Question and where you think the enquiry will go from here.

Teacher hat: Discuss using the questions as prompts:

- *What is different about this question?*

- *What kind of a response will it provoke in students?*

- *What might happen in the first lesson?*

- *How might the inquiry develop?*

- *Are there characteristics of this question that you could apply to a Fertile Question for your own subject?*

- *What prior knowledge will students require?*

- *What is the core conceptual understanding underpinning the question?*

ii.   *The London Olympics: A blessing or a curse?* (Geography)

Student hat: Discuss the Fertile Question and where you think the enquiry will go from here.

Teacher hat: Discuss using the questions as prompts:

- *What is different about this question?*

- *What kind of a response will it provoke in students?*

- *What might happen in the first lesson?*

- *How might the inquiry develop?*

- *Are there characteristics of this question that you could apply to a Fertile Question for your own subject?*

- *What prior knowledge will students require?*

- *What is the core conceptual understanding underpinning the question?*

iii. *Can texts capture experiences?* (English)

Student hat: Discuss the Fertile Question and where you think the enquiry will go from here.

Teacher hat: Discuss using the questions as prompts:

- *What is different about this question?*

- *What kind of a response will it provoke in students?*

- *What might happen in the first lesson?*

- *How might the inquiry develop?*

- *Are there characteristics of this question that you could apply to a Fertile Question for your own subject?*

- *What prior knowledge will students require?*

- *What is the core conceptual understanding underpinning the question?*

iv. *Is it ever alright to break the law?* (RE)

Student hat: Discuss the Fertile Question and where you think the enquiry will go from here.

Teacher hat: Discuss using the questions as prompts:

- *What is different about this question?*

- *What kind of a response will it provoke in students?*

- *What might happen in the first lesson?*

- *How might the inquiry develop?*

- *Are there characteristics of this question that you could apply to a Fertile Question for your own subject?*

- *What prior knowledge will students require?*

- *What is the core conceptual understanding underpinning the question?*

v. *What made Cromwell 'tick'?* (History)

Student hat: Discuss the Fertile Question and where you think the enquiry will go from here.

Teacher hat: Discuss using the questions as prompts

- *What is different about this question?*

- *What kind of a response will it provoke in students?*

- *What might happen in the first lesson?*

- *How might the inquiry develop?*

- *Are there characteristics of this question that you could apply to a Fertile Question for your own subject?*

- *What prior knowledge will students require?*

- *What is the core conceptual understanding underpinning the question?*

What lessons have you learnt from this about designing Fertile Questions?

Benefits	Traps

Now you have looked at different ways of thinking about designing questions, cut up and match the questions below to the principle.

Open		*'Should we pay tax?'* (Mathematics)
Undermining		*'Does more muscle mean a higher level of fitness?'* (PE)
Rich		*'How does use of colour transform a painting?'* (Art)
Connected		*'How could the Holocaust have happened?'* (History)
Charged		*'What is love? What is hate? Can science explain it?'* (Science)
Practical		*'What makes a good parent?'* (Sociology)

The point here is to realize that not every Fertile Question will fulfil all six principles and that is OK.

You have now done enough thinking to be able to go ahead and design your own Fertile Questions.

Thinking about your own Fertile Questions (Part 1 – in isolation)

Think about a unit of work you are going to teach. Now use the planning framework below to teach that unit through a Fertile Question.

Curriculum area/core content	
i. *What is the target knowledge you want students to learn?*	
ii. *How are you going to assess what they have learnt?*	
iii. *What is the key concept the question helps students to understand?*	
iv. *How does this question prepare students for future questions?*	
v. *What are possible Fertile Questions that allow the above to happen?*	

Thinking about your own Fertile Questions (Part 2 – in groups)
Swap your planning grid with someone else and reflect on each other's planning. Provide feedback on the following:

i.   Use the six principles on page 79 to test out the fertility of their questions.

ii.   Which question is most fertile?

iii.   Does the question clearly connect to the concept they wish students to understand?

iv.   Does the question engage and create a problem to be solved?

v.   Does the question mimic how experts in the real world 'do' the subject?

vi.   Does the question try to do too much?

vii.   Does the question appear to be trying 'too hard'? Does it actually fit with the target knowledge?

viii. Does the assessment resolve the problem posed by the question?

Thinking about your own Fertile Questions (Part 3 – using the feedback)
Return the planning grids:

ix. Look at your feedback. Choose the 'most fertile' question and use it to plan a sequence of lessons using the table below.

x. Now look at the eight stages below (also on page 77). How would you plan a journey through this Fertile Question?

Stage of Fertile Question	What this looks like in action
i. Introduce the new Fertile Question – engage and motivate pupils, discover what they already know and check out their existing preconceptions. Make this known to the pupils.	
ii. Allow pupils to decide what research question(s) they might like to formulate that answers the Fertile Question or outline to the students the journey you have already planned.	
iii. Start the process of enquiry – *what small questions do we need to answer to formulate a response to the BIG question, can we divide the BIG question up, what happens if we disagree, where might we go for information, what will we do if we get stuck, how will we know if we are on the right track, how much information do we need, how do we turn the information into knowledge, how are we going to display our thinking, what are the success criteria, who is the intended audience, what is the purpose of this piece of learning?*	

iv. Come back as a whole class to discuss findings so far and any problems that have arisen.	
v. Create an initial response to the question in groups or individually – tentative answers and provocative feedback to encourage deeper reflection (oral rehearsal).	
vi. Follow this with peer review and redrafting in light of feedback.	
vii. Ask groups/individuals to give a concluding performance.	
viii. Organize a class concluding performance and feedback/review.	

Thinking about your own Fertile Questions (Part 4 – mapping across a Key Stage)
Now you have had a chance to practice designing and testing Fertile Questions it is time to have a go at mapping out a series of Fertile Questions across several year groups. (Complete the following table.)

Remember to be guided by the following ideas:

i.   *How do you plan to expose your students to the same concept over a Key Stage – remember the idea of the spider's web?*

ii. *How will their knowledge of this concept and ability to use it as a tool for explaining ideas grow across the Key Stage?*

iii. *How do your Fertile Questions connect across a year and Key Stage?*

iv. *What is the overall aim of your curriculum plan – what does it enable students to be able to do by the end?*

v.   *How does the Learner Profile (discussed next) help you in your planning?*

vi. *How will you assess understanding at the end of each Fertile Question? Have you used the Harpaz table on page 57 to help plan for progression?*

	Year 7 Fertile Questions	Year 8 Fertile Questions	Year 9 Fertile Questions
Autumn 1			
Autumn 2			
Spring 1			
Spring 2			
Summer 1			
Summer 2			

Stage 6: The Learner Profile

Now that we have looked at the planning approach we can address the last (but arguably most important) aspect the whole-school curriculum must possess: a Learner Profile. This is an idea of what a learner in your school looks like – the characteristics and qualities they possess. It complements the whole-school model described so far; the curriculum and the Learner Profile gear together to accelerate student progress.

By sharing the profile with students you can develop in them the habits they will need for enquiry-based learning. The profile should be communicated to students not just in lessons but through all aspects of school life: assemblies, tutor times, parents' evenings, reports, enrichment sessions and so on.

A Learner Profile can be created by answering the questions below:

- *What does a learner look like in this curriculum?*

- *What habits of mind or dispositions do they develop?*

- *How do they make connections between learning experiences?*

- *What language do we use to talk about learning?*

- *How does this learning connect to the wider-world and what does it prepare me for?*

- *How does this learning connect to the way experts in the different fields think about and construct knowledge?*

- *How do I view problems and challenges?*

- *How do I respond to mistakes?*

Our Learner Profile maps out the different types of thinking a learner develops through their studies. Because it shows exactly *how* medium- and long-term plans draw out the qualities and attributes we desire in students, it forms a planning framework across subjects, year groups and key stages. It provides all members of the school community – teachers, support staff, parents, students and governors – with a common language with which to talk about learning, and it allows everyone to take responsibility for getting better at learning.

The Learner Profile is both a planning tool and a framework for school reports. It should underpin the behaviour and rewards system in the school. By using the structure and language of the profile in all discussions about learning, you can ensure all learners have a clear understanding of how their work at any given point fits into their overall path or direction. The Learner Profile is also future-proof and corresponds with the desired attributes employers look for.

In order to be used effectively it needs to permeate all aspects of school life: be displayed in public spaces, be talked about in lessons, assemblies and meetings, and be reviewed as part of the school's self-evaluation. The profile should form the heart of the school and the essence of its purpose. It will become meaningful to students if it is a living thing, made concrete through students' day to day experience. Many schools claim to have something akin to a Learner Profile, but few can say it is fully embedded. The best people to explain the profile are the students themselves; you can tell if you have successfully implemented it when they can explain it back to you in their own words. You will find they will be far more eloquent than the teachers.

The Learner Profile is not a tool for labelling students. It is not different types of intelligence or ways of learning. It simply maps out what the desired dispositions are for a student to possess to be able to operate successfully in a changing and uncertain world, and is used as a planning, evaluating and reporting tool at whole-school level. It provides a common framework and language for talking about learning and progression.

The Learner Profile: We are becoming…[29]

A critical thinker	Collaborative	Adaptable	An entrepreneur	A communicator	Analytical	Creative
• They learn to identify and clarify situations. • They learn to make predictions and generate hypotheses. • They learn to draw conclusions and give reasons. • They learn to evaluate and check how well a solution solves a problem.	• They learn to work with others and listen to reasons. • They learn to build on and combine ideas. • They learn when to take the lead and when to take a step back. • They learn to decide on a course of action and review the consequences. • They understand the advantages of working in teams and that the best solution is rarely arrived at on their own.	• They learn to deal with multiple possible solutions. • They learn to not look for one answer. • They learn to deal with new situations and new experiences. • They learn to try out ideas and solutions and modify them if they do not solve the problem.	• They learn to take the lead and not rely on being given the solution. • They learn to create their own answers and solutions. • They learn to take multiple perspectives. • They learn to see failure or critical feedback as an opportunity to improve. • They learn to not expect instant gratification for a successful solution.	• They learn to communicate ideas and solutions clearly and concisely. • They learn to speak with passion to persuade others. • They learn to use energy to persuade others on their course of action. • They learn to sum up clearly and with purpose. • They learn to be convincing and speak in an appropriate style with confidence.	• They learn to filter and sift information to help make decisions. • They learn to synthesise information to understand what is relevant and what is not for the task at hand. • They learn to sequence, order and rank information to help decide on a course of action. • They learn to generate and research their own questions.	• They learn to get beneath the surface of a problem. • They learn to ask good, pertinent and productive questions. • They learn to use mental rehearsal and mental simulations to see what might happen. • They learn to look at problems from different perspectives.

Figure 1.14 The Learner Profile

TRAINING ACTIVITY

The Learner Profile:

i.   What does your Learner Profile currently look like in school? (This question is especially important if there is not a coherent model already.)

ii. Does it create a holistic picture?

iii. Do the students know about the Learner Profile?

iv. Do teachers use the Learner Profile to inform and shape their long-term planning?

v.   Does the way you assess and give feedback match up with your Learner Profile?

vi. Does the way you report back to parents and talk to them about learning and progress match with your Learner Profile?

Stage 7: Medium-term plans – frameworks for progression in understanding

Deciding on the journey through the Fertile Question

We have offered you many frameworks and templates for planning Fertile Questions. None are presented as prescriptive – in practice the framework that works best for you may be one that you have adapted from the versions above. They are being offered here as guidelines that can help you to construct and organize your ideas.

The two case studies so far have shown that each lesson within an enquiry forms part of the journey through the overarching Fertile Question. Individual lessons work best when they are framed by smaller questions which help students build up their ability to resolve the main problem posed.

The easiest way to do this is to work backwards from the desired outcome and experiment with different 'mini-questions' to see which ones help students develop the knowledge and conceptual understanding necessary to create a meaningful answer to the overall Fertile Question. The sequence through a Fertile Question has been outlined above.

Pick the Fertile Question you were working with earlier on and start to think about the individual lesson questions. There is (yet another) grid below to help you in your planning.

Fertile Question template

Fertile Question:

Lesson question	Main themes and outcomes

Possible planning matrix for all Fertile Questions

Once the principles are fully understood and embedded at classroom and department level it is possible (and probably desirable) to move to a less 'heavy-handed' planning grid. Some examples of these are at the end of this section. For now this grid gives the structure required.

Medium-term planning template		
Fertile Question:	**Connections to previous enquiry or prepares pupils for:**	
Year group:	**Duration of scheme of work:** *(No. of lessons)*	
Objectives of the enquiry/unit: *By the end of the enquiry ALL pupils will be able to:* i. ii.	**Assessment/end product:**	
	Assessment Objectives: *(Link to NC, GCSE, etc.)* i. ii.	
Core concept being explored:		
Core content and target generalizations: *By the end of the enquiry ALL pupils will demonstrate understanding of:*	**AfL opportunities:** *(Convergent and/or divergent)*	

Principal tasks/stages of the enquiry:

Metacognitive questions we want students to grapple with: (See *disciplinary planning grid from Peter Lee*)

Language focus:

i. *What genre/way of communicating do pupils need to understand or demonstrate?*

ii. *Opportunities for reading:*

iii. *Opportunities for speaking and listening:*

Use of ICT to deepen understanding:

How will students use the Visual learning Environment (VLE)?:

Purpose of Homework:

Medium-term planning template – exemplar from one of the Fertile Questions above

Fertile Question: *What made Cromwell tick?* Did Cromwell's vision for England stay the same throughout his rule?

Connections to previous enquiry or prepares pupils for:
Links back to previous enquiry on causes of the Civil war and historical perspectives on leadership.

Year group: 8

Duration of Scheme of Work: *(No. of lessons)* 6

Objectives of the enquiry/unit:
By the end of the enquiry ALL pupils will be able to:

i. Reflect on the nature of change and continuity with regards to the construction of historical accounts.

ii. Construct a response to the enquiry question.

Core concept being explored:

Change and continuity – the change lurking within the continuity.

Core content and target generalizations: *By the end of the enquiry ALL pupils will demonstrate understanding of:*

i. Cromwell's reign and his relationship with Parliament.
ii. The relationship between Cromwell and his religion.
iii. The status of religion in England at this time.

Assessment/end product: Pupils giving 5 minute university-style lecture to rest of class in pairs.

Assessment Objectives: *(Link to NC, GCSE, etc.)*

i. Pupils examining the extent and nature of change.

ii. Pupils reflecting on the criteria needed to make judgements and beginning to ask their own questions.

AfL opportunities: *(Convergent and/or divergent)*

Divergent – flexible planning driven by students in developing their own research questions and criteria for assessment.

Convergent – summative feedback on final performance against agreed criteria.

Principal tasks/stages of the enquiry:
- Introduce the Fertile Question and discover what pupils already know/think about Cromwell and Parliament.
- Outline the BIG picture and end product of the enquiry.
- Introduce Robert's article on Cromwell and analyse.
- Deconstruct article and look at genre-specific mode and tenor.
- Students use article as a framework for mapping out change and continuity.
- Students develop own research question and work towards answering it. Development of success criteria.
- Peer review of their draft lectures.
- Concluding performance.

Metacognitive questions we want students to grapple with:
- Are change and/or continuity constant?
- Is change happening for all groups or just a few?
- Is the change/continuity determined by agents or accidental?

Language focus:
i. *What genre/way of communicating do pupils need to understand or demonstrate?*

University lecture

ii. *Opportunities for reading:*

Roberts' lecture from Cambridge.

iii. *Opportunities for speaking and listening:*

Draft and concluding performances.

Use of ICT to deepen understanding:
- **Synthesize** – ICT used to engage and help learners to structure their final performances – starting to get them to see how technology can help them present complex ideas in a clear format.
- **Purpose** – ICT used to give the concluding assessment or resolution of the problem meaning through creating an audience for the piece.

How will students use the VLE?:
- Article and all resources – timeline, etc. – on VLE.
- Students use VLE for homework to communicate with each other and to upload work for the following lesson.

Purpose of Homework:
- Consolidate and build on lesson time. Homework is for individual work and preparation for working in pairs each lesson.
- At the end of each lesson the pair will set themselves homework based on where they are and what needs to be done next.

Let's look again at the disciplinary planning grid for this Fertile Question – how does it map onto what we have looked at so far?

Fertile Question (based around a conceptual understanding)	Core content and target generalizations to be taught	Target ideas to be taught about core conceptual understanding	Preconceptions to be checked out	Key conceptual understandings to be taught	Metacognitive questions we want pupils to develop/grapple with
For example, if it is a 'how do we know' type question then the teaching will need to focus on the concept of evidence relevant to that subject domain.	Residual knowledge – in six months' time what things do we want pupils to remember/feel about the topic? What knowledge do they need in order to be able to apply it to new settings later on in the curriculum?	What are we aiming for in terms of conceptual progression? For example, an evidence focused enquiry might have a target of enabling pupils to see that explanations of why people do things are not always the same as explanations of why things happen.	What likely preconceptions might we encounter about the conceptual understanding that will need to be addressed before we can continue with our target focus? For example, many pupils believe that we can only know what happened if we were there or if we read the eyewitness account of someone else.	What is the core concept? What will mastery look like?	What questions do pupils need to ask themselves to monitor their own progress through the enquiry?

What made Cromwell tick?					
	i. Cromwell's reign and his relationship with Parliament. ii. The relationship between Cromwell and his religion. iii. The status of religion in England at this time.	To enable pupils to see that change does not always lead to progress. To enable pupils to see that continuity for one group in society can mean change for another.	Change means progress and as we progress through time things change for the better. Change is the intentional outcome of human actions.	Change and continuity – the change lurking within the continuity. Mastery = analysing the extent and nature of change for different groups and the locomotive for that change.	Are change and/or continuity constant? Is change happening for all groups or just a few? Is the change/continuity determined by agents or accidental?

Letter received from Cambridge University about the Fertile Question above that was taught to a Year 8 class in a complex urban school in East London

Mr Oliver Knight
St Angela's Ursuline School
St George's Road
Forest Gate
London
E7 8HU

25 February 2009

Dear Mr Knight

Thank you very much indeed for sending me the examples of work from your **Year 8** history class. I was astounded at the sophistication of their thinking about change and continuity, their detailed knowledge of Cromwell's activities (many A Level students are not so secure in their knowledge and understanding!), their understanding of a work of scholarship by a leading historian (David Smith) and their ability to marshal ideas and evidence into their own arguments. The 'sense of period' in the form of a grasp of the wider narratives of the 17th century also came through strongly.

This work is a model of the high standards we should be aiming for with 12 and 13 year-old students. I will be using it to show both my trainee history teachers, and experienced history teachers who come on our other courses at Cambridge, just how exciting, knowledge-rich and energising the finest historical learning can be. It also convincingly demonstrates that we should not patronise Year 8 by only ever giving them easy texts and tiny source gobbets to read. It is clear that these students have both read and thought about a long, difficult and scholarly paper, and that they have made meaning out of a complex political narrative. The big ideas of historical 'change' and 'continuity' have clearly also been effective intellectual tools in helping them to think rigorously and critically.

Thank you again for sending me this inspirational work and please pass on my admiration of your Year 8's work and my warmest congratulations.

All good wishes

Yours sincerely,

Christine Counsell
Senior Lecturer

This letter demonstrates that teaching through Fertile Questions is the best way of enabling ALL students to develop disciplinary thinking and to make progress in academic areas that perhaps are more usually reserved for A-level or university students. By taking a careful approach to planning, by using scientific concepts as the framework and by believing that engagement comes through carefully managed challenge rather than simplifying learning down to recital, excellence can be achieved by every teacher. This is what school should be about – transcending our everyday experiences and ways of understanding the world and learning instead to think using disciplinary or scientific concepts to see how 'experts' make sense of and construct the world around them and how that in turn influences how we see and act. This is the true goal of twenty-first century schooling.

Conclusions

The approach to medium- and long-term planning outlined in this chapter is based on what the research suggests is the most efficient way to ensure both progression in thinking and progression in understanding.

The planning is at first labour-intensive, but this is offset by the gains it creates in the classroom. To get the most from Fertile Questions you may need a complete curriculum rethink (as demonstrated in Case Study 2). Once the approach to the planning becomes embedded it is of course possible to strip it down, but the hard work and hard thinking at the beginning are vital.

To sum up, the key points of the planning approach are:

- Plan backwards from degree level and KS5 – what does success look like and how can you prepare for this. How do experts 'practice'?

- Teach for understanding not recitation – use enquiries to ensure students are operating on the knowledge they have been given, not passively receiving it.

- Work out what the core concepts are that students need to understand in order to make sense and organize what they are being taught and foreground these in your teaching.

- What are the key dispositions or ways of thinking a student needs to master in order to replicate the way experts in the field think? Reinforce the Learner Profile at every opportunity.

- Design the curriculum around a series of Fertile Questions that pose meaningful puzzles that mirror the way experts think and authentic problems in the real world, and provide 'apprenticeships in thinking'.

- Design the curriculum around ideas of target knowledge and conceptual thinking, and consider how you can escalate the complexities in knowledge and concepts over time. How does one Fertile Question prepare students for the next?

- Teach the 'whole game' of your subject. How do the conceptual understandings students are developing connect with the 'whole game' (or a junior version of it)? How does one Fertile Question re-enforce earlier learning and help students apply it to new settings?

- Ensure that the approach is developing academic language and enabling students to move from highly spoken forms of communication to academic writing. (See Chapter 3 later on for a full explanation of this.)

- As the approach to planning becomes second-nature, scale it back so it does not become burdensome but ensure it still maintains the same focus.

Appendix to Chapter 1: Model examples of different long- and medium-term plans using the principles from Chapter 1 (reproduced from Ark Academy curriculum documents)

History Department: Scheme of work overview (long-term plan – one year, Year 7 2010–2011)

Half Term	Fertile Question	Concept	Description	Formative Assessments	Summative Assessments	Links to GCSE Requirements
Autumn 1	**How English are the English?**	Change and Continuity	**Focus:** *Enabling students to orientate themselves in time and space to allow for meaningful analysis of the past.* They will begin with an enquiry on skeletons from Maiden Castle to introduce the concept of historical investigation. Students will then analyse a timeline of the last 2000 years of the UK and reflect on the changing nature of English national identity.	Peer review of hypothesis. Paired critique of Professor Knowall. Oral presentation	i. Written explanation of their outcomes. ii. Explanation of the changes and continuities between 2 way-markers.	AO1 AO2
Autumn 2	**Did all roads ever lead to Rome?**	Historical Diversity	**Focus:** *Exploration of the concept of empire to prepare students for later studies.* Students will investigate a depth study on the Roman Empire to analyse the reasons for the development of empires and the extent to which they are homogeneous.	Peer review of draft essay. Evaluation of model analysis.	Essay – Did the Roman Empire do more harm than good?	AO1 AO2
Spring 1	**Can we know what happened without being there?**	Evidential understanding + Causation	**Focus:** *The battle of Hastings and how historical accounts are created.* Students will explore the reasons for the battle of Hastings and then evaluate different stances on the battle to help develop a more powerful understanding on the nature and status of historical accounts.	Analysis of two different accounts of the Battle of Hastings.	Obituary on William the Conqueror.	AO1 AO3

© 2014, Creating Outstanding Classrooms, Oliver Knight and David Benson, Routledge

		Focus			
Spring 2	**Could a King do whatever he liked?**	Causation	**Focus:** *The nature of power in medieval Britain.* Students will begin with a look at the role and expectations of a medieval King. They will then go on to investigate the rebellion against King John as a case study in power.	Example paragraphs and critique of exemplar pieces of writing	Essay – "Why did the Barons rebel against King John?"	AO1 AO2 AO3
Summer 1	**Why could no-one ignore the Church?**	Historical Significance	**Focus:** *The role of the Church in the medieval period.* Students will explore the ways in which the Church had power over people's lives and at the same time offered them spiritual hope and practical help.	Oral presentation of draft game for peer review.	Board game on the enquiry question.	AO2 AO3
Summer 2	**Was Henry VIII too cool for school?**	Change and Continuity	**Focus:** *The changing nature of ideas.* Students will start with a case study on the Renaissance and its impact on European thought. They will then evaluate the reign of Henry VIII against these criteria.	Example paragraphs and critique of exemplar pieces of writing.	Essay – "Was Henry VIII really a 'Renaissance Man'?"	AO1 AO2 AO3

Figure 1.15 History Department: Scheme of work overview (long-term plan – one year, Year 7 2010-2011

Assessment objectives for GCSE (OCR History B)

AO1

Recall, select, use and communicate their knowledge and understanding of history.

AO2

Demonstrate their understanding of the past through explanation and analysis of:

- key concepts: causation, consequence, continuity, change and significance within a historical context;
- key features and characteristics of the periods studied and the relationships between them.

AO3

Understand, analyse and evaluate:

- a range of source material as part of an historical enquiry;
- how aspects of the past have been interpreted and represented in different ways as part of an historical enquiry.

Maths KS3 curriculum map: Long-term plan (three years)

Year 7	Autumn 1	Autumn 2	Spring 1	Spring 2	Summer 1	Summer 2
Fertile questions and core concept (brackets)	Does speaking a different language mean that we count differently? (Number)	Is life fairer because of maths? (Number)	Is beauty mathematical? (Geometry)	Are there different ways to represent the same number? (Number	Are there numbers big enough and small enough to measure everything? (Number)	Are there equations with no solutions? (Algebra)
	Can the perimeter and area of a shape ever be equal? (Geometry)	Could a world without algebra survive? (Algebra)	What's in your bowl...Can maths help you figure out your food choices? (Statistics)	How do we use 2D shapes to understand 3D shapes? (Geometry)	How can you create a fair game? (Statistics)	How is a geometry problem constructed? (Geometry)
Year 8	**Autumn 1**	**Autumn 2**	**Spring 1**	**Spring 2**	**Summer 1**	**Summer 2**
	Is your guess as good as mine? (Statistics)	Are mortgages fair? (Number)	What's so special about congruent shapes? (Geometry)	What does simple mean in maths? (Number)	Is it possible to draw a journey? (Algebra)	How many ways are there to solve an equation? (Algebra)

Year 9	Autumn 1	Autumn 2	Spring 1	Spring 2	Summer 1	Summer 2
	Does enlargement affect length, area and volume in the same way? (Geometry)	Can you always predict the next term in a sequence? (Algebra)	Does jail work? (Statistics)	How do you decide where to put a fire escape? (Geometry)	What are the chances of winning at 21? (Number)	Is there always a connection between the side lengths of a shape and the angles inside? (Geometry)
	Can you solve an equation that isn't equal? (Algebra)	How do insurance companies make money? (Number)	Is volume always based on area? (Geometry)	How do we answer a Number exam question? (Number)	How do we answer a Statistics exam question? (Statistics)	Can a number be irrational? (Number)
	How has Pythagoras influenced mathematics? (Geometry)	Can you graph a goal? (Algebra)	What is the difference between probability and statistics? (Statistics)	How do we answer an Algebra exam question? (Algebra)	How do we answer a Shape and Space exam question? (Number)	How can Pythagoras' Theorem help us understand non right angled triangles? (Number)

Figure 1.16 Maths KS3 curriculum map: Long-term plan (three years)

The key point here is to look at how the GCSE inventory is mapped out across KS3 with the students encountering concepts and engaging with them at a deeper and deeper level across the 3 years.

English Department: Medium-term enquiry plan, Year 7

Fertile Question:	Length of Enquiry: 6 weeks Original Author: JKI Revised By: JDO
Is it possible to paint a picture with words?	

	Key questions
Synopsis This enquiry focuses on descriptive writing and how writers create images in readers' heads using language. **As a way into this, the enquiry uses photography and paintings as a stimulus for their writing. They will look at how to explore both characters and settings in an effective way, investigating and trying out a range of techniques. There will also be a strong focus on literacy this half term, particularly ones that will aide their descriptive writing – there will be a one hour dedicated literacy lesson each week. The writing process also stands – students will learn how to plan creative pieces, perform and proofread effectively.**	What makes an effective piece of creative writing? How do I write about characters? How do I write about settings? How can I use language to create an effective description? How can I use structure to help construct an effective description? How can I engage a reader? What strategies can I use to improve the accuracy of my writing?

KEY ENGLISH FOCUS: Writing	**GENRE:** Creative / Descriptive Writing?

Key Objectives of the Enquiry		
Core Learning Objectives and Actions	Assessment and Technical Skills	Resources & Texts
• Students will analyse a range of texts to see what makes them successful in engaging a reader so that they can emulate this in their writing. • Students will learn how to write descriptively about characters	*Students will learn and develop their technical writing skills during this unit of work. The key things they will learn for this kind of writing are:* • paragraphing (and how to paragraph for effect) • different kinds of sentence structure and how these can be used for effect.	• character postcards • setting based postcards and photographs • the paintings of L.S. Lowry • the paintings of Van Gogh • examples of descriptive writing from *Jane Eyre, Hard Times, The BFG, Why the Whales Came*

- past and present tense and first, second and third person writing.

Students will also cover the basic writing skills, including:

- sentence punctuation including capital letters, full stops and other end of sentence punctuation.
- using commas correctly
- apostrophes
- semi-colons and why they are used
- spelling strategies, particularly homophones, basic spellings and complex spellings.

Some students will need small group and individual support in improving their writing skills with things like:

- tense / subject verb concord
- prepositions, articles and connecting words
- irregular spelling patterns
- handwriting

- Students will learn how to write descriptively about setting

Students will attempt to create their own engaging writing. To this end:

- Students will learn about and use a variety of language techniques for description such as:
  o similes, metaphors and personification
  o vocabulary (adjectives, adverbs, descriptive verbs)
  o Show Don't Tell
- Students will learn about and use a variety of structural techniques for description, such as:
  o 'Snapshots'
  o 'Zoom'
  o using sentences and paragraph for effect.
  o when and when not to use ellipsis (…)
- Students will learn about different narrative techniques such as:
  o withholding information[33]
  o the five senses
  o dual narratives
  o cliffhangers
  o stream of consciousness
  o etc.
- Students will learn about the writing process – planning, performing and proofreading. Refer to bookmarks.

Links to the National Curriculum: 2.3 A-J, S, P, T-W
Links to GCSE and Beyond: Creative writing is assessed through both examination and coursework at GCSE level

Key words and phrases:
Simile, metaphor, personification, narrative, structure, complex, vocabulary, character, setting,

Assessment	
Formative Assessment	Summative Assessment
The paintings of Van Gogh Write a descriptive piece based on one of the Van Gogh paintings that you have been given.	**The paintings of L.S. Lowry** Write a descriptive piece based on one of the paintings of L.S. Lowry

Outside of Lessons
Homework
WEEK 1: Spellings + Literary techniques worksheet **WEEK 2: Spellings + Write a description of the character in the photograph you have been given.** **WEEK 3: Spellings + Write a description of the setting you have been given in the photograph**
WEEK 4: Spellings + Find an interesting painting or photograph. Stick it in your book and come up with five interesting sentences about it. **WEEK 5: Spellings + Create two revision cards based on your target areas.** **WEEK 6: Shakespeare based homework ready for next Fertile Question.**

Week	Focus	Core Objectives	Possible activities
1	What's the difference between creative and non-fiction writing? What makes an effective piece of creative writing? How do I write about characters?	• Students will learn the difference between non-fiction writing that they have done previously (such as newspaper and persuasive writing) and creative writing. • Students will analyse a range of texts to see what makes them successful in engaging a reader so that they can emulate this in their writing. • Students will learn how to write descriptively about characters • Students will learn about and use a variety of language techniques for description such as: 　o similes, metaphors and personification 　o vocabulary (adjectives, adverbs, descriptive verbs) 　o Show Don't Tell	• comparing and contrasting examples of non-fiction texts in terms of PAF. • making a table of differences. • examining texts where the description of a character is particularly effective • introduce imagery techniques such as similes, metaphors and personification through match up activity. • play a 'taboo' game to demonstrate Show-Don't-Tell. • using character postcards to write their own character descriptions
2	What makes an effective piece of creative writing? How do I write about characters? How do I write about settings? How can I use language to create an effective description?	*Continue with last week's work on character and then move onto setting.* • Students will learn how to write descriptively about setting • Students will learn about and use a variety of structural techniques for description, such as: 　o 'Snapshots' 　o 'Zoom' • Students will learn about different narrative techniques such as: 　o the five senses	• Use further examples of good descriptive writing, this time of settings. Annotate and highlight. • Teach Zoom and Snapshot techniques using examples scenes. • Use postcards and photographs of places to inspire creative writing. • Complete descriptive writing carousel.

3	How can I use language to create an effective description? How can I use structure to help construct an effective description?	**FORMATIVE ASSESSMENT TO TAKE PLACE AT THE END OF THIS WEEK: Students given one of five of Van Gogh paintings in pairs. Plan and write a description using the painting as a stimulus.** • Students will learn how to write descriptively about characters • Students will learn how to write descriptively about setting *Students will attempt to create their own engaging writing. To this end:* • Students will learn about and use a variety of language techniques for description • Students will learn about and use a variety of structural techniques for description, such as: • Students will learn about different narrative techniques	• Use Van Gogh painting to practice planning and writing about it. • Re-cover any writing techniques that haven't been used for a while. • Spend one lesson planning formative assessment.
4	How can I engage a reader? What strategies can I use to improve the accuracy of my writing? What makes an effective piece of creative writing?	• Paragraphing (and how to paragraph for effect) • Different kinds of sentence structure and how these can be used for effect. • Past and present tense and first, second and third person writing. Also cover any areas not covered above or that need covering as a result of formative assessment.	• Complete full review of formative assessment, including completing self reflection. • Use student examples to demonstrate exemplary or weak practice. • Lots of redrafting and rewriting work.

© 2014, Creating Outstanding Classrooms, Oliver Knight and David Benson, Routledge

5	SUMMATIVE ASSESSMENT TO TAKE PLACE DURING THIS WEEK: Students given one of five of L.S. LOWRY paintings in pairs. Plan and write a description using the painting as a stimulus.	• Use one Lowry painting to practice planning and writing about it. • Re-cover any writing techniques that haven't been used for a while. • Spend one lesson planning summative assessment.
6	REVIEW WEEK	• Complete full review of summative assessment, including completing self reflection. • Use student examples to demonstrate exemplary or weak practice. • Lots of redrafting and rewriting work. • Complete new golden ticket for this half term and writing.

Figure 1.17 English Department: Medium-term enquiry plan, Year 7

Show Don't Tell is a technique you use to develop students' descriptive writing skills. It is about them showing the reader a feature of a landscape or character rather than telling them – e.g. Telling is 'She had long brown hair'. Showing is 'Her chestnut locks tumbled over her shoulders and down her back'.

Snapshots is a great way to describe settings. Students imagine they are using a camera looking on a setting. They take four photographs of key parts of the landscape. A paragraph is dedicated to describing each 'snapshot'.

Zoom is similar to Snapshots, in that the students imagine they are using a camera, however this is where students imagine they have zoomed in on a part of the setting. This small part of the setting is described in one paragraph, and then the 'camera' zooms out a bit and describes the things around it, then it zooms out some more and describes those things. For example, if students are describing a beach they might focus on a child with a bucket and spade at first, then on the sunbathing women around it, then on the ice-cream sellers wandering around the sun beds, then on the sea lapping up against the beach.

This is where a writer does not reveal a key bit of information about a character, situation or place and leaves the reader with questions or a false impression of a situation.

© 2014, Creating Outstanding Classrooms, Oliver Knight and David Benson, Routledge

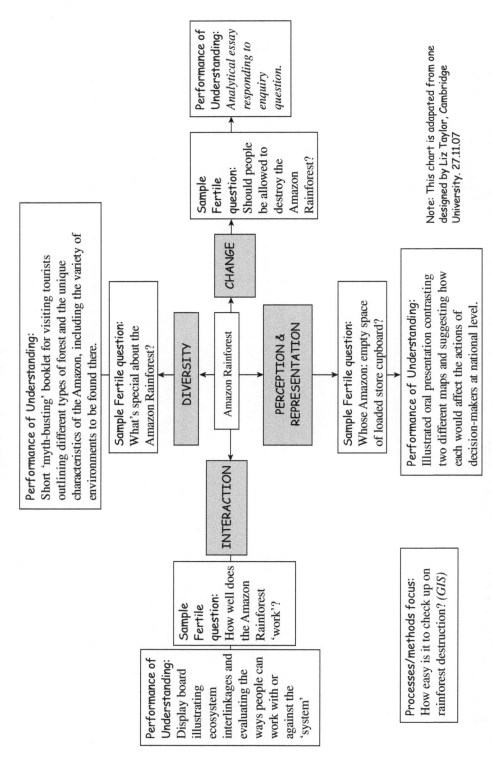

Figure 1.18 Possible approaches to teaching the Amazon Rainforest through structural concepts in Geography

Notes

1 Oates, T. (2010) *'Could do better': Using international comparisons to refine the National Curriculum for England*, National Curriculum – 18 Nov 2010: Cambridge Assessment.
2 See Counsell, C. (2000) 'Historical knowledge and historical skills: a distracting dichotomy' in Arthur, J. and Phillips, R. (eds) *Issues in History teaching*: Routledge.
3 Young, M. (2008) *Bringing knowledge back in*: Routledge.
4 Oates, T. (2010) *'Could do better': Using international comparisons to refine the National Curriculum in England*, National Curriculum – 18 Nov 2010: Cambridge Assessment.
5 Donovan, M.S. and Bransford, J.D. (2005) *How students learn*: The National Academies Press.
6 Example from Perkins, D. (2008) *Making learning whole*: Jossey-Bass. Perkins is at the forefront of developing teaching for understanding and we have used his Newton example in full here.
7 This example is taken from Perkins, D. (2008) *Making learning whole*: Jossey-Bass.
8 Bruner, J. (1962) *The process of education*: Harvard University Press.
9 Perkins, D.N. and Salomon, G. *'The science and art of transfer'*, https: //learnweb. harvard.edu /alps/thinking/docs/ trancost.pdf
10 Geary, D., Wade Boykin, A., Embretson, S., Valerie Reyna, V., Siegler, R., Berch, D.B. and Graban, J. Chapter 4, 'Report of the task group on learning processes', http:// www2.ed.gov/about/bdscomm/list/mathpanel/report/learning-processes.pdf
11 Ideas adapted from Gardner, H. (2000) *The disciplined mind*: Penguin.
12 Bereiter and Scardamalia, quoted in Erik De Corte, Lieven Verschaffel, Noël Entwistle and Jeroen van Merriënboer (eds) *Powerful learning environments: Unravelling basic components and dimensions*: Pergamon; 1st edition (2003)
13 Bruner, J. (1960) quoted in Donovan, M.S. and Bransford, J.D. (2005) *How students learn*: The National Academies Press.
14 Willingham, D.T. (2007) 'Critical thinking. Why is is so hard to teach?', *American Educator*, Summer 2007
15 Gardner, H. (2000) *The disciplined mind*: Penguin.
16 Wiliam, D. and Leahy, S. (2008) *Beyond the national strategy: Sustaining assessment for learning with teacher learning communities*: SSAT.
17 Peter Lee (2002) Institute of Education.
18 Scardamalia, M. (2002) 'Collective cognitive responsibility for the advancement of knowledge' in B. Smith (ed.) *Liberal education in a knowledge society*: Open Court Publishing.
19 Adapted from Smith, M. and Wilhelm, J. (2006) *Going with the flow*: Heinemann.
20 Lefstein, A. (2003) *Design heuristics for a community of thinking*.
21 Lefstein, A. (2003) *Design heuristics for a community of thinking*.
22 Image initially from http://www.elearningcouncil.com/content/overcoming-ebbinghaus-curve-how-soon-we-forget
23 Adapted from Tokuhama, (2010) *Mind, brain, and education science: A comprehensive guide to the new brain-based teaching*: W.W. Norton & Co.

24 Guy Claxton (2009) 'Cultivating positive learning dispositions': University of Bristol.

25 Ark Academy Teaching and Learning policy.

26 Adam Lefstein and Yoram Harpaz 'Communities of thinking', http://yoramharpaz.com/publications-en/thinking/communities-of-thinking/

27 Mercer, N. (1995) *The guided construction of knowledge*: Multilingual Matters Ltd. Mercer, N. (2000) *Words and Minds:* Routledge.

28 Guidance provided to Ofsted Inspectors on judging attainment and progress – www.ofsted.gov.uk

29 Adapted from Wagner, T. (2008) *The global achievement gap: Why even our best schools don't teach the new survival skills our children need – and what we can do about it*: Basic Books and Claxton and Lucas (2010) *New kinds of smart: How the science of learnable intelligence is changing education*: Open University Press.

2

Teacher practices –
the nuts and bolts

2

Teacher practices

The nuts and bolts

We have looked, in some depth, at how to write medium- and long-term plans. It is right to begin with the big picture: real understanding will only be secured if all teachers in the school are operating within the planning frameworks outlined above. Without this lessons become isolated and individual displays, divorced of links and connections. Deep understanding will not be developed and progress will be limited and patchy.

However, these plans are just that – plans. They are a starting point for what the teaching in your school might look like. What happens during the lessons will depend on teachers' ability to fully exploit those plans through their interactions with students. So this next section is crucial – how to go from the big picture to specific lesson activities; from macro to micro.

This chapter is broken down into three small 'chunks'. Each chunk is a core practice that has a direct impact on student understanding. More has perhaps been written on 'hints and tips' for teachers than most teachers could ever read. We have therefore only included what is most important as this is a handbook for embedding a whole-school approach rather than a guide to 'surviving' in the classroom – whatever that means!

These three chunks are:

i.   Lesson structure and planning

ii.   Questioning

iii. Mindsets and classroom culture

One option for using this chapter is to build on the Fertile Questions you have sketched out in the previous section, and add individual lesson plans using the four-part lesson structure detailed below.

Lesson structure and planning

The simplest way to ensure consistency across all lessons is to use a common planning framework. It is our experience that the best frameworks are both simple and challenging. This book is a handbook for teachers and school leaders and as such requires a whole-school approach to lesson planning; not just some teachers in some classrooms but *all* teachers in *all* classrooms.

Below is an outline for planning a four-part lesson. It is simple and clear for all teachers to use. But the outline challenges teachers to think through the purpose of each episode in the lesson. It is not just four rows on a table, a case of 'Starter > Main 1 > Main 2 > Plenary'. Instead the plan helps teachers and learners know what they are trying to do, how they will do it, and what success will look like. As such the four-part lesson is a developmental tool.

We know that now Ofsted have removed their jackboot the new Inspection Framework does not require inspectors to see lesson plans; only that lessons be well planned. However, it would be a foolish school or department that thought that having a tight framework for lesson planning was no longer important. The framework outlined in this chapter allows teachers to be creative and consistent whilst at the same time allows for Senior Teams to check quality and eradicate in-school variance: both in terms of student progress and teacher expertise. Whilst Ofsted inspections will definitely look for these three elements: teachers effectively checking pupil's understanding and intervening where necessary, high quality ongoing constructive feedback and students tackling challenging activities; a clear approach to lesson planning will ensure that in every lesson all students are making progress, levels of challenge are high and language is not a barrier to learning.

Above this the framework here also provides a clear and supportive structure for teacher professional learning and embedding of the model. Once the approach has become second nature schools may think about scaling back the amount of individual lesson plans they see and discuss but initially a tight regime ensures rapid and consistent implementation.

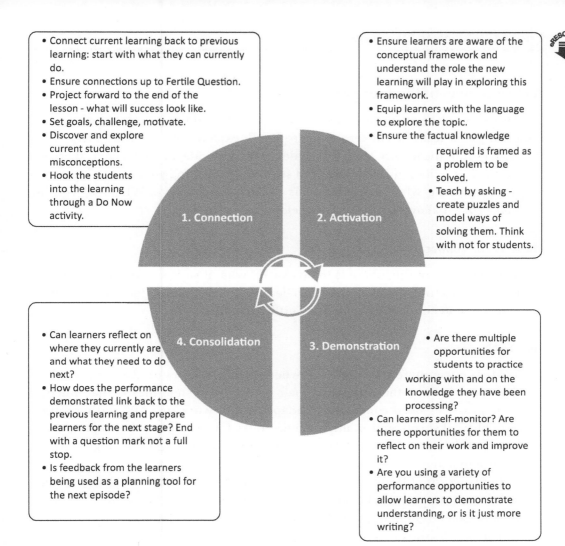

- Connect current learning back to previous learning: start with what they can currently do.
- Ensure connections up to Fertile Question.
- Project forward to the end of the lesson - what will success look like.
- Set goals, challenge, motivate.
- Discover and explore current student misconceptions.
- Hook the students into the learning through a Do Now activity.

1. Connection

- Ensure learners are aware of the conceptual framework and understand the role the new learning will play in exploring this framework.
- Equip learners with the language to explore the topic.
- Ensure the factual knowledge required is framed as a problem to be solved.
- Teach by asking - create puzzles and model ways of solving them. Think with not for students.

2. Activation

4. Consolidation

- Can learners reflect on where they currently are and what they need to do next?
- How does the performance demonstrated link back to the previous learning and prepare learners for the next stage? End with a question mark not a full stop.
- Is feedback from the learners being used as a planning tool for the next episode?

3. Demonstration

- Are there multiple opportunities for students to practice working with and on the knowledge they have been processing?
- Can learners self-monitor? Are there opportunities for them to reflect on their work and improve it?
- Are you using a variety of performance opportunities to allow learners to demonstrate understanding, or is it just more writing?

Figure 2.1 The four-part lesson[1]

A clearer view of the four parts

This section is not concerned with issuing hints and tips for snazzy starters or great plenaries. It is concerned instead with explaining what has to happen at each part of the lesson. How it is achieved is individual to the teacher; there are probably a million different ways of starting and ending your lesson, the key is understanding what each section is designed to achieve. Whatever you do, make sure it allows for the points below to be achieved.

Phase 1: The connection

The main aim of this phase is to do exactly what it says – *connect*. This means both connecting *back* to previous learning, connecting *forward* to future learning and connecting *up* to the Fertile Question.

The Do Now

We first encountered the 'Do Now' when visiting a series of Charter Schools in the States. Whilst the context of their education system means that much of their practices need considerable adaptation to work in a UK setting – their love of worksheets and multiple choice tests for example – their approach to classroom culture is exceptional and the Do Now is a great example of that culture in action.

In the words of Doug Lemov: 'Students should never have to ask themselves, "what am I supposed to be doing?" when they enter your classroom, nor should they be able to claim not to know what they should be doing.'[2]

The best lessons get off to a flying start.

The Do Now is simply an activity that the students can complete as soon as they enter the room - either written up on the board or on their desks – that ensures that every minute of the lesson is focused on learning. To make it effective the Do Now should:[3]

- be able to be completed with minimal help or direction from the teacher;
- take three to five minutes to complete;
- require stretches of thinking and language;
- preview/foreground the learning they are about to encounter.

The worst way to start a lesson has to be to have students sat there whilst you call out the register. In order to maximize learning the Do Now is an instant start to the lesson and the register can be taken silently by you (if required) whilst the Do Now is completed. Another horror show is watching a teacher dictate, or get students to copy down, the 'learning objectives', with no further explanation. WALT (what are we learning today) and WILF (what I am looking for) need to be consigned to the scrapheap; a more intellectually appropriate way of foregrounding learning follows:

Connect current learning back to previous learning experiences

It is essential that in the first part of the lesson the learning students are about to encounter is connected back to what has gone before. The context for the lesson must be established, and latent knowledge students have should be activated. Consider the difference between these two Do Nows from an English lesson.

Students will have some knowledge of personification – it first appears in the curriculum during early Key Stage 2. The second Do Now elicits this knowledge, involving students in the discussion. The first one tells them the answers.

If all lesson planning starts with the answer to the question 'What can my students currently do?' then the answer to that question needs to be revisited from lesson to lesson. As we saw earlier with the Ebbinghaus curve of forgetting, failure to review previous learning and to connect new learning to that results in a severe drop-off in terms of 'remembering'.

As well as foregrounding where the lesson is going the Do Now can also connect back to previous learning.

Monday 5th November Poetic techniques DO NOW: Copy down this definition: *Personification is when you give human characteristics to an inanimate object.*	Monday 5th November DO NOW: What do you notice about this description? Discuss with your partner. *The desk screamed as it was dragged across the floor.*

Ensure connections up to the Fertile Question

Building on what has just been said, it is essential that the Fertile Question is revisited, talked about and the BIG picture restated. This can take any number of forms but the essential thing is to ensure that all learners are aware of how what they are doing today fits into and helps resolve the BIG problem that the Fertile Question poses.

Project forward to the end of the lesson

Just as foregrounding is central to helping the development of academic language, so is foregrounding important in helping students make sense of how what they are learning fits together and what the journey through that learning looks like. Students need to be aware of what they will be able to do by the end of the lesson that they could not do at the start and have a model of what success looks like. This does not mean copying down learning objectives!

Discover and explore current student misconceptions

This is one of the core principles on which this approach is built – new understandings are built on a foundation of existing understandings – and so it is vital that these existing understandings are checked out. This works at both a deeper conceptual level and a more superficial knowledge level. If student misconceptions are not discovered and corrected at this stage then the entire learning episode will be lost.

An example of a conceptual misconception from History is that many pupils believe we can only know what happened if we were there or if we read the eyewitness account of someone else. This needs to be challenged before new learning can take place. Otherwise all new learning is built on shaky foundations. Some readers may know the story of 'Fish is Fish' by Leo Lionni – it is a great example of what happens if new learning is not placed in a robust conceptual framework.

Phase 2: The activation

Again, the role and focus for this part of the lesson is clear – to activate new learning and provide all students with the information they need to solve the problem posed at the start. This phase also provides opportunities for feedback and redrafting prior to the demonstration phase.

Ensure learners are aware of the conceptual framework and understand the role the new learning will play in exploring and expanding on it

As we saw earlier on with the master and novice chess players, concepts form an organizing or structural framework that allows students to move beyond information acquisition to knowledge application and creation.

If the students in your classroom are not aware of the concept they are working with and have no picture in their own minds of how it works they are simply going to place any new information into a box that does not connect with the other boxes. It is vital that in the activation phase attention is drawn to the conceptual framework of the Fertile Question and how the learning they are about to experience helps shape and expand their understanding of this concept.

Equip learners with the language to explore the topic

As you will see in Part 3 of this chapter, language plays a central role in understanding. It is imperative that the specific language demands of the Fertile Question are known and that access to this language is planned for. In the words of Vygotsky: 'Thought undergoes many changes as it turns into speech. It does not merely find expression in speech; it finds reality and form.'[4]

Ensure the factual knowledge required is framed as a problem to be solved

The brain likes problems and it likes beginnings. A key part of this phase of the lesson is to ensure that the lesson is posed as a problem to be solved. That problem in turn must form part of the wider solution to the BIG problem that the Fertile Question poses.

Phase 3: The demonstration

The key focus of the demonstration phase is to provide multiple opportunities for all students to demonstrate understanding. This demonstration takes the form of posing a solution to the problem they have been working on. This phase also provides opportunities for feedback and peer review – *how are we doing, what do we need to do next?*

The crucial design structure in this phase is to ensure that opportunities for self-monitoring are built into the activities

By self-monitoring we simply mean allowing the learners to take control of their own learning. This means giving them opportunities to set their own learning targets and assess their progress towards these targets.

A clear example of self-monitoring is requiring self-explanation – that is requiring students to explain *how* they solved a problem or *how* they applied knowledge to an unseen question to answer it. During the demonstration phase activities that require students to explain *how* as well as *what* are crucial to developing deeper conceptual understandings.

Are there multiple opportunities for students to practice working with and on the knowledge they have been processing?

During the demonstration phase students need to be presented with opportunities to practice applying the new learning (or indeed to design their own). They should demonstrate mastery of the new knowledge they have acquired.

The importance here is to build into this phase language acquisition, so that students are having to use different types of academic language to explain, justify and amend their thinking.

Are you using a variety of performance opportunities to allow learners to demonstrate understanding?

Learning for understanding means thinking flexibly, not regurgitating small chunks of information – however 'snazzily' that information has been presented.

This phase has to require students to do something 'new' with the learning. What will they do to demonstrate progress? How will you know they actually understand?

Phase 4: The consolidation

The primary focus of the consolidation phase is to provide opportunities for the new learning that has taken place to be 'fitted' into the Fertile Question.

How does the performance demonstrated link back to the previous learning and prepare learners for the next stage?

Are students aware of the BIG picture? Can they see how this lesson connects to the next lesson and builds on what they have already done? Are students designing their own pathway through the question?

Can learners reflect on where they currently are and what they need to do next?

Is there time built in to reflect on where we currently are and where we need to go next?

Is planning flexible enough to allow for this? In other words, does lesson and medium-term planning change based on student feedback and responses?

Does every student know what they are doing and why they are doing it?

Is feedback from the learners being used as a planning tool for the next episode?

Is there a role for the students themselves to decide what they need to do next?

Are there questions posed by the students that can take the form of the next lesson question? (See later section on questioning for this.)

The four-part lesson summarized

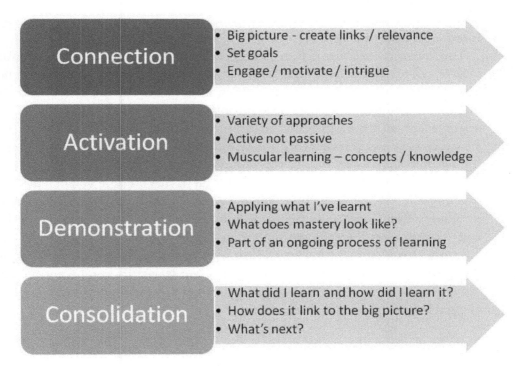

Figure 2.2   The four-part lesson summarized

How does a four-part lesson structure connect with an enquiry-based learning approach?

The four-part structure is a planning tool, which allows for consistency across all departments and disciplines. The difference between outstanding and satisfactory lessons is often the extent to which students are engaged in their learning and the ways in which they are challenged to think and interact with the information being presented. Key questions for observers are: *Are they demonstrating progress in their thinking? Can they do something with the information at the end of the lesson that they could not do at the beginning? Have they applied the knowledge they have been given, or just acquired information?*

The four-part lesson structure emphasizes the centrality of understanding – and Performances of Understanding – in the learning process. This means moving beyond simply reframing information in their own words or reciting formulae to creating real opportunities for learners to work with and on knowledge; to question its construction and use. Learning in a four-part lesson is active not passive.

The four-part structure is fluid enough to be used as an open-ended planning tool. It can stretch over several hours or even days of learning and does not have to start and end with the arbitrary time frame of the school day. By building in planned review sessions during each phase and by ensuring that all learners are aware of the BIG picture created by the Fertile Question, the structure becomes a framework for ensuring progress happens rather than a rigid grid to squeeze chunks of content into.

By utilizing the learning objectives later on in this section, you can plan for learning and review by having tangible markers of success at various stages through the enquiry. By starting out knowing what success looks like at the end, and sharing this picture with your students, you are instantly giving everyone involved in the journey a clear view of the destination and how to get there. Anyone who is heading off on a different trajectory can be noticed and brought back on track swiftly and easily through the use of the guiding markers of success – both short- and long-term.

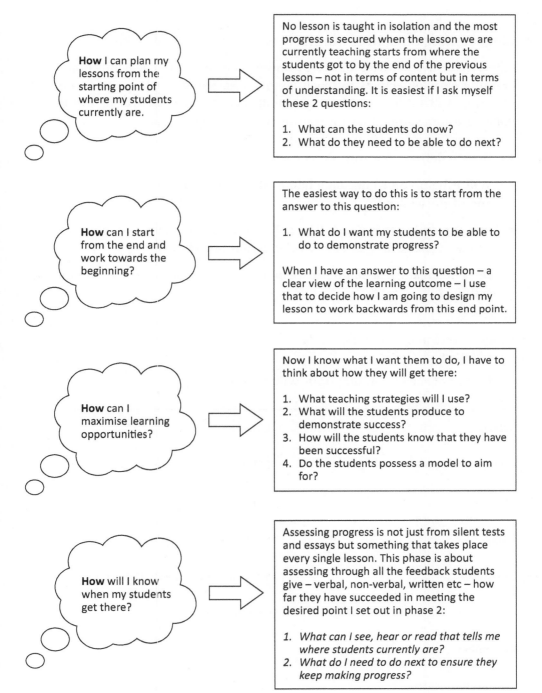

How I can plan my lessons from the starting point of where my students currently are.

No lesson is taught in isolation and the most progress is secured when the lesson we are currently teaching starts from where the students got to by the end of the previous lesson – not in terms of content but in terms of understanding. It is easiest if I ask myself these 2 questions:

1. What can the students do now?
2. What do they need to be able to do next?

How can I start from the end and work towards the beginning?

The easiest way to do this is to start from the answer to this question:

1. What do I want my students to be able to do to demonstrate progress?

When I have an answer to this question – a clear view of the learning outcome – I use that to decide how I am going to design my lesson to work backwards from this end point.

How can I maximise learning opportunities?

Now I know what I want them to do, I have to think about how they will get there:

1. What teaching strategies will I use?
2. What will the students produce to demonstrate success?
3. How will the students know that they have been successful?
4. Do the students possess a model to aim for?

How will I know when my students get there?

Assessing progress is not just from silent tests and essays but something that takes place every single lesson. This phase is about assessing through all the feedback students give – verbal, non-verbal, written etc – how far they have succeeded in meeting the desired point I set out in phase 2:

1. *What can I see, hear or read that tells me where students currently are?*
2. *What do I need to do next to ensure they keep making progress?*

Figure 2.3 Revisiting the Teaching and Learning cycle (from Chapter 1)

Framing learning objectives: Knowing what mastery looks like

Often an unsuccessful lesson can be traced back to confused learning objectives. Framing clear objectives for each lesson is essential – it helps to focus your planning and understand how you will measure the success of the lesson. Below are some guidelines for writing learning objectives:

- Does it define a learning outcome?

- Will it help you to decide whether the pupils have learnt anything at the end of the lesson?

- Is it something that you will be able to see, hear or read (i.e. you must have a way of checking that you have *met* your objectives)?

- Does it create a meaningful response and prepare for the culminating activity?

Some useful words and phrases that will give you the precision you need in a learning objective

By the end of the lesson *all* pupils will be able to:

Select...	Extract...
Give examples of...	Relate...
Choose...	Connect...
Link...	Explain...
Illustrate...	Show the relationship between...
Explain the relationship between...	Comment upon...
Remember...	Recall...
Ask questions about...	Choose questions that...
Prioritize...	Create headings...

Refine headings...	Justify...
Justify their thinking concerning...	Explain their thinking concerning...
Compare...	Contrast...
Define...	Analyse...
Join up...	Shape...
Organize...	Reconsider...
Reflect...	Support...
Support a view that...	Evaluate...
Weigh up...	Create/construct...

Below is a suggested template for designing a four-part lesson, followed by some exemplars. They should illustrate some of the principles of lesson planning discussed so far in this chapter.

A scaffold not a cage – using a lesson planning proforma to ensure consistency across every classroom

LESSON PLAN

Teacher:	Subject:	Set/year:
Lesson: 123456	Class & room:	Number on roll:
Focus of lesson: *(Concept and target knowledge)*	Date:	Student data: (Numbers) G&T: SEN: EAL:
	Lesson question:	

Links to prior learning:	Lesson objectives:
	By the end of the lesson *all* pupils will be able to:

Time	Lesson structure
	Starter – connections to prior learning and lesson focus: *(Engage, intrigue, motivate.)*
	Main body of the lesson – activation phase: *(Input and accessing new information.)*

© 2014, Creating Outstanding Classrooms, Oliver Knight and David Benson, Routledge

Main body of the lesson – demonstration phase: *(Learners demonstrating understanding of new knowledge – Mastery.)*

Plenary – review and consolidate: *(Pupils seeing the progress they have made, seeing their learning in a new light, placing their knowledge into the big picture – making connections.)*

Assessment/homework

Building on/consolidating learning or preparing pupils for new knowledge: (Vague bits of finishing off, leaving some pupils with nothing to do is unacceptable.)

Intervention strategies

Targeted pupils	EAL, SEN, G&T, etc.	Level	Nature of intervention (Based on IEP strategies where appropriate)

Pupil progress and engagement: *Reflect on the lesson before discussing the lesson with the person observing. Include in this section any pupil misconceptions or miscues that will need to be addressed at the beginning of the next lesson.*

WWW	EBI

LESSON PLAN

Teacher:	Subject: Mathematics	Set/Year: 7
Lesson: 3	Class & room:	Number on roll: 30
Focus of lesson: *(Concept and target knowledge)* During this lesson students will learn how to *simplify* expressions with one and *two* variables.	Date: 24 November 2010	**Student data:** (see seating plan for more detail) G&T: 20/30 SEN: SA: 1/20; SA+: 1/30 EAL: 12/30
	Lesson question: *What are the key words we need to understand to use algebra to solve problems?* *What strategies do we use when simplifying expressions?*	

Links to prior learning:	Lesson objectives:

In the previous lesson, students looked at the questions:
Could a world without algebra survive?
This lesson was an introduction to algebra and students learnt how to form and substitute into formulae.
 	
This is the first lesson on simplifying expressions and students will be progressing from simplifying expressions with one *variable* to simplifying expressions with *two variables*.
	By the end of this lesson, *all* students will be able to:
	
	i. Explain the meaning of and give an example of
	    • a variable
	    • an expression
	    • an equation/formula
	ii. Simplify expressions with one or two variables.
	    Level 5

Time	Lesson Structure

12 minutes	**Starter – connections to prior learning and lesson focus:** (*Engage, intrigue, motivate.*) Line up silently outside, enter and stand behind chair. Take out pencil case, planner and water bottle, say pledge and then sit. Teacher takes register when students are doing the 'Do Now'/activation.
3 minutes	**Do Now** **IKEA shopping**
7 minutes	Students are introduced to the idea of mix-and-match purchases at IKEA. Students work in pairs to discuss the problem and then to construct a formula to represent the price of a table when the table top and table legs are all sold separately. Once they have constructed the formula they are asked to work out the cost of the table given a price for the table top and each table leg. This activity allows for the teacher to assess the students' understanding of forming and substituting into formulae, which was covered in Monday's lesson. The students have an opportunity to assess their own understanding.
2 minutes	If necessary students will be asked to explain how they got their answer. This will either be used to address a misconception or to facilitate peer learning.
10 minutes	**Main body of the lesson – activation phase:** (*Input and accessing new information.*)
7 minutes	Students note today's lesson title. Students are introduced to the key words that they need to understand, in order to use algebra to solve problems. The definitions of these key words are stuck into their books.
3 minutes	**Sorting activity** Students are selected, using cold calling, to answer questions as part of a sorting activity that checks their understanding of the key words that have just been introduced. **Discussion** (30 seconds to share their ideas) Students are shown a picture of two shapes and two expressions where the side lengths are represented by either one or two variables. Students are asked to discuss the following question:

How would you…
i. *find the perimeter on these shapes?*
ii. *simplify the below expressions?*

Teacher to move around the room to monitor, encourage and, where necessary, aid student discussions. Students are selected to share their ideas using lollypop sticks

23 minutes	**Main body of the lesson – demonstration phase:** *(Learners demonstrating understanding of new knowledge – mastery.)*
7 minutes	**Teacher modelling** The teacher models how to write and simplify an expression for the perimeter of the two shapes and also how to simplify the two abstract expressions. Students are asked to note the examples onto their worksheet.
13 minutes	Students start their **10 Minute Challenge.** Students work through a set of questions independently. There are two sections to the worksheet with the second being more challenging than the first. A **challenge activity** is provided for any students who finish before the end of the 15 minutes. The challenge activity requires that students construct and simplify their own expressions. They can work with the teacher and co-teacher to construct a unique expression and to simplify it.
3 minutes	The teacher will move around the room to support and encourage students whilst they are completing this task. Students are also encouraged to help each other. Answers will be displayed on the IWB and students are to mark their own work and assess their own progress in the lesson so far.
15 minutes	**Plenary – review and consolidate:** *(Pupils seeing the progress they have made, seeing their learning in a new light, placing their knowledge into the big picture – making connections.)*
13 minutes	**Matching activity** Students are selected, using lollypop sticks, to come to the board and match the statement with its correct algebraic expression. Students must explain their reasoning but if unsure they can 'phone a friend' (ask someone else in the group to help them).

2 minutes	Students pack away to the sound of our pack away song: Magnum PI!

Assessment/homework

Building on/consolidating learning or preparing pupils for new knowledge: (Vague bits of finishing off, leaving some pupils with nothing to do is unacceptable.)

Student's homework tonight is set individually based on the work they have produced in the topic which ended on Friday. (They did not have a lesson yesterday). Students need to complete the reply on their learning review sheet and then work on their targets. They can meet the teacher at lunch time to discuss any problems areas and are also encouraged to work together if they get stuck. Homework is due tomorrow.

Intervention strategies

Targeted pupils	EAL, SEN, G&T, etc.	Level	Nature of intervention *(Based on IEP strategies where appropriate)*
	EAL		Seating plan indicates EAL students in the class. Students work in pairs/groups throughout the lesson. *(Discussion instructions on display and in student's book for group work.)*
			Students also supported by teacher during individual work (detail indicated on lesson plan – though there is no co-teacher in this lesson).
			All keywords/terms relating to algebra are displayed on the board and referred to throughout the lesson. Students have explanations of the terms stuck into their book for reference.

SEN	SA (BESD+ OTH) SA+(OTH)	Examples are copied down to support students when working independently. Students supported by teacher during individual work and by other students at other parts of the lesson (see seating plan for more details).
G&T		Students have the opportunity to complete work of increasing difficulty during the simplifying expressions tasks. A **Challenge activity** is provided for any students who finish before the end of the 15 minutes. The challenge activity requires that students construct and simplify their own expressions. They can work with the teacher and co-teacher to construct a unique expression and to simplify it. Students are set individual and challenging targets for homework including Level 7 'find the original amount' percentage questions

Pupil progress and engagement: *Reflect on the lesson before discussing the lesson with the person observing. Include in this section any pupil misconceptions or miscues that will need to be addressed at the beginning of the next lesson.*

WWW

EBI

LESSON PLAN

Teacher:	Subject: History	Set/year: 7A2
Lesson: 2	Class & room: G08	Number on roll: 30
Focus of lesson: (Concept and target knowledge) **Causation** – why did something happen?	Date: 8/6/11	**Student data:** (Numbers) G&T: 6 SEN: 4 EAL: 14
	Lesson question: *What was a medieval king supposed to do?*	

Links to prior learning:	Lesson objectives:
This is their second lesson on the new Fertile Question. Last lesson they were given the narrative overview of the topic and we discussed the focus of the case study. **Fertile Question:** *Could a Medieval king do whatever he liked?*	By the end of the lesson *all* pupils will be able to: i. Justify their thinking concerning the lesson question. ii. Reflect on the different demands made on a Monarch. iii. Construct a reasoned response to the lesson question.

Time	Lesson structure

© 2014, Creating Outstanding Classrooms, Oliver Knight and David Benson, Routledge

10 minutes	**Starter – connections to prior learning and lesson focus:** (*Engage, intrigue, motivate.*) i. Do Now – Ranking exercise on seven jobs of a medieval monarch. ii. Use the feedback from this to shore up any misconceptions arising from their prior learning and link back to the new Fertile Question. iii. Outline lesson focus and outcomes. iv. Get lesson question into their books.
20 minutes	**Main body of the lesson – activation phase:** (*Input and accessing new information.*) i. Look at six things a king does – students must summarize the information into five words to explain what the king is doing and why. ii. Students now have to evaluate the priorities and decide which one was the trickiest, the easiest, the most important and why they think that.
20 minutes	**Main body of the lesson – demonstration phase:** (*Learners demonstrating understanding of new knowledge – Mastery.*) i. Introduce the next layer to the Fertile Question – what constituted power in Medieval England. ii. Students now complete the king's thought bubbles. iii. Feedback – is the king in total control of the country? How has your thinking changed/moved on from the beginning of the lesson?
10 minutes	**Plenary – review and consolidate:** (*Pupils seeing the progress they have made, seeing their learning in a new light, placing their knowledge into the big picture – making connections*) i. What was a medieval king supposed to do? ii. Do you think that the church would be eager or reluctant to rebel against a king? Why? iii. Do you think the barons would be eager or reluctant to rebel against a king? Why? iv. What else do we need to look at to be able to answer the Fertile Question?

Assessment/homework

Building on/consolidating learning or preparing pupils for new knowledge: (Vague bits of finishing off, leaving some pupils with nothing to do is unacceptable.)

N/A – not hwk week.

Intervention strategies

Targeted pupils	EAL, SEN, G&T, etc.	Level	Nature of intervention (Based on IEP strategies where appropriate)
6	EAL	ABL	These students are supported through the visuals on the IWB and the group talk activity. The nature of the tasks means that students talk about the lesson question before moving into writing. The IWB supports thinking through visual scaffolding and their own copy of the thought bubbles helps them capture their thinking.
8	EAL	NCL4	All students have an end of year target of L5. They are strong orally but some struggle with getting their thoughts down on paper. The visual nature of the tasks and the seating plan helps students access the higher-level thinking through having the language of justification scaffolded for them.
1	SA	MLD	xxxxxx is supported through the group work and the partners he is working with. xxxxxxx is keen to participate and the structured and oral approach of the demonstration activity enables him to demonstrate understanding before moving into writing.

| 2 | SA | BESD | xxxxxxx is eager and is making good progress. His seat allocation and the clear expectations set help him stay within the prescribed boundaries. xxxxxx is supported through the fact that the lesson has many beginnings and is 'chunked' into short activities. The demonstration activity allows her to grapple with the lesson question. This prepares her for next lesson when she will be required to construct a written response. The IWB scaffolds her thinking and means she can focus on responding to the questions rather than having to remember them. |
| 6 | G&T | KS2 SATS | These six students have an end of year target of L5a/6c or above. They need an extra challenge to stretch them. This is provided through the nature of the questions they are asked – probing rather than clarifying at the end of each activity. This requires them to be more reflective rather than to recall. This will be evident in the next lesson when they move from a love–hate line to a piece of extended writing. |

Pupil progress and engagement: *Reflect on the lesson before discussing the lesson with the person observing. Include in this section any pupil misconceptions or miscues that will need to be addressed at the beginning of the next lesson.*

WWW

EBI

TRAINING ACTIVITY

Planning a lesson in four stages

Using the two model lesson plans as a guide, complete the blank lesson plan proforma to plan the first lesson of one of your new Fertile Questions.

Answer these questions first:

- *What can the students do now?*

- *What do they need to be able to do next?*

- *What do you want your students to be able to do to demonstrate progress (that you can see, hear or read)?*

- *What knowledge do students need to acquire to get to the desired place?*

- *How do students need to apply that knowledge – what is the problem they are solving?*

- *What is the concept that underpins the problem?*

- *How will you know when your students get there?*

- *How will they know – can they answer the three key questions: Where am I going, where am I now, what do I need to do next?*

- *How does what they are learning to do link to what they have done before and prepare them for what they need to do next?*

Now plan the lesson using the proforma below

LESSON PLAN

Teacher:	Subject:		Set/year:
Lesson: 123456	Class & room:		Number on roll:
Focus of lesson: *(Concept and target knowledge)*	Date:		Student data: (Numbers) G&T: SEN: EAL:
	Lesson question:		

Links to prior learning:	Lesson objectives:
	By the end of the lesson *all* pupils will be able to:

Lesson structure	
Time	
	Starter – connections to prior learning and lesson focus: *(Engage, intrigue, motivate.)*
	Main body of the lesson – activation phase *(Input and accessing new information.)*

Main body of the lesson – demonstration phase (*Learners demonstrating understanding of new knowledge – Mastery.*)

Plenary – review and consolidate: (*Pupils seeing the progress they have made, seeing their learning in a new light, placing their knowledge into the big picture – making connections.*)

Assessment/homework

Building on/consolidating learning or preparing pupils for new knowledge: (*Vague bits of finishing off, leaving some pupils with nothing to do is unacceptable.*)

Intervention strategies

Targeted pupils	EAL, SEN, G&T, etc.	Level	Nature of intervention (*Based on IEP strategies where appropriate*)

Pupil progress and engagement: *Reflect on the lesson before discussing the lesson with the person observing. Include in this section any pupil misconceptions or miscues that will need to be addressed at the beginning of the next lesson.*

WWW

EBI

Questioning and creating a culture of inquiry

Now that the structure or route through the learning is created at the level of an individual lesson it is possible to look at *questioning*. Teachers are only as good as the questions they ask, and in this section we consider how to use different types of questions to help learners make meaning out of information, and to convert information to knowledge - how to move from acquisition to application.

If we know that learning is a two-way process and that the learner has to be actively involved at all stages, how can we guarantee learner engagement whilst using a planning framework that is teacher-led? This is where the use of the question comes in.

The enquiry and problem-based approach enshrined in this book is only made possible if everything starts and ends with questioning. By creating a culture of enquiry at all levels of school life, it is possible to create independent and resilient learners whilst allowing them to grapple with powerful knowledge. It is here that Michael Young's definition of what constitutes powerful knowledge is most useful.[5]

> Schooling is about providing access to the specialised knowledge that is embodied in different domains. The key curriculum questions will be concerned with:
>
> (a) The differences between different forms of specialist knowledge and the relations between them;
> (b) How this specialist knowledge differs from the knowledge people acquire in everyday life;
> (c) How specialist and everyday knowledge relate to each other; and
> (d) How specialist knowledge is pedagogised [communicated through teaching activities].

Keeping Young's four questions in mind it is possible to look at how different layers of questioning can move students from everyday to academic ways of thinking; or in the words of Vygotsky: 'moving from the known to the unknown'.

If learning therefore is a relatively enduring change in one's ideas about the world then, in the words of Lefstein, surely a critical condition of learning is *'perplexity or cognitive disequilibrium'* (author's italics). Or, in other words 'the experience of a question'.

The following section is in three parts:

- **Part 1** explores some of the current problems with much current practice.
- **Part 2** goes on to look at some intermediate strategies and practices to try and solve the problems outlined in Part 1.
- **Part 3** explores an approach that goes beyond participation and focuses on inquiry and student questioning.

TRAINING ACTIVITY

What is the current problem with much practice of questioning in the classroom?[6]

Questions:

The information below is well-known but worth reminding ourselves of (this could be the basis of a training input on questioning):

- *How many questions do teachers ask in 30 minutes?*

- *How many questions are asked by students?*

- *What kinds of questions are asked by each?*

- *What is the significance of these questioning practices?*

Answers:

- Teachers ask 45–150 questions per half-hour lesson…

- …but estimate asking 12–20 questions.

- 67–95 per cent of the questions involve straight recall.

- Students ask two or fewer questions per lesson.

- Teacher recall questions are negatively correlated with student questions.

- Most questions posed in the classroom do not promote deep or searching intellectual activity.

- Despite increased awareness of 'wait time' – most teachers still find it impossible to tolerate increased thinking time.

- Two-choice questions – can be answered by a single word.

- Wh-type questions (sometimes dressed up in the language of Socrates) again controls where the discourse is going. Pupil responds and then becomes silent again.

What does a student look like in this environment?

- gives short responses;

- asks few, if any, questions;

- seldom elaborates on their answers to any questions addressed to them;

- talks to their peers infrequently;

- seldom volunteers their own thoughts;

- shows frequent signs of confusion;

- rarely develops the language of the discipline or talks like a ...;

- tries to guess the answers to these questions.[7]

A more worrying look at much current practice

Try to guess the answers to the questions about the text in the following exercise.

Text #1 – Questions from a US Scholastic Aptitude Test (SAT), following a reading passage (not supplied here):

1. The main idea of the passage is that

    (A) a constricted view of [this novel] is natural and acceptable

    (B) a novel should not depict a vanished society

    (C) a good novel is an intellectual rather than an emotive experience

    (D) many readers have seen only the comedy [in this novel]

    (E) [this novel] should be read with sensitivity and an open mind

2. The author's attitude toward someone who 'enjoys' [this novel] and then remarks 'but of course it has no relevance today' (lines 21–22) can best be described as one of

   (A) amusement

   (B) astonishment

   (C) disapproval

   (D) resignation

   (E) ambivalence

3. The author [of this passage] implies that a work of art is properly judged on the basis of its

   (A) universality of human experience truthfully recorded

   (B) popularity and critical acclaim in its own age

   (C) openness to varied interpretations, including seemingly contradictory ones

   (D) avoidance of political and social issues of minor importance

   (E) continued popularity through different eras and with different societies

The 'correct' answers:

1. (E) [this novel] should be read with sensitivity and an open mind;

2. (C) disapproval;

3. (A) universality of human experience truthfully recorded.

i. *What does this tell us about much questioning in schools?*

ii. *What does this tell us about classroom culture?*

Does teacher-led questioning improve student thinking?

When students set about answering a question they begin to construct ideas, apply knowledge, absorb new information and demonstrate understanding. This is why skillful and considered questioning is a pre-requisite of outstanding teaching, and a fundamental part of our whole-school model. Open, rich, responsive questions should be consistent features of the classrooms in your school, and when the questioning falls below this standard it should stick out like a sore thumb. The problem is that, in our experience, closed, narrow questions appear too frequently in UK classrooms, and even the highly vaulted open or 'higher-level' question too often is nothing more than a way of teachers checking for surface understanding.

The extract below is taken from one of the most influential papers on teacher questioning and its impact on student thought and cognition. It explores the psychology that lies behind the current practice. If, as Dillon[8] argues here, most teacher-led questioning has little impact on cognition – it might allow students to demonstrate acquisition but rarely allows them to demonstrate application – how can we design classrooms that allow for meaningful progress to both be made and demonstrated?

> Considered alone as a sentence, a question has first an expressive function, serving to state something on the part of the asker. For example, a question-sentence may be said (in some cases) to express perplexity and to state a request for information. On grounds of this ipsative function, questions have long been held functional in the thinking process of the questioner. They would not, however, on that account be said to stimulate thinking in the respondent, versus: 'Individual [teacher] questions spur students to think'. Similarly, various kinds of questions may function to express given kinds of perplexity, to motivate given kinds of thinking, and to request given kinds of information. But they would not be said to cause given kinds of thinking in the respondent, versus: 'Different questions not only seek different answers, but they also cause the students to go through different mental processes in responding'.
>
> From an analytic viewpoint, then, A's question functions to stimulate A's thought. How might it function to stimulate B's thought? Analysis does not have a ready account for that case, versus this account: Since thinking begins with a problem, one way for the teacher to encourage pupils to think is to pose a problem in the form of a question. Thus, the aim of teaching is to stimulate and shape the pupil's cognitive responses. The teacher stimulates and directs the response by posing a problem that initiates the

pupil's thinking; that is, he asks a question that requires an answer. (BELLACK, A.)

But, since thinking begins with a problem, student thinking begins with a student's problem; since questions stimulate thought, student questions stimulate student thought. How might the teacher's question become, by proxy, the student's question, so that its ipsative function has a causal effect? Analysis readily accounts for this case. To share the same question both parties would have to experience the perplexity which it expresses and feel the same need for the information which it requests. The act of merely hearing another party's question does not of itself entail experiencing the perplexity; neither does the fact of not knowing the answer of itself entail needing the information. In any event, teachers are rarely perplexed about the questions they ask, so there are small grounds available for sharing the question and little chance of stimulating anyone's thought on either side....

Research would determine the still unresolved empirical matter; whether, as presumed in pedagogical theory, higher-level teacher questions stimulate higher-level student thought. Logico-linguistic theory does not presume them to have this effect. Analysis of the procedures which manuals use to classify teacher questions reveals a matrix of displaced inferences among question and response; function and effect; expression and cognition; teacher and student. Beginning with some question-sentence, one procedure first projects a hypothetical response; next it makes an inference as to the cognition of any student who might speak it; and then, by retrojection, attributes to the question the quality of the presumed response. In this fashion questions are labelled 'thought-provoking' because they are presumed to provoke thought.

Taking the same question-sentence, another procedure first posits a hypothetical questioner; next takes a guess at the intents and meanings of any teacher who would speak the question; and then, by projection, assigns to the putative response the inferred cognition of the hypothetical questioner. In this fashion questions are labeled 'creative', because they encourage creative answers or 'convergent' because, having only one thing in mind, they can only be answered in one way. The first procedure defines the function of a question by presuming its effect; the second defines the effect of a question by presuming its function. Having thus circularly erected a linear taxonomy, the manuals propose to use questions as 'cognitive levers' for moving at least a third of student thought to successively higher rungs. Ask a foolish question, get a foolish answer; 'ask a higher-level question, get a higher-level answer'.

From an analytic perspective, a high-level question would characterize the talk, perhaps the thought, of the questioner, not the respondent. It makes a request, not elicits a response, for information, not for cognition. It might be said to express a high-level thinking, but it does not cause it in the respondent. Thus, teacher questions would not be said to stimulate student thought, nor higher questions higher thought.

Part 2: The intermediate solutions

Much has been done to try and overcome these problems and we have termed these strategies and practices 'intermediate questioning approaches'. These are the strategies you might train on and embed if taking a teacher from 'requires improvement' to 'good'. They do not promote deep or searching intellectual activity within the student but they do start to alter the relationship in the classroom so that the teacher is doing less of the work. Geoff Petty has done a lot of excellent work in this area and the table overleaf is a summary of some of the strategies he believes in. It is a step in the right direction and gives teachers a structure to help them ask fewer, better questions.

Look at the table below and fill it in using the key. The first line has been done for you.[9]

Key: *** Excellent   ** Good   * weak   !! poor

Questioning strategy: (Students anticipate these in advance.)	Participation rate	Students' feedback and dialogue	Teacher's feedback	Student comfort	Thinking time
1. Q&A: Volunteers answer Students volunteer to answer questions.	!!	!!	!!	***	!!
2. Q&A: Nominees answer Students nominated by teacher to answer questions.					
3. Buzz groups: Volunteers answer Students work in small groups to answer a thought-provoking question. Teacher asks each group in turn to contribute part of the answer. A volunteer answers for their group.					
4. Buzz groups: Nominees answer As above but the teacher nominates the student in each group who will contribute that groups answer after the group discussion.					

5. Assertive questioning				
Groups work on a thought-provoking question. Teacher asks individuals to give their group's answer, and then asks the rest of the class to discuss and agree a 'class answer'.				
6. Pair checking				
Teacher asks a question, then students work alone to answer it. Pairs then compare their answers; giving their partner one good point and one way their answer could be improved. The teacher then gives the correct answer. Pairs suggest another improvement to their partner's answer.				

There is also a lot of talk in education circles at the moment about teacher-led questioning strategies such as 'Hinge Questions' or 'Pose, pause, pounce, bounce'. These types of strategy are often cited as 'the way' to move from Good to Outstanding and 'If only I had known about this technique five years ago…'. Whilst there is no doubt that such strategies can help the Satisfactory teacher do less work and get their students to do more; these teacher-led methods are still problematic in that they are driven more by participation than thinking. There is an approach and range of strategies that enable a more powerful learning environment to be created. As much of the research currently suggests, the creation of a learner-centred environment that encourages risk-taking and collaboration is vital in enabling students to take control of their learning; which in turn is a powerful lever on progress.

Part 3: Questioning and interactive teaching – creating a culture of inquiry

The aim of this approach is to create a powerful learning environment rather than give a list of instructional tools. If, as we have seen, transfer rarely happens and the 'thinking-skills' approach is limited, how do we design classrooms that create powerful learning and allow students to apply and create new knowledge?

> We take it that the actual belief among most learning scientists is that only in the basic academic skill areas of reading, writing, and elementary mathematics do we know how to teach cognitive skills with fair confidence that they will transfer to a wide range of situations. Yet we must respect the demands of society for the schools to turn out people who, in addition to being proficient in these basic skills, will be prepared to learn new things, collaborate in the solution of novel problems, and produce innovations in areas that presently may not even exist. In the absence of tested methods, how do we do this? The time-honored and still the only promising way is immersion. If you do not have an effective way of teaching a foreign language, then place the students in an environment where that is the dominant language and trust that their natural adaptive abilities will lead them to master the language. By the same reasoning, if we want students to acquire the skills needed to function in knowledge-based, innovation-driven organizations, we should place them in an environment where those skills are required in order for them to be part of what is going on.[10]

In order to be effective then, questioning needs to be seen as being more than just asking questions – it is a cultural shift where the question is the start and end point of a process of students' thinking. Otherwise, despite all the rhetoric to the contrary, questioning remains teacher-led and teacher dominated. The strategies in Part 2 are a middle ground and whilst being a useful training aid for developing teacher practice, they are not an end destination.

Questioning has been the focus of much teacher training in recent years. But for us it has to be more than 'wait time', 'no hands' and 'lollipop sticks'. These and hundreds of other so called 'Assessment for Learning' strategies are mainly mechanisms for increasing participation. This is an important stage for teachers to get to and the work of Wiliam and others has been invaluable in moving teachers forward. We know that students tend to only try to answer questions to which they already know the answer and the strategies in Part 2 are a remedy to this. However, we have taken this a step further and we outline this approach below.

Part 3 then looks at an approach that builds the lesson around the question and uses student questions as a driver for the direction and pace of the learning journey.

Questioning then has to be part of a different classroom culture. Questioning that:[11]

i.   Requires students to form constructs – that is, requires them to form their own meaning or interpretation of the material being studied.

ii. Allows the learner and the teacher to detect misconceptions, errors and omissions in learning and correct these.

iii. Allows for student questions to inform the planning process and to demonstrate student thinking and perplexity.

What does this look like in practice?

It is important to remember that the entire sequence of lessons is built around the BIG Fertile Question and that each lesson is framed through a smaller question that helps lead to the resolution of the BIG question (problem). What this section is about is how to use different types of question to enable learners to explore problems and solutions without being hand-held or led through the process by the teacher. As explained earlier on, the role of the teacher is a shifting one and the types of question posed will shift as the stages of the enquiry are moved through. This is all about creating powerful learning environments.

Questioning: Examples of putting the principles into practice

Example 1: Using the classroom as a market place

This first example is taken from a sequence of lessons on the First World War. The Fertile Question was *'Did one bullet lead to twenty million deaths?'*[12] The example is taken from halfway through the enquiry where students are beginning to work on their individual Performances of Understanding. At this stage they are introduced to a conceptual diagram and asked to deconstruct it before creating their own first draft diagram and seeking peer feedback. The *concluding Performance of Understanding* for this Fertile Question is the individual construction of a conceptual diagram that answers the BIG question. This outcome clearly requires students to operate on and with knowledge, and draws out the underpinning historical concepts.

Stage 1: Introducing a model of what their performance will eventually look like

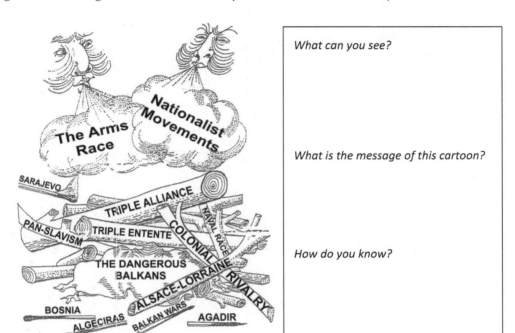

Figure 2.4   A conceptual diagram of the causes of the First World War[13]

Stage 2: Getting students to think more deeply about the model Performance of Understanding they have been presented with

- Pick a cause of the First World War from the diagram in front of you.

- You now have five minutes to find out about that cause.

- You will then have to explain the role that cause played to the rest of the class without mentioning it by name.

Stage 3: Linking factual knowledge to conceptual thinking

The concept underpinning the Fertile Question was that of causation – why things happen – or more precisely '*How do historians explain why things happened in the past?*' The model performance presented to the class has a clear conceptual argument. Students now need to be able to weave together the knowledge of the causes they have studied with the conceptual knowledge of causation that they are developing in order to begin to create a model with real explanatory power.

- In groups of four you have to convert the causes of the First World War into a diagram or picture like the one in Stage 1.

- We will then open a market place for you to compare and contrast the class' diagrams.

Stage 4: Creating meaningful opportunities to allow learners to express knowledge and criticize and create knowledge

Market place – how it works

- One person presents their group's ideas on their market stall as the rest journey around the other stalls.

- Other group members go to another group, listen and ask:

    i.   clarifying questions (at the end of the presentation) and

    ii. probing questions (on post-its).

- If you cannot answer the question, write it down – it has become a probing question.

Probing questions:	Clarifying questions:
• They are intended to help the presenter *think more deeply* about the issue at hand; • They are designed to help the person you are asking understand and think through their own ideas; • The *answers will usually be longer*, and require thinking time.	• They are designed to help you (the questioner) understand more. • They usually *check factual details*. • The *answers will usually be short and easy* to give.

Example 2: Allowing learners to create their own Fertile Questions from little prior learning

- Using BIG questions to predict and hypothesize;

- Getting students to generate their own questions;

- Using student questions as the framework for the new learning.

Stage 1: Introducing the problem to be solved through a snippet of text and a simple question

> Enabling learners to generate hypotheses, make connections to previous learning to see where they could be going next, and enabling them to create links between different curriculum areas.

> 'From this filthy sewer pure gold flows.' (Alexis de Tocqueville 1835)

> *What are we going on to explore next?*

> Discuss in pairs then summarize your ideas to the class.

Stage 2: Introducing a longer body of text to allow context to be generated and to allow learners to create their own questions

> This will highlight initial misconceptions and relevant prior learning that can then be addressed before the new learning begins.

> A thick black smoke covers the city. The sun appears like a disc without any rays. In this semi-daylight 300,000 people work ceaselessly. A thousand noises rise amidst this unending damp and dark labyrinth...the footsteps of a busy crowd, the crunching of wheels of machines, the shriek of steam from the boilers, the regular beat of looms, the heavy rumble of carts, these are the only noises from which you can never escape in these dark half-lit streets....The homes of the poor are scattered haphazard around the factories. From this filthy sewer pure gold flows. In Manchester civilised man is turned back almost into a savage. (Alexis de Tocqueville 1835)

> - What questions do you have about this passage?

> - What is our new topic?

Stage 3: Going deeper into the topic to allow learners to generate their own Fertile Questions that help frame the journey they will undertake on the topic selected

> *The bitter cry of outcast London*[14]

> - Read the passage below, pupils close their eyes and listen.

> - Read the passage again, pause every now and then, pupils jot down key ideas/themes.

- Pupils draw a picture of what they think it is about.

- Pupils generate their own BIG questions about the topic.

> Every room in these rotten and reeking tenements houses a family, often two. In one cellar a sanitary inspector reports finding a father, mother, three children and four pigs! In another room a missionary found a man ill with small pox, his wife just recovering from her eighth confinement, and the children running about half naked and covered with dirt.
>
> Here are seven people living in one underground kitchen, and a little dead child lying in the same room. Elsewhere is a poor widow, her three children, and a child who had been dead thirteen days. Her husband, who was a cabman, had shortly before committed suicide. Here lives a widow and her six children, including one daughter of 29, another of 21, and a son of 27. Another apartment contains father, mother and six children, two of whom are ill with scarlet fever. In another nine brothers and sisters, from 29 years of age downwards, live, eat and sleep together.
>
> Here is a mother who turns her children into the street in the early evening because she lets her room for immoral purposes until long after midnight, when the poor little wretches creep back again if they have not found some miserable shelter elsewhere.

Stage 4: Using student-generated questions to frame a learning journey

Go back to the market place idea outlined in Example 1. Students present their own Fertile Questions to the class and a review of each is carried out using probing and clarifying questions. Once the process is complete, a series of votes takes place to choose the Fertile Question that most engages the learners but that also connects with how academics within that domain operate and construct knowledge. For example, students may generate questions about change and progress, society and fairness, or any area that is of interest to them and links to their prior understanding.

Example 3: Scaffolding group discussion through posing questions

These two separate activities come from the 'launch' lesson of a new Fertile Question in Maths: one (a) about geometry: *Can the perimeter and area of a shape ever be the same?* and the other (b) looks at a different way into a bigger question: *'How can you create a fair game?'*

(a) Divide the class into groups of four. Each person in the group is given one question card. The group should use these questions to help them explore our new Fertile Question:

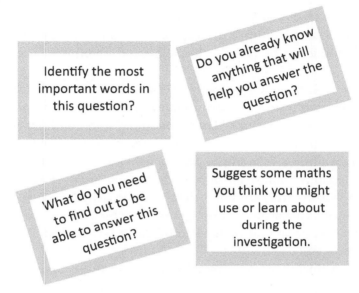

Figure 2.5 (a)   A set of questions cards to help students explore a Fertile Question

(b) Divide the class into pairs to discuss these questions.

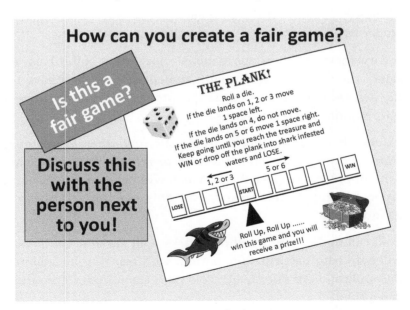

Figure 2.5 (b)   Looking at a different way into the bigger question *'How can you create a fair game?'*

Conclusions

Questioning, considered as it has been here, takes on roles different and more complex than those usually associated with the word. By removing the role of the question from sole control of the teacher (whilst ensuring the questions still remain framed within a disciplinary framework) genuine Performances of Understanding can be created that allow for meaningful progression to take place.

If there is a mismatch between the questions teachers ask – generally for recall – and the questions students have then this creates a significant problem. If, as we have seen earlier, all lesson planning starts with what the learner can currently do then the evidence of what that is, normally collected through the use of questioning, is going to be problematic at best. If we are asking the wrong questions then we are getting the 'wrong' answers and so in turn we are planning lessons that are mismatched to the actual current level of student performance. It is hardly surprising then that by the time we get to Year 11 this mismatch is so great that we have to fill Saturdays and holidays with non-stop intervention and catch-up!

The key principle here is that *effective questioning extends thinking:*

The problem (Part 1 summarized):

- Thinking begins with a problem, so 'student thinking begins with a student's problem'.[15]

- If we want to use questions to model expert ways of thinking, and to engage rather than instruct, then, 'both [student and teacher] have to experience the perplexity which [a question] expresses and feel the same need for the information which it requests'.[16]

- Extended periods of whole-class questioning, where a teacher stands at the front selecting individual students to answer questions (the traditional Initiation/Response/Feedback model) will not generate this kind of higher-order thinking. In fact episodes like this sap pace and challenge from the lesson.

- Cold calling/No hands/Lollipop sticks – all variants on the same theme – will help with participation, but not with teaching for understanding and the application of knowledge. To do this a culture shift around questioning is required.

Intermediary solutions (Part 2 summarized):

- The devil is in the detail with questioning. Subtle tweaks of the language make all the difference. Consider these two options:

  i. *'Alfie, why is the opening sentence of this article so effective?'*

  ii. 'Everyone read the opening sentence of this article (wait). *Why is that such an effective opening?* (wait). *Alfie, what do you think?* (take response). *Who else wants to say something about this?'*

- The best teachers use devices to ensure every child is engaged in answering the question – not just the one they have selected: *'What is 25 per cent of eighty?* Everyone write down the answer on your "show me" board' or 'Mohamed thinks it's twenty – put your hand up if you agree with Mohamed'.

- Instead of asking lots of shallow, surface-recall type questions, pose just a few rich, open, provocative questions. Students could then work in groups to puzzle out answers before a spokesperson from each group feeds back. The case studies above explore this idea.

- Expert teachers script their questions in advance, and replay them in their heads before the lesson to see if they will deepen students' understanding.

- Think on your feet! When you pose a question and are met with 30 blank faces, can you quickly rephrase it to open it up? NOTE: This does not mean make the question easier – amplify by saying the same thing in different ways, do not simplify by substituting an easier question.

- Wait time – one of the easiest changes to make. If all teachers in your school add three seconds to their wait time it will deepen students' responses and give them more time to construct their thinking. Have the confidence to wait – if students sense the teacher is impatient they stop thinking (because they know they are about to be let off the hook).

Creating a culture of inquiry (Part 3 summarized):

- Pupils can ask questions and provide explanations too – not just the teacher. This is the biggest conceptual shift, and the most important learning point to take from this section.

- Through engaging with BIG questions students take on roles and argue viewpoints different from their own.

- Each sequence in the learning is planned through a driving question and the question in turn creates 'relevance' and makes the learning real and purposeful.

- The culture of questioning encourages metacognition and reflection as well as enabling new learning to always be placed in a clear conceptual framework.

- The approach allows learners to replicate the ways of thinking and meaning making that experts in that particular field follow.

- The approach allows learners to develop the particular language requirements of the discipline and immerse themselves in more 'scientific' ways of thinking and understanding the world.

TRAINING ACTIVITY

Planning a lesson(s) around questioning

Using the ideas talked about in the three case studies above,

Either:

- Complete another blank lesson plan proforma to plan a lesson or series of lessons for one of your Fertile Questions.

The planning focus is on building the lesson(s) around questioning that goes beyond lollypop sticks or wait time.

Or:

- Work in department teams and plan a one hour training session for a group of teachers to introduce them to the ideas and ways of questioning this section outlines. The most effective way of doing this is to create your own examples of deep questioning and get the teachers you are training to actually carry out the tasks as if they are in a lesson and then to reflect on the learning experience and how this can inform their teaching in turn.

This will require a lot of thinking but as every teacher knows – teaching others is probably one of the best ways of developing understanding and working through problems.

Mindsets – creating the climate for excellence in every lesson

> Students may know how to study, but won't want to if they believe their efforts are futile. If you target that belief, you can see more benefit than you have any reason to hope for. (Dweck 2006)

We discussed earlier the idea of a 'Learner Profile': a set of desirable qualities and characteristics which are reinforced with students through their lessons and the wider school ethos. This is a key component of the whole-school model. The Learner Profile is a living, meaningful concept that must be communicated to students on an ongoing basis, in ever more varied and engaging ways. It is not a dry thing which is 'done to' students. It should be a planning tool for teachers, and provides all members of the school community with a language for talking about learning. If the Learner Profile is fully implemented, students will never feel their 'efforts are futile'.

The work of Carol Dweck is of such importance to what we are trying to achieve that we have relied heavily on her ideas in this section. Her research has transformed the thinking around 'excellence' and life-long success and happiness and her concept of the 'growth mindset' is what we are aiming for.

MINI TRAINING ACTIVITY[17]

Read each statement and decide if you agree or disagree with it.

i.   Your ability is something very basic about you that you cannot change very much.

ii. You can learn new things, but you cannot really change how 'clever' you are.

iii. No matter how much ability you have, you can always change it quite a bit.

iv. You can always substantially change how 'clever' you are.

The views we have on intelligence, ability, potential, all shape the way we interact with students – both in the classroom and around the school – as well as the conversations we have about them in the staffroom. Having the belief that intelligence is static and you are born with a certain amount of it is the opposite to what we are trying to achieve. The 'science of learning' is transforming the way we view intelligence and the ways in which it can manifest itself within school. The next part of this book looks at exploring ways in which we can design classrooms to maximize learning through sending positive messages to all students that harness the power of positive psychology and motivation. This is really the only thing schools need to concern themselves with in terms of classroom environment. All the glass and rotating tables in the world will not make any difference if students still feel that effort in your classroom is futile and that you and they have a fixed view of their intelligence and 'ability'.

Moving beyond 'ability' – brain as a bucket or a muscle?[18]

The two boxes below are a simple way of presenting the research and approaches that follow. The box on the left can perhaps be termed the 'traditional' approach to viewing learning and the brain – ability is fixed, some people are more intelligent than others and there is little that can be done to change it.

The box on the right can then in turn perhaps be termed the 'research-based' approach in that the research is currently suggesting that the brain is more like a muscle and can be 'grown'. There is a lot of research to support the idea that the plasticity of the brain gives endless capacity to learn and that:

> This capacity to learn and to advance which our brain gives us is individually acquired. This means a single generation without access to education, libraries, computers, etc. will be back in the Stone Age. We are narrowly detached from our distant evolutionary past. Everyone has to reacquire everything that has been learned through the adaptation of an individual's brain. (Prof. C. Blakemore)

Therefore an approach to education based on the premise that the brain is a changing 'organ' and needs to be cultivated requires a shift in the way we talk to and about students and about learning in general.

Bucket:	Muscle:
• fixed ability	• expandable ability
○ born smart	○ get smarter
• proving	• improving
• conservative learning	• adventurous learning
• failure/mistakes bad	• failure/mistakes useful
• effort aversive	• effort pleasurable
• ignores information	• focuses on information
• fragile – depressive	• resilient – determined
• shirk/blame/cheat	• try/commit/be open
• comparative/competitive.	• collaborative/generous

Speaking at the Centre for Confidence in Glasgow in September 2008, Carol Dweck referred to *the important difference between self-esteem and self-efficacy*. She made the following points:

- Private education buys the 'empty self-belief' of confidence of superiority over others.

- Fixed-mindset self-esteem is about feeling good about yourself, often in relation to the perceived lower achievement of others.

- Growth-mindset self-esteem is about having the courage and determination to address weaknesses.

- Confidence and self-efficacy comes from *mastery of problems through resilience*, not from false self-esteem.

- The growth-mindset teacher says: 'I am not interested in judging how good your work is, I am interested in the quality of your learning and the strategies you use'.

Cultivating a lifelong learner…how?[19]

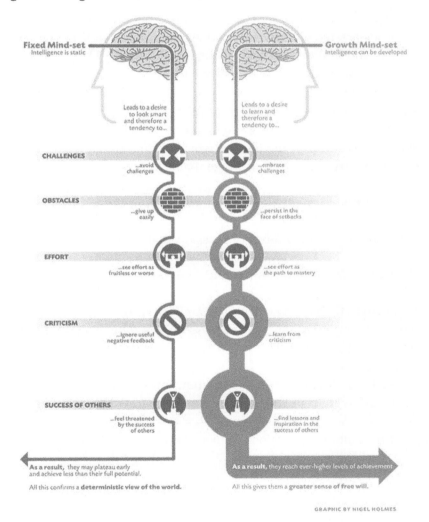

Figure 2.6   Cultivating a lifelong learner…how?[20] (*continued on next page*)

Figure 2.6 *(continued)*

Stanford University psychologist Carol Dweck has carried out decades of research on achievement and success. Her findings can be boiled down to a simple idea – the *growth mindset*.

In a growth mindset people believe that their most basic abilities can be developed through dedication and hard work – brains and talent are just the starting point. This view of the brain creates a love of learning and a resilience that is the basis of great accomplishment in every area.

In opposition to this, in a *fixed mindset* people believe that their basic qualities are fixed. They spend their time documenting or judging their talents and abilities instead of developing them. They also believe that talent alone creates success, without effort.

How do we develop growing minds?
Every word or action sends a message. It tells children how to think about themselves and how to view the world around them.
It can be a fixed-mindset message that says:

'*You have permanent traits and I am judging them.*'

Or it can be a growth-mindset message that says:

'*You are a developing person and I am interested in your development.*'

In a nutshell: Praising children's intelligence harms their motivation and harms their performance. *If success means they are smart, then failure means they are stupid.*

Instead, our focus is on teaching our students to love challenges, to be intrigued by their mistakes, to enjoy effort and to keep on learning.

Figure 2.6 Cultivating a lifelong learner...how?

How do you create a culture of excellence within all aspects of school life?

> There truly is no scientific justification anymore – if there ever was – for labeling children as having different amounts of 'intelligence', 'ability', or even – the new weasely euphemism – potential. (Lucas and Claxton 2010)[21]

If Senior Leaders want a school full of students who possess growth mindsets, then a fully integrated approach is required. The message that challenges should be embraced, and that mistakes represent opportunities for new learning, needs to be communicated at all levels and by all parties. This philosophy should underpin the curriculum; the classroom teaching; the approach to homework; the culture and ethos of the school as communicated via assemblies, tutor period and the visual environment; the behaviour and rewards system; and communication and reporting to parents. Without a single-minded focus on each student as a developing individual, all the other strategies, systems and approaches are worthless.

There are five areas we will look at here which link with creating a school and classroom culture that builds a growth mindset:

i.   how we give feedback to students;

ii. how we create learner expectations;

iii. how we talk to students about their learning;

iv. how we encourage parents to talk to their children about learning;

v.   how we design the curriculum to model lifelong learning.

How we unwittingly give feedback every second

Every action, gesture and comment in the classroom sends a message from teacher to student and from student to student. A raised eyebrow at a question we do not think is relevant; moving on and not responding to a student's response or question – these interactions give feedback and send a message. This messaging in turn influences how a student feels in your classroom and dictates the level of effort and engagement they commit to learning in your classroom. We therefore need to be super-conscious of what messages our actions are sending to students.

Think about your own classroom interactions and consider these questions:[22]

● *What messages does our feedback give:*

i.   'You have permanent traits and I am judging them.'; or

ii. 'You are a developing person and I'm interested in your development.'

iii. Do we praise intelligence and talent and use these words as fixed points when talking with students? What messages does this send?

iv. How do we present new material to students – do we lower standards to ensure success or raise standards but offer no way of meeting them?

Added to our unconscious messaging, too often, our explicit teacher feedback focuses on the student at a personal (or self) level. According to Hattie, this is the least effective of all feedback types. Personal feedback (for example phrases such as 'Good girl' or 'Great effort') usually contains little task-related information and is rarely converted into more engagement, commitment to the learning goals, enhanced self-efficacy, or understanding about the task.

So, feedback to students has to focus on the learning objectives shared with students earlier on. Feedback that focuses on learning goals or success criteria is more likely to lead to greater engagement and progress and does not attach personal value judgements to it. (This is expanded on in the assessment section.)

Making the most of expectations[23]

Dweck outlines four key things we can do to ensure that the expectations we create in our classrooms maximize student engagement and progress. These four areas are easy to execute and with a bit of thought every classroom can be designed to fulfil their requirements.

i.   climate – a warm, welcoming social and emotional classroom climate;

ii. feedback – not performance but learning orientated;

iii. input – attempts to teach more material and more difficult material through realistic and carefully planned Fertile Questions. The idea of 'junior versions' explained earlier;

iv. output – more opportunities to respond; both student to teacher and student to student.

Teacher behaviours that signal expectations:[24]

David Perkins of Harvard University has been influenced by the work of Dweck and he builds on her work by outlining some very clear ways in which teachers – often unwittingly – signal to students what our expectations of them are. When you take the time to stop and think about the examples below it is clear to see how we are all guilty at times of signalling to a student that we do not have the time – or the belief in them – to listen to their thoughts and responses!

- *Is there a student the teacher never asks?*

- *Is there a student the teacher always asks?*

- *Do you wait for the student to get the answer or quickly move on?*

- *How do you pair students up with one another?*

- *Do you praise for solving easy problems?*

- *What do you praise – effort or easy success?*

Being aware of this and shining the spotlight on our signals is the only way to stop them. Creating a classroom that supports growth through high expectations of all students and a belief that they are all growing and developing people is central to maximizing progress for all students. We so often hear excuses from schools and teachers about their students – 'they cannot do that', 'so and so is on the SEN register', etc. As soon as the excuses and labelling starts, the progress and attainment ends. 'Labelling and limiting' has been a core principle of NLP (Neuro-Linguistic Programming) for some time and although there is debate about the evidence-base for some of the ideas within NLP, there is no doubt that labelling a child as *lazy, stupid, slow, nasty*, is instantly placing a set of expectations on them that they will inevitably fulfil. Why not create a school full of classrooms that have the highest beliefs and set of expectations for every learner – imagine the power of that.

How we talk to students about their learning

There is a whole section of this book dedicated to feedback, but the quote below from Hattie gives helpful guidelines on the kind of feedback we should be giving to students:

> A problem occurs when feedback is not directed toward the attainment of a goal. Too often, the feedback given is unrelated to achieving success on critical dimensions of the goal. For example, students are given feedback on presentation, spelling, and quantity in writing when the criteria for success was 'creating mood in a story'. Students' attributions about success

or failure can often have more impact than the reality of that success or failure. There can be deleterious effects on feelings of self-efficacy and performance when students are unable to relate the feedback to the cause of their poor performance. Unclear evaluative feedback, which fails to specify the grounds on which students have met with achievement success or otherwise, is likely to exacerbate negative outcomes, engender uncertain self-images, and lead to poor performance.[25]

So the feedback we give to students is only as useful as their response to it, and their response is determined by cultural factors in the school as well as the teaching activities we build around the delivery of the feedback. Establishing the growth mindset is key: 'Helpless children react as though they have received an indictment of their ability, but mastery orientated children react as though they have been given useful feedback about learning.' (Elliott and Dweck)[26]

How we encourage parents to talk to their children about learning[27]

It is vital for effective schools to engage parents in the learning process. However there is often a mismatch between the messaging a student receives in school and the messaging they receive at home. Therefore for a school to really embed a 'growth-mindset approach', parental engagement and training is necessary. Parents often base the questions they ask their child around their own experiences of the school system and are often much happier with quick and easy success rather than development over time. (This is not blaming parents but ensuring that schools are conscious of this mismatch.) Schools need to actively engage with this, challenging parent–child conversations that focus on quick wins or that see failure as negative or demonstrating fixed traits and abilities.

The three examples below are used by Dweck to highlight some simple ways that schools can train parents to respond and engage with their child's learning in a different way.

i. **Show your child that you value learning and improvement, not just quick, perfect performance**. When your child does something quickly and perfectly or gets an easy A-Grade in school, you as a parent should not tell your child how great they are. Otherwise, your child will equate being smart with quick and easy success, and they will become afraid of challenges. Parents should, whenever possible, show pleasure over their children's learning and improvement. Do not expect them to be good at something straight away but enjoy talking to them about their learning journey.

ii. **Do not shield your children from challenges, mistakes and struggles**. Instead, parents should teach their children to love challenges. When sitting at home discussing their homework they can say things like 'This is hard. What fun!' or 'This is too easy. It's no fun.' It is vital that parents teach their children to embrace mistakes and to see failure as an inevitable part of the learning process. The conversations parents have with their children should focus on the strategies they deployed when they were stuck and how they overcame a difficulty. This is equally important when they are reading at home as well as when they are working on their Maths homework.

iii. **Finally, stop praising your children's intelligence.** Research has shown that, far from boosting children's self-esteem, it makes them more fragile and can undermine their motivation and learning. Praising your child's intelligence puts them in a fixed mindset, makes them afraid of making mistakes, and makes them lose their confidence when something is hard for them. Instead, parents should praise the process – your child's effort, strategy, perseverance, or improvement. Then your children will be willing to take on challenges and will know how to stick with things – even the hard ones.

TRAINING ACTIVITY

Analysing your messaging to students

As shown above, all feedback and action in the classroom sends a message and, according to Dweck, that message tends to be one of two things – *you have fixed traits and I am judging them* or *you are a developing person and I am interested in your development*.

Much of this feedback is unconscious and difficult to change without having a light shined on it. The training activity below is designed to help every teacher in the school take a look at what messages they are sending to their students in every lesson and then how this can be changed to fit in with the theory of a growth mindset.

The training activity below relies on all teachers in the school taking part in a process of videoing and reviewing their lessons.

Stage 1: Partnering up

This training activity works best if teachers are partnered up in threes (triads) outside their normal department or subject area. Three is a helpful number: if it is just one person watching another they may not pick up on all of the subtle messages the teacher is giving students through their feedback. Sometimes if you are too familiar with a teacher's style you might miss the finer details.

Stage 2: The observation timetable

A timetable needs to be drawn up that enables the triad to observe each other at least twice. Each observation should be with a different age group and should be at least two days apart. This will require careful planning at whole-school level.

Stage 3: The observation focus

The focus of the observation is not to look at student progress or learner engagement but to watch the teacher and make a note of all the messages they are sending to their students using the grid below.

Stage 4: The analysis of the feedback

Each observer pair in the triad should spend at least 45 minutes going through their observation grids and summarizing the types of feedback they witness – not feedback on progress – but feedback on the type of mindset the teacher is wittingly/unwittingly creating and the classroom climate. This should be compared, collated and compiled using the feedback grid below.

Stage 5: Sharing the analysis

The observation triad should meet up once the cycle of observations is complete and each person in turn should be given the feedback and then discussed with suggestions as to how to move it forward.

Stage 6: Making the change

In sport coaches regularly talk about something called 'paralysis by analysis'. This is where you are given so many points to change and improve on that you do not know where to start and so nothing changes. In order to avoid this, it is recommended that each teacher only be given two points they can work on within the next two weeks. The training in this section and Dweck's own writing will be of help here.

Stage 7: Revisiting the change

Three weeks after the feedback meeting, the triads should again observe each other. This time for only one lesson and with one of the original classes they saw in Stage 2. The focus of this observation is to compare the feedback being given to students and the climate and culture of the classroom. *Has the feedback from the analysis in Stage 5 been actioned, can you notice a change, what might you suggest next to keep that change?*

Focus of observation:	To observe teacher–student interactions and teacher habits to analyse whether they are creating a growth-mindset or a fixed-mindset environment.
Teacher being observed:	Date of observation:
Class:	Room:

What you are looking for: (examples)

Fixed mindset:	**Growth mindset:**
• Teacher comments that talk about talent or ability. • Teacher comments that label a child. • Children that the teacher never asks. • Children the teacher always asks. • Teacher moving on before fully responding to a question or answer. • No sense of challenge. • Feedback to student responses not developmental but judgemental. • Mistakes laughed at or ignored. • Atmosphere in the classroom that creates individuals.	• Teacher comments that encourage and reward effort. • Teacher comments that encourage mistakes. • Opportunities created for students to talk about mistakes. • Opportunities for students to talk about what they currently find difficult. • Opportunities created for students and teacher to discuss possible strategies to overcome difficulties. • Atmosphere in the classroom that promotes collegiality and mutual support.

What did you see in the lesson?

Examples of fixed mindset:	**Examples of growth mindset:**

Feedback: What three things could change to move the environment to a growth-orientated one?

Mindsets feedback grid

Name of teacher being observed:		
Lesson 1: Agreed examples and developmental feedback		
Fixed mindset examples:	**Growth mindset examples:**	**What could change?**
Lesson 2: Agreed examples and developmental feedback		
Fixed mindset examples:	**Growth mindset examples:**	**What could change?**

Conclusions

The approach to teaching and lesson design as outlined in this section is concerned with only three major elements: the structure of each lesson, the way that questioning can become something more than just asking questions and the central role that the learner plays in the learning process.

To sum up, the key points of this part of the approach are:

- The simplest way to ensure consistency across all lessons is to use a common planning framework.

- This requires a whole-school approach to lesson planning; not just some teachers in some classrooms but *all* teachers in *all* classrooms.

- Lesson planning must answer these questions:

  - *What can the students do now?*

  - *What do they need to be able to do next?*

  - *What do you want your students to be able to do to demonstrate progress (that you can see, hear or read)?*

  - *What knowledge do students need to acquire to get to the desired place?*

  - *How do students need to apply that knowledge – what is the problem they are solving?*

  - *What is the concept that underpins the problem?*

  - *How will you know when your students get there?*

  - *How will they know – can they answer the three key questions: where am I going, where am I now, what do I need to do next?*

  - *How does what they are learning to do link to what they have done before and prepare them for what they need to do next?*

- Questioning, considered as it has been here, takes on roles different and more complex than those usually associated with the word. By removing the role of the question from sole control of the teacher (whilst ensuring the questions still remain framed within a disciplinary framework) genuine Performances of Understanding can be created that allow for meaningful progression to take place.

- The key principle here is that effective questioning extends thinking.

- As set out in Principle 3 of our approach (see Figure 0.2), the burden of learning does not fall on the teacher alone – even the best teaching will be successful only if the learner can make use of the opportunity to learn.

- Therefore an approach that focuses on developing a growth mindset and creating a climate of mutual respect is vital.

- The way a student conceptualizes themselves in relationship to their learning dictates how successful any lesson or learning experience is.

- It does not matter how expert the teacher, if the student does not feel they are valued as a learner, then no new learning will take place.

Notes

1   Young, M. (2008) *Bringing knowledge back in*: Routledge.
2   Review of research by Susskind, discussed in Sarason (1996) *Revisiting the culture of the school and the problem of change*: Teachers College Press.
3   Questions and activity taken from: Lefstein, A. (2008) Talk at SSAT National Conference.
4   Dillon, J.T. (1982) 'The effect of questions in education and other enterprises', *Journal of Curriculum Studies*, 14:2, 127–152.
5   Table taken from Petty, G. *Evidence-based teaching*: Nelson Thorne.
6   Lucas, B. and Claxton, G. (2010) *New kinds of smart*: OUP.
7   Dweck, C. (2006) *Mindset, the new psychology of success*: Ballantine.
8   Dweck, C. (2006) *Mindset, the new psychology of success*: Ballantine.
9   Perkins, D. (2010) *Making learning whole*: Jossey-Bass; 1st edition.
10   Hattie, J. (2008) *Visible learning*: Routledge.
11   In Kruglanski, A. and Higgins, E. (eds) (2003) *Social psychology: A general reader*: Psychology Press Ltd.
12   These three ideas are taken from Dweck, C. (2006) *Mindset, the new psychology of success*: Ballantine.
13   Picture originally found at http://en.wikipedia.org/wiki/File:WWI-Causes.jpg
14   Mearns, A. (1883) *The bitter cry of outcast London: An inquiry into the condition of the abject poor* (Pamphlet).
15   Dillon, J.T. (1982) 'The effect of questions in education and other enterprises', *Journal of Curriculum Studies*, 14:2, 127–152.
16   Dillon, J.T. (1982) 'The effect of questions in education and other enterprises', *Journal of Curriculum Studies*, 14:2, 127–152.
17   Questions taken from Dweck, C. (2006) *Mindset, the new psychology of success*: Ballantine.
18   The two boxes are taken from Claxton, G. (2010) in presentation to group of teachers.
19   Adapted from http://mindsetonline.com/whatisit/about/index.html

20 Nigel Holmes, in Carol Dweck (2012) *Mindset: How you can fulfil your potential*: Robinson.

21 Lucas, B. and Claxton, G. (2010) *New kinds of smart*: OUP.

22 Dweck, C. (2006) *Mindset, the new psychology of success*: Ballantine.

23 Dweck, C. (2006) *Mindset, the new psychology of success*: Ballantine.

24 Perkins, D. (2010) *Making learning whole*: Jossey-Bass; 1st edition.

25 Hattie, J. (2008) *Visible learning*: Routledge.

26 In Kruglanski, A. and Higgins, E. (eds) (2003) *Social psychology: A general reader*: Psychology Press Ltd.

27 These three ideas are taken from Dweck, C. (2006) *Mindset, the new psychology of success*: Ballantine.

3

Every teacher is a teacher of language

Every teacher is a teacher of language

So far we have looked at medium- and long-term planning and then at core teacher practices which are manifest from lesson to lesson. This section cuts across both. It covers the central role that *language* plays in students' learning.

The section is broken down into three parts to make it easier to embed:

- **Part 1: Every teacher a reading teacher** looks at the role of reading in the curriculum and wider life of the school.

- **Part 2: Talk is how learning happens** looks at the role of talk in learning.

- **Part 3: The writing process** looks at the writing process and how it is informed by reading and talking.

Once these three parts have been outlined they are illustrated further through two case studies. The first is a case study looking at developing and embedding a whole-school approach to reading, and the other is looking at how one school group wanted to embed a coherent approach to language acquisition across four academies.

The way we recommend you use this section is to carry out the training activities in this section first. Once these activities have been completed and discussed you should then move into the planning phase. The most effective way of doing this is to take several Fertile Questions you have already planned and then build in approaches to language acquisition to them. This is straightforward as there are guiding questions in the planning matrices for this. So, by the end of this chapter, you have just to look at assessment before you have a complete approach planned for and mapped out.

This chapter is informed by the following set of beliefs about language.

Key beliefs:

i. **Every teacher is a teacher of language.** This is the overriding principle. The teaching of all subject areas should address the language demands of that area. *All teachers* have a responsibility for this.

ii. **All areas of the curriculum challenge students.** All pupils have an entitlement to a full curriculum. The most effective way to raise standards is to increase the skill set of teachers to enable this to happen.

iii. **Reading is key to a young person's future.** There is a strong emphasis on *reading* in the approach. The view is that any writing done by pupils must be informed by reading widely, critically and in depth. The view is also that speaking and listening inform reading and writing and that the language skills are integrated.

iv. **Talk is how learning happens.** Effective learning takes place through dialogue. There should be an emphasis on the value of dialogic talk in the classroom, seeing questions as part of this dialogue; that is, questions that are cumulative, exploratory and to which, in some cases, there are no answers.

v. **All areas of school life develop language.** The approach is designed to enable language acquisition to happen in every space of the school. For this to happen it has to be deliberate and planned; structuring opportunities for every learner to talk using formal, academic language.

Part 1: Every teacher a reading teacher

There's a conundrum facing many secondary schools in the UK today. On the one hand the Key Stage 3 curriculum requires students to be able to read at an age-appropriate level. On the other there are large numbers of students arriving in Year 7 with very weak reading skills. In some London boroughs over 30 per cent of students achieve below Level 4 in the end of Key Stage 2 Reading SATs – meaning they are weak readers, who will struggle to access the subject texts they will encounter in Year 7 and beyond.

The only sensible response to this for a secondary school is to become good at teaching reading. The best secondarys have effective 'catch-up' programmes that provide intensive support for students who join with very low attainment in English and Maths, and get them back on track as quickly as possible.

What we are arguing here is that the best catch-up strategy starts by placing reading at the heart of the school, and training all teachers to be reading teachers. It is not the job of the English Department to teach reading, or the 'Literacy Coordinator'. Instead we believe teachers of all subjects can teach reading. Whilst this may sound quite scary, there are some very clear ways of embedding reading and reading development into your Fertile Questions.

Indeed, if we are really interested in social justice and the achievement gap, then reading is the most important skill a child can develop. The quote below outlines the problems teachers in some schools face:

> It also involves a tale of two children, both of whom must acquire hundreds upon hundreds of words, thousands of concepts, and tens of thousands of auditory and visual perceptions. These are the raw materials for developing the major components of reading. Owing largely to their environments, however, one child will acquire these essentials, and the other will not. Through no fault of their own, the needs of thousands of children go unmet every day. Learning to read begins the first time an infant is held and read a story. How often this happens, or fails to happen, in the first five years of childhood turns out to be one of the best predictors of later reading. A little discussed class-system invisibly divides our society, with those families that provide their children environments rich in oral and written language opportunities gradually set apart from those who do not, or cannot. A prominent study found that by kindergarten, a gap of 32 million words already separates some children in linguistically impoverished homes from their more stimulated peers. In other words, in some environments the average young middle-class child hears 32 million more spoken words than the young underprivileged child by age 5.[1]

So reading is absolutely vital, and bringing all students up a proficient level in reading is a key task for any school. The pages that follow look at how schools can best teach reading. This section is broken down into four stages:

- **Stage 1** looks at what the research currently says about reading.

- **Stage 2** looks at what this looks like in practice.

- **Stage 3** outlines two reading models.

- **Stage 4** looks at designing a training session on teaching reading as a way of assessing understanding.

Stage 1: What does the research currently say?

i. '"Reading for pleasure outweighed every social advantage, including parent's income, in the future success of the child". Children's success in life depends not on whether they can read, but on whether they do – and derive enjoyment from doing so.' (Progress in International Reading Literacy Study, PIRLS 2006)

ii. 'Reading is much more than the decoding of black marks on a page: it is a quest for meaning and one which requires the reader to be an active participant.' (English 5–16, 16.2)

iii. In a European-wide study, English children came third in the study of reading achievement but ranked thirty-fourth out of thirty-five in relation to the enjoyment of reading.

iv. In order to become engaged in reading and writing pupils need a curriculum which goes *beyond* functional literacy and sees reading and writing as a transformative, personal experience.

v. What appears to matter most to boys in their literacy learning is the possession of the 'invisible difference' of passion, commitment and caring. Teachers that pay attention to their students as people and as learners appear to enable their pupils to make greater gains. To make seismic shifts in their literacy learning learners need to move beyond the functional approach and have teachers who are committed to student engagement and teacher engagement through the exploration of real problems that are relevant to students and significant in the world.[2]

vi. If there are no genes specific only to reading, and if our brain has to connect older structures for vision and language to learn this new skill, every child in every generation has to do a lot of work. As the cognitive scientist Steven Pinker eloquently remarked, 'Children are wired for sound, but print is an optional accessory that must be painstakingly bolted on'. To acquire this unnatural process, children need instructional environments that support all the circuit parts that need bolting for the brain to read. Such a perspective departs from current teaching methods that focus largely on only one or two major components of reading.[3]

vii. Adolescents entering the adult world in the twenty-first century will read and write more than at any other time in human history. They will need advanced levels of literacy to perform their jobs, run their households, act as citizens, and conduct their personal lives. They will need literacy to cope with the flood of information they will find everywhere they turn. They will need literacy to feed their imaginations so they can create the world of the future. In a complex and sometimes even dangerous world, their ability to read can be crucial.[4]

Stage 2: What does this look like in practice?

The reading process

Secondary teachers do not need to become specialists in teaching reading, but they do need an overview of the process, and a basic understanding of the theories behind teaching reading.

There are two important points to the reading process:[5]

i.   Reading is not a precise sequential process involving careful attention to every word and letter. Readers can dispense with much of the graphic information on the page. They select only as much information as is necessary: the more familiar the language and content, the less graphic information the reader needs.

ii. The reader uses a number of cueing systems or strategies in order to process this graphic information:

- **Information about meanings** (semantic information): both how we use our understanding of the world to bear on our reading – the more we know about a subject, the easier we will find the text; and also our understanding of the text itself – as we understand more of the text, the easier we are likely to find it;

- **Information about language structures** (grammatical information): how we use the grammatical structures of the language: not just at sentence level but how we use our knowledge of the structure of larger units of text to predict, for example, the likely beginnings and endings of a fairy tale;

- **Information about the sounds of language** (phonological information);

- **Information about language in print** (graphological information).

In order to become a successful reader – not just a successful decoder – we must understand and utilize all four systems above.

Stage 3: What strategies can we use in the classroom?[6]

There are probably as many approaches to teaching reading as there are teachers – and each approach has a weight of support behind it. We have chosen to look at implementation models for getting reading into every classroom. The first model outlined below is used because it is simple, clear, easy to embed and assess uptake and has worked in a number of different schools with different contexts. The second model is used because it punches well above its weight – a simple strategy that yields powerful results.

One of the problems with reading is that it can be seen as a scary word. There is usually very little focus in Initial Teacher Training for secondary teachers on reading, and most schools seem to leave it up to the English Department to do (with very few complaints from other subjects).

This is exactly the wrong thing to do. All subjects necessarily involve teaching the language of that subject, so all teachers need an awareness of how language is developed through reading (and speaking and writing). The model below allows all teachers to become reading teachers. There is of course scope to take this principle much further, and the first case study at the end of this section looks at one academy that did just that. However, for the purposes of embedding a whole-school approach and ensuring that every classroom addresses the reading demands of its subject discipline, the model below is the best place to start.

Model 1: Strategies for more fluent readers or when using texts in-line with current reading ability

This approach follows the three-stage model outlined below:

i. **Building field knowledge** – what is the text about?

ii. **Interacting with texts** – reading for a purpose;

iii. **Responding to texts** – making meaning out of what has been read.

These three stages represent very clear stages in the planning cycle. The key thing for the individual teacher to think about is where in the Fertile Question each stage happens. Once this has been worked out the actual mechanics of the individual lesson plans are simple to create and implement.

The model used here also allows for progression in 'skills' to be increased over time. The careful planning of a curriculum-based reading programme from Year 7 to Year 11 will allow for escalation in terms of the type of text being used, the depth of use for the text and the increased metacognition of students in directing their own reading and the understandings they develop from this.

Building field knowledge

Before using a text in a Teaching and Learning session it is vital to ensure that all students have a useable knowledge of the topic the text is about, so that they can draw on this 'field knowledge' to access the text. This phase is almost identical to the Connection Phase in a four-part lesson. The idea is to find out what students already know about the topic and to give them the context and fingertip knowledge they need in order to make sense of the text in its correct context.

You would also follow the same structure when looking at visual literacy in Art or when explaining the process of solving a mathematical problem. There are of course hundreds of ways of finding out what students already know and we have listed a few ideas below.

This group of strategies includes:

- **Brainstorming** – Brainstorming is a means of activating and recording information about current knowledge, range of vocabulary and perceptions of a given topic. This information can include vocabulary, questions, known facts, predictions, links and ideas.

- **Predicting** – Predicting involves readers or viewers considering what they expect a text to contain or what might happen next in a text. The stimulus for predicting could be a title, a picture or reading or viewing part of the text.

- **Creating a map or timeline of the key events the text deals with** – This visual aspect includes diagrams, flow charts, illustrations, graphs, timelines.

- **Introducing key words** – To prepare students for reading or viewing it is necessary to familiarize them with any words from the text that might hinder their understanding.

Although these strategies can be used at any point throughout the Fertile Question, they are particularly valuable in providing support for students early in a learning sequence as they encourage students to:

- recall and draw upon their existing knowledge about information contained within a text or a text type being studied;

- use their background knowledge to predict the meaning of the text;

- examine other aspects of the text that will assist understanding, i.e. key words, visual representations, titles.

Interacting with texts

Students need to have an understanding of the purpose for reading and viewing particular texts before they commence. Teachers can assist students to clarify the purpose of reading by asking the questions:

- *Why are you reading this text?*

- *Are you reading for enjoyment, to retell, to answer questions, to gain information, for research?*

Once a purpose for reading is established, students can be directed about which method of reading will best achieve that purpose. These methods for reading include:

- **skimming**: reading to gain an overall understanding of the content of the text;

- **scanning**: reading to locate specific information;

- **rereading**: reading to confirm meanings and understandings, and to clarify details;

- **note-making**: reading and completing a simple data-capture grid.

Again, close attention needs to be paid to when in the Fertile Question this stage is planned for, how the activities will be introduced to students, and how expertise will be developed over time. The aim is that over time students will develop the knowledge to select their own methods for interacting with a text and assessing their own understanding as they go along.

Responding to texts

Once a text has been used in the classroom, it is important that students have the opportunity to respond to the text. This response is crucial as it is about assessing understanding and using that new understanding to solve the problem posed by the Fertile Question.

i. **Note-making**

Its purpose could be to assist understanding, to identify key concepts, to plan speaking or writing, to assist recall of information or to express ideas clearly and succinctly.

ii. **Converting**

Students should be given the opportunity to convert the ideas in the text into a different form – a diagram, a mind map, a flow-chart, a story-map. This gives a clear indication of understanding and enables the information to be applied to a problem in a useable format.

iii. **Ordering information**

Ordering information involves:

- anticipating the structure of the text by using knowledge of the text type, e.g. if it is a recount, information is likely to be ordered chronologically, with key words being time words and phrases and dates;

- identifying key points, e.g. events, facts, opinions or steps, pertinent to the reader's needs;

- sequencing these points in order to enhance understanding of text content.

iv. **Synthesizing**

Synthesizing means giving students the opportunity to summarize and pull together all of the main ideas that the text deals with into a manageable whole. The ability to synthesize information from a number of texts into one document is a valuable skill that should be planned for.

v. **Criticizing and deconstructing**

A very difficult skill to develop is the ability to deconstruct in an intellectually honest form the basis of the text. This means enabling students to begin to:

- give reasons for the knowledge created by the text;

- find contradictions with other texts they have read;

- expose the assumptions of the author;

- formulate counter-arguments to the text.

Again, the aim is that over time students move to becoming more independent in terms of the activities they choose to use to respond to the text and when they choose to deploy them.

Model 2: Strategies for enabling struggling or reluctant readers to engage with meaningful texts in the classroom

What is reciprocal teaching?

Reciprocal teaching or reciprocal teaching of comprehension has become an increasingly popular way of helping struggling readers to develop their comprehension ability. Part of the reason for its popularity has to be down to its impact. Hattie, in his meta-analysis of different interventions on student outcomes gives it an effect size of 0.74 and it ranks in the top ten interventions (Hattie 2008). Below is a very simple model, adapted from the original and highly important work of Palinscar and Brown[7] that works either as small group work or as a whole-class model. In order to be successful, as with anything, time has to be invested up front in outlining to students the ground rules and approach.

The reason why reciprocal teaching is so effective is because it does what most strategies do not: it enables transfer of skills. Thus the skills it teaches you can be applied to any subject area and with correct teacher prompting the metacognitive aspect remains embedded. In other words, 'the strategy trains students in a manner that helps them achieve and maintain high levels of comprehension over time, to generalize those skills across settings, and to transfer those skills to other conceptual domains'.[8]

Another crucial reason as to why this approach is so successful is because it works – and really does work – in any subject area. In fact, it seems to be especially powerful in Maths and Science where the four stages are used to help students make sense of and self-regulate whilst solving complex mathematical and scientific problems. There is no excuse for not using this approach in every classroom and it is not just relevant to reading.

What is the process?

The implementation into the classroom of this strategy follows four stages and needs to be seen as part of a long-term plan. You have to accept that you will need to front-load time at the beginning to model to students the process and the thinking and allow them to slowly gain control by removing the scaffolding in planned stages.

The diagram opposite demonstrates the 'flight path' from teacher to student-led operating of reciprocal teaching.

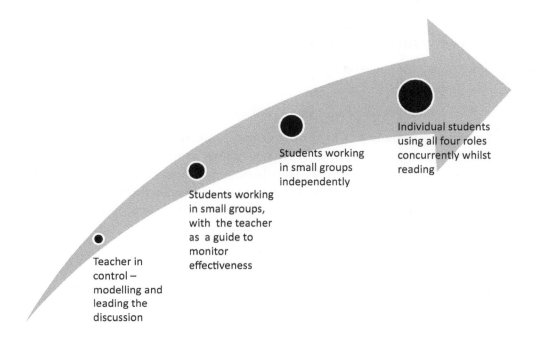

Individual students using all four roles concurrently whilst reading

Students working in small groups independently

Students working in small groups, with the teacher as a guide to monitor effectiveness

Teacher in control – modelling and leading the discussion

Figure 3.1   A 'flight-path' model of reciprocal teaching

Teacher in control: Modelling the process and thinking aloud

Teacher selects a meaningful piece of text – aimed at the chronological age of the students, not their actual reading age. So, students in Year 11 should be reading text appropriate for a 16-year-old. The text should be around 1500 words. Ensure that the students have the prior knowledge and context to access the main ideas and themes of the text.

i.   All students in their groups of four silently read a paragraph.

ii. The teacher asks a main idea or BIG question about the paragraph. The question should be one of the five Ws – who, what, where, etc.

iii. The groups discuss and agree a group answer.

iv. Then the groups contribute and everyone agrees a 'class' answer.

v.   The teacher discusses and evaluates the answers and clarifies any misconceptions and may ask further questions.

vi. Each group then summarizes the paragraph in two sentences or uses the prompt 'What would you tell someone who has just walked in what the main point of this paragraph was?'

vii. Then each group predicts what they think they might be reading about next: what the main point of the next paragraph will be.

viii. Finally the teacher summarizes the paragraph and starts the process all over again.

Teacher monitoring: Students begin to develop independence

Students, especially in KS3, find it very hard at first to play 'teacher' and know how to structure 'main idea' or BIG questions as this requires them to have a firm grasp of the content they have just read. To overcome this, it is worth for the first couple of times really structuring the cycles. Do this by putting students into *groups of four* and giving each student in the group one of the following roles:

- Summarizer

- Questioner

- Clarifier

- Predictor

The structure of these initial 'practice runs' is as follows:

i.   Give each student a copy of Handout 1.

ii. Have students read a paragraph of the assigned text selection.

iii. At the end of the paragraph the students complete their part of the handout with you leading the process – telling each role in turn when to speak, etc.

- The *Summarizer* will highlight the key ideas up to this point in the reading.

- The *Questioner* will then pose questions about the selection:

  ○ main points of the text;

  ○ five Ws rule – *why, who, what, when, where, how?*

  ○ connections to other concepts already learnt.

- The *Clarifier* will address confusing parts.

- The *Predictor* can offer predictions about what the author will tell the group next.

iv. The group then has a five minute discussion about the text they have just read. The teacher (you) journeys around the class listening to the discussions, intervening with additional questions and prompts where necessary to help them 'understand' the text.

v. The roles in the group then switch one person to the right, and the next selection is read. Students repeat the process using their new roles. This continues until the entire selection is read.

Throughout the process, the teacher's role is to guide and nurture the students' ability to use the four strategies successfully within the small group. The teacher's role is lessened as students develop skill.

Handout 1: Student roles

Predictor:	**Clarifier:**
• *Based on what you've read and what you know, what do you think will happen next?*	• *Was there a word you weren't sure about?*
	• *What can we guess it means?*
• *What clues helped you to think about what will happen next (I think... I predict... My guess is that...)?*	• *How can we check it?*
	• *Were there any ideas that were confusing to you or that you didn't understand?*
Questioner:	**Summarizer:**
• *Who/what was the paragraph about?*	• *What are the most important ideas or events?*
• *Why did the author choose to tell you about this?*	• *What does the author want you to remember or learn from this?*
• *When/where did the events in the paragraph take place?*	• *What is the most important information in this passage?*

Students working independently: – For older students – KS4/5

For older students it should be possible to go straight into the process outlined at the beginning. However, as the students are meant to be engaging with text that is in-line with their age rather than their current achievement, they may need to follow the roles above initially to ensure they can access the thinking.

The classic lesson looks like this:

i.   Students are divided into groups of five: one lead pupil, four roles.

ii. One pupil acts as teacher and asks the group to predict what they might be about to read.

iii. That pupil then either reads the section aloud or the group reads it in silence.

iv. The lead pupil then asks W questions about what they have just read to check for understanding.

v.   The lead pupil asks them to list unfamiliar words or phrases or to outline parts of the paragraph they are unsure about.

vi. The group then works together to clarify these words, etc.

vii. The lead pupil then asks the group to summarize the paragraph in two sentences.

viii. A new lead pupil is chosen and the cycle starts again.

This process works particularly well at KS4/5 when deconstructing model answers – both perfect and deficient – and getting students to talk about the answers and then compare them to the success criteria. The reason this works so well is that it makes the choices of the author and the structure of the answer clear and is an excellent way of modelling the thinking process behind A Grade answers. It is not about ability!

Training students before starting

Students will need to be trained first and the rules made explicit.

●   Questioners will need to practice how to ask BIG questions: *who, what, when, where, why, how, etc.*

- Clarifiers will need to practice how to ask questions about the meaning of words and phrases so that the meaning of the paragraph can be reached, even when they do not understand the meaning of every word.

- Summarizers will need to practice how to boil down a paragraph into its main idea.

- Predictors will need to practice how they can use the clues from the text to guess what is likely to happen or be said next.

Remember, the impact of reciprocal teaching does not come from the act of questioning or clarifying but from the quality of the interactive talk that the structure enables. The aim is that by modelling the thinking process students, over time, can become autonomous and control their own learning as they carry out the four roles concurrently and on their own. It requires clear initial planning and a belief that slowing down the process initially will lead to greater gains in the long run.

Stage 4: Looking at designing a training session on teaching reading as a way of assessing understanding

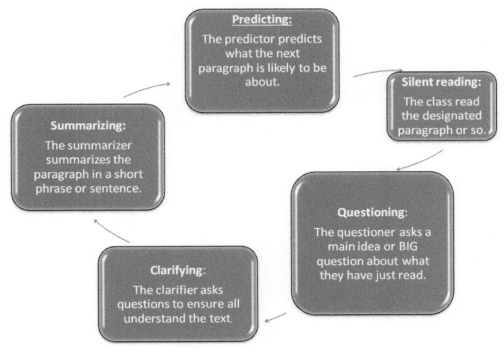

Figure 3.2 A cycle of the five stages of the reciprocal questioning process

TRAINING ACTIVITY

Planning a training session on building reading into the subject classroom

As everyone knows, the best way to check understanding is to apply that knowledge to an unseen problem. With that in mind this training activity seeks to use the approach to reading outlined above to devise a training activity for a group of teachers.

So, your job is to work with two or three other teachers and plan an imaginary training activity for a new group of teachers coming to start at the school. You will need to follow this process:

i.   Your training session focus will be on enabling this group of teachers to have an understanding of the reading model and how they can build this into their Fertile Questions and three and five year plans.

ii.   It will require some proper thinking and planning if they are to be able to use the model in the classroom and see how the model allows for greater reading 'skill' to be developed over time as a student moves from Year 7 through to Year 11.

Use the space below to map out your initial ideas before finalizing them and hopefully then having an opportunity to deliver the training.

Part 2: Talk is how learning happens

One of the fundamental beliefs of the approach outlined in this book is that *language plays a central role in learning and meaning making.* It is impossible to secure outstanding progress without having an understanding of how language advances understanding, and the difficulties students have in developing the language demands of each discipline. So often we hear about the importance of language or teachers and school leaders talk about co-constructivism and neo-Vygotskyism, but rarely does that same teacher or school leader have a clearly thought-out view of what this looks like in practice and how all teachers can follow their lead.

This section maps out an approach to language acquisition based on talk. Students' talk output is as important as teachers' talk input – it is how students construct ideas, build understanding and apply knowledge. It is vital to acknowledge the role of talk in learning, but also to be skeptical about much current practice. In many classrooms there are plenty of opportunities for group and paired talk, however much of the time this talk is not collaborative, not necessary for task completion, and not requiring stretches of language and thinking. It is as if the talking is a by-product and a bolt-on rather than a central component.

So engaging with this section will require the desire to look deep at your own practice and be prepared to acknowledge that not all talk-based activities are successful.

Again, to help make this easier to understand, this section is broken down into five stages:

- **Stage 1** looks at what academic language is.

- **Stage 2** looks at the role language plays in learning.

- **Stage 3** looks at how to build this into lesson planning.

- **Stage 4** looks at building talk into Fertile Questions.

- **Stage 5** looks at embedding talk at whole-school level.

Stage 1: What is academic language?

Before we can think about extending students' language from the everyday usage to the academic we need to be clear what we mean by *academic language.* The most useful definition we have found for defining academic language and making it easy for all teachers to understand is that of Edwards.

Subject–register: The 'language' of academic subjects[9]

What is a subject register?

- A set of linguistic features associated with a situation or activity. For example sports journalism or parliamentary debate.

- Any special language – criminal argot, schoolboy slang, occupational jargon – serves two main functions. It facilitates common action by providing words which have precise meanings for fellow specialists, and it reinforces group feeling and group loyalty.

- This double function is apparent in the use of academic languages.

Why is it important?

- The distinctive terms associated with a discipline can be seen as essential tools of the intellectual trade, discriminating between and classifying phenomena in ways which are not available in everyday language.

- Usage of academic language is not just a semantic striptease but essential for mastery of a discipline. As a person employs technical language 'properly' – that is in ways in which his fellow specialists can recognize and accept – so he reinforces his sense of belonging to that field of knowledge.

- By insisting on the 'right' word the teacher is transporting students' move from the everyday to the academic; they are changing the students' reality. A Science teacher might say: 'This is part of the reality we call Chemistry and this is how we talk about it. For the next 40 minutes, other forms of reality don't matter, and you must see things, and try to talk about them, in the appropriate way'.

- Academic terms and language cause problems either because they are assumed to be part of pupils' general knowledge and so need no teaching, or because the teacher acts as though their context-specific meaning will simply be picked up as they go along.

So, if we are to create an approach based on disciplinary thinking we need to maintain a focus on the language of those disciplines and ensure that students and teachers converse in ways appropriate to the discipline they are immersed in.

Stage 2: What role does language play in learning?

Learning takes place through dialogue

> It is not an exaggeration to suggest that classroom talk determines whether or not children learn, and their ultimate feelings of self-worth as students. Talk is how education happens![10]

If you ask teachers how they feel about group-work or discussion-based tasks, some may give a negative response. They may talk about behaviour management problems, or a lack of collaboration on the part of students, or how it is quicker and safer to get through the material using more orthodox methods.

For us, discussion and group work are not flashy activities that can be bolted on to an observation lesson to impress; optional accessories that some teachers take up and others ignore. They are a fundamental part of our philosophy of teaching. All classrooms in your school should be talk-based classrooms, and students should become familiar with the process of discussing problems collaboratively. In fact, the more consistently this is done in a school the easier it becomes, as each lesson reinforces the routines of the last. However, at the same time it is easy to believe that just because students are talking that they are learning. This is obviously not the case and it is important that classroom dialogue follows the principles outlined below.

Talk is important because it is how learning takes place. According to Wallace[11] educators make a difference between *monologic* and *dialogic* talk. Most classroom discourse is monologic, that is centred around the teacher's agenda; even if students respond fully they are converging on the 'expected' response. Dialogic talk is 'that in which both teachers and pupils make substantial and significant contributions and through which pupils' thinking on a given idea or theme is helped to move forward' (Mercer 2003). It is at this stage that it is useful to think back to the role we see new technologies playing in learning. If technology can help students encounter surface understanding and content, then the role of structured talk is central in turning that surface understanding into deeper or more conceptual understandings and ways of thinking.

So, effective classroom dialogue rests on five key principles:[12]

- **Collective:** teachers and children address learning tasks together, whether as a group or as a class;

- **Reciprocal:** teachers and children listen to each other, share ideas and consider alternative viewpoints;

- **Cumulative:** teachers and children build on their own and each others' ideas and chain them into coherent lines of thinking and enquiry;

- **Supportive:** children articulate their ideas freely, without fear of embarrassment over 'wrong' answers; and they help each other to reach common understandings;

- **Purposeful:** teachers plan and steer classroom talk with specific educational goals in view.

Learning takes place through dialogue – an anecdote from David's life

I am terrible at drilling holes in walls. I have never owned a drill, do not know what wall plugs are; basically I am hopeless. I have inherited it from my parents who never went near a toolkit. Fortunately, my father-in-law is pretty expert in this area. Recently he came round to help me put up some hooks in our hallway. His approach to teaching me this was to do it himself, with me watching, and to narrate what he was doing as he went along. It was a *monologic* approach. By the time he finished his lesson all the hooks were up and I may (or may not) have acquired some knowledge of how to do this.

The problem came several weeks later, when I attempted to put up another set of hooks elsewhere in the house. I remembered little or nothing about how to do it. I got halfway through the first hook and abandoned the task, before I caused serious damage to the wall, and promised myself that next time I would try to actually *do* some drilling in my father-in-law's company; thereby applying the knowledge he was teaching me and discussing it with him, rather than passively listening and assuming I was learning (which I evidently was not).

Stage 3: How can I plan for this in my lessons?

Creating a talk-based classroom

Planning for discussion-based activities requires some training; it is not a case of giving students a question and telling them to talk about it for 20 minutes. Being able to effectively set up discussion activities so that all students are participating, stretches of language and thinking are taking place, and there is a real sense of purpose and engagement is a hallmark of an expert teacher. When talk-based activities are effective they are powerful tools in developing more complex ideas and ways of expressing this.

We will not attempt to list a series of great discussion-based tasks for your classroom here,[13] but rather try and outline the principles behind effective group work and discussion.

The role of talk in learning:

i. Producing language encourages learners to process the language more deeply than just listening to that language.

ii. Learners need to be placed in a context where they are required to focus on the ways they are expressing themselves.

iii. So, learners should have the opportunity to focus not just on *what* they are saying but also on *how* they are saying it.[14]

Designing collaborative activities:

Pauline Gibbons (1991) has six criteria that activities must meet if they are to be truly collaborative. Group work and discussion tasks will only develop language and thinking if they are meeting these criteria:

Collaborative activities – six criteria (adapted from Gibbons 1991)[15]

i. **Do participants have to talk to enable them to complete the activity?** Group work is not group work if the problem can be solved by an individual without any need to talk and shape the solution with others. Talking whilst doing an activity is not the same as thinking aloud through an activity.

ii. **Are all participants involved in the activity in some way?** By this we mean meaningful involvement – it is hard to see how a scribe or a timekeeper can be useful to developing or enabling complex cognitive moves. All participants should play a part in designing the solution to the problem posed by the activity – either by having information that is required that no other participant has or by helping the group reach a solution collaboratively.

iii. **Are participants using stretches of language?** One word responses are not helpful in developing thinking and language. The design of the task should require participants to have to talk at length and actively listen to others also talking and using their information and ideas to shape the solution.

227

iv. **Are participants having to think?** Is the task cognitively challenging as well as linguistically challenging – do not feel tempted to 'dumb it down' to ensure your students can talk. Change the approach but maintain the standards and expectations – not expectations in terms of behaviour but expectations in terms of what students can think and do.

v. **What kinds of language are participants having to use?** Make sure that the task develops subject-specific and high-cognitive language to enable all students to play the bourgeois game of job interviews and university admissions interviews.

vi. **Which curriculum areas does the activity involve?** The activity has to relate to a specific area of the curriculum and ideally should replicate the way a group of experts in that field might converse, argue and adapt their thinking as they build on one another's ideas.

TRAINING ACTIVITY

Developing higher-order language[16]

Another way to think about what makes effective discussion tasks is to question the types of language students are using in their discussion. We have said they should be moving from everyday to academic language, but you can also think about the degree of cognitive challenge inherent in the language. For example, is it the language of description or repetition, or the language of evaluation and prediction?

Low Cognitive	High Cognitive
Repeating	Arguing
Reproducing	Justifying
Naming	Analyzing
Matching	Predicting
Sequencing	Hypothesizing
Identifying	Inferring
Explaining	Evaluating

Figure 3.3 Language demands for different outcomes

Using the information above:

i.   Look back at the lessons you have planned already. Did you design some paired or group work?

   ● Pick one of the activities you designed and assess it against Gibbons' six criteria above.

      ○ How collaborative is your activity?

      ○ How could you amend it to ensure it meets all six points?

ii. Think about how to develop higher-order language: Choose a Fertile Question you have planned and now add in a series of activities that will move students to high-cognitive language skills.

Stage 4: Building talk into my Fertile Questions

Now that the role of talk in the learning process has been explored and how to design activities that create opportunities for meaningful talk to happen has been analysed, the final piece of this part of the jigsaw is to look at planning talk into the medium-term plans of your Fertile Questions.

This can be done in a number of ways. Perhaps the most useful thing to do is the following:

i.   Take several lesson plans you have constructed and tweak them so that they include collaborative activities.

ii. Take one of your Fertile Questions and answer the following questions:

   ● What are the particular language demands of the Fertile Question? How might experts in that particular field talk and express their ideas – both tentative and final?

   ● Planning backwards from the end point of the Fertile Question, what stages will you need to take the students through to get them to meet those demands? How can you help them move from talking in everyday language to talking in more formal academic language using the target terms and criteria?

   ● Where will these stages occur in the learning process?

   ● What will individual lessons look like?

iii. Revise the Fertile Question on the back of these answers so that the planning represents a journey through the language acquisition required.

TRAINING ACTIVITY

Is talk enabling learning?

This activity is similar to the triad observation schedule outlined in the previous chapter, but this time with a focus on the talk-based classroom.

Stage 1: Partnering up

This training activity works best if teachers are partnered up in threes (triad) outside their normal department or subject area. This is so that any technical language is more explicit to the untrained ear.

Stage 2: The observation timetable

A timetable needs to be drawn up that enables the triad to observe each other at least twice. Each observation should be with a different age group and should be at least two days apart. This will require careful planning at whole-school level.

Stage 3: The observation focus

The focus of the observation is to look at the types of language demands the lesson is making on the students and to assess these demands using the grid below.

Stage 4: The analysis of the feedback

Each observer pair in the triad should spend at least 45 minutes going through their observation grids and summarizing the types of language developed and the success of the approaches seen. Use Gibbons' six criteria to measure the success of any discussion-based tasks.

Stage 5: Sharing the analysis

The observation triad should meet up once every member of the triad has been observed by the other two members and each person in turn should be given the feedback and then this discussed with suggestions as to how to move it forward. This meeting should focus particularly on sharing ideas for how discussion tasks can work best.

Stage 6: Making the change

As with the mindsets approach, no more than two development points should be given.

Stage 7: Revisiting the change

Three weeks after the feedback meeting, the triads should again observe each other. This time for only one lesson and with one of the original classes they saw in Stage 2. The focus of this observation is to assess the language demands now observed and whether the feedback given has been acted upon.

Language observation grid

Focus of observation:	To observe: i. The impact of teaching activities in developing literacy. ii. The impact of students' literacy skills on their achievement. (Focus on groups of students.)
Teacher being observed:	Date of observation:
Class:	Room:

What you are looking for: (examples)

i. The structure of the activities – are they truly collaborative?
Give examples of:
- opportunities for language at an appropriate cognitive level and related to a specific area of the curriculum;
- all students given opportunities to talk about the task and demonstrate appropriate skills for completion of task (speaking, listening, reading, writing);
- groups of students engaged in their learning through talk;
- students required to make longer and more complex interactions, not just single words or phrases – for example, through questioning and feedback;
- students required to think in order to complete the task, rather than operate on a mechanical level.

Evidence:

ii. The type of language demand the observed activities make

- Describe the language skills that students are required to use during activities – low-cognitive or high-cognitive.
- Describe the kind of thinking and possible progression that is taking place.

Low Cognitive	High Cognitive
• Repeating • Reproducing • Matching • Sequencing	• Arguing • Justifying • Analysing • Evaluating

Evidence:

iii. How is the pupils' language extended at each stage of this lesson?

- Does it start by enabling students to explain their current thinking in everyday language?
- Are students helped to move from everyday to more formal language?
- Do students have an opportunity either to read aloud formal written texts or to write using the formal language they have been talking with?
- Are the language demands made on the student resulting in:
  - greater engagement, focus and concentration that leads to enjoyment of learning;
  - low-level disruptive behaviour/off-task chatter?

Evidence:

Feedback: What three things could change to improve student progress in the lesson?

© 2014, Creating Outstanding Classrooms, Oliver Knight and David Benson, Routledge

Part 3: The writing process

The final section of this chapter now looks at the writing process. It has been placed last for a particular reason: writing is informed and strengthened by reading and talking and the knowledge developed in the previous two sections underpins the approach to developing student writing outlined below.

Again, as with talking, there are numerous approaches available and many resources to help. However, many of the approaches and resources currently in use are more a reflection of what the teacher thinks and believes about a subject than what the student does. Many writing frames and other support mechanisms have become so mechanistic that they are more of a cage than a scaffold. It is often the teacher that has 'got a Level 5' rather than the student.

So, the approach below maps out a whole-school approach to embedding the writing process into every classroom that will enable all students to make outstanding progress.

Again, to help make this easier to understand, this section is broken down into five stages:

- **Stage 1** looks at Language progression and the Mode Continuum.

- **Stage 2** looks at academic language acquisition.

- **Stage 3** looks at the three stages of the writing process.

- **Stage 4** looks at building writing into Fertile Questions.

- **Stage 5** looks at developing independence in your students.

Stage 1: Language progression and the Mode Continuum

In order to ensure progression for all pupils, regardless of baseline data and previous experiences, pupils need to be taught and to understand the language choices required to produce an appropriate text for an appropriate task and the teacher needs to support pupils in developing those language choices.[17]

The journey through a Fertile Question should be planned to move from talk as process through to written text on the basis that writing is informed by and strengthened through talking. The three stages outlined above are a very simple way of helping build language acquisition into your planning. We have already looked at talk and its role in developing meaning. The process above maps that onto the approach to developing written expertise.

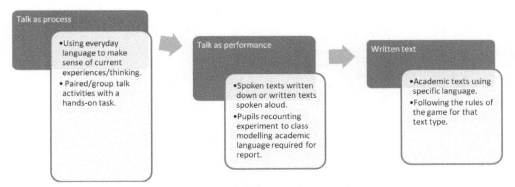

Figure 3.4 The journey through a Fertile Question from talk as process to written text

During the first few lessons of the Fertile Question there should be multiple opportunities for students to talk to each other and to the teacher about their thinking. They should be allowed to use everyday language to explain and justify. Paired and group tasks should be designed that create meaningful reasons to talk about the learning. The genre and its attendant rules need to be foregrounded at this stage so that the resolution of the Fertile Question is created following those rules.

As the lessons progress and as students share and respond to draft answers talk should be planned as a performance. This means either writing down answers in everyday language or reading aloud more academic language. Feedback should be planned that means the learners have to speak to one another about their current thinking and understanding and where they need to go next.

The resolution of the Fertile Question should then focus on using the more formal academic register of that subject discipline. This can either be through written texts that follow the rules of the game for that genre or spoken texts that are formal.

Creating a talk-based classroom

Using the Mode Continuum to scaffold language progression – an example from Science[18]

The diagram below represents how the Mode Continuum could be used to help students move from talking using everyday language through to writing in formal academic language about an experiment they have carried out. As the student progresses through the lessons, the language demands increase.

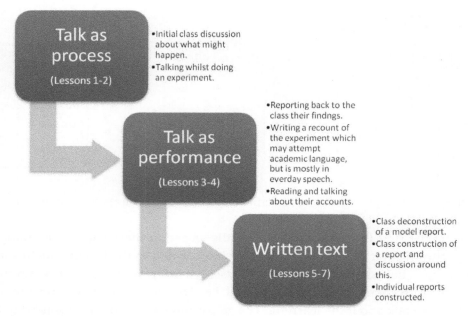

Figure 3.5 Using the Mode Continuum to scaffold language progression in Science

What might the journey look like in Maths?

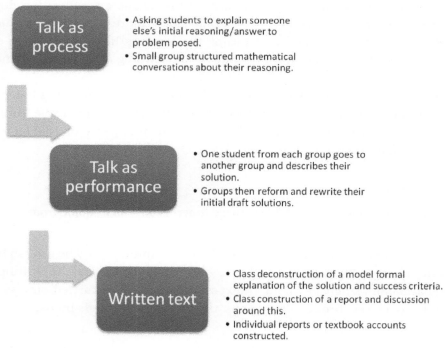

Figure 3.6 Using the Mode Continuum to scaffold language progression in Maths

Or History?

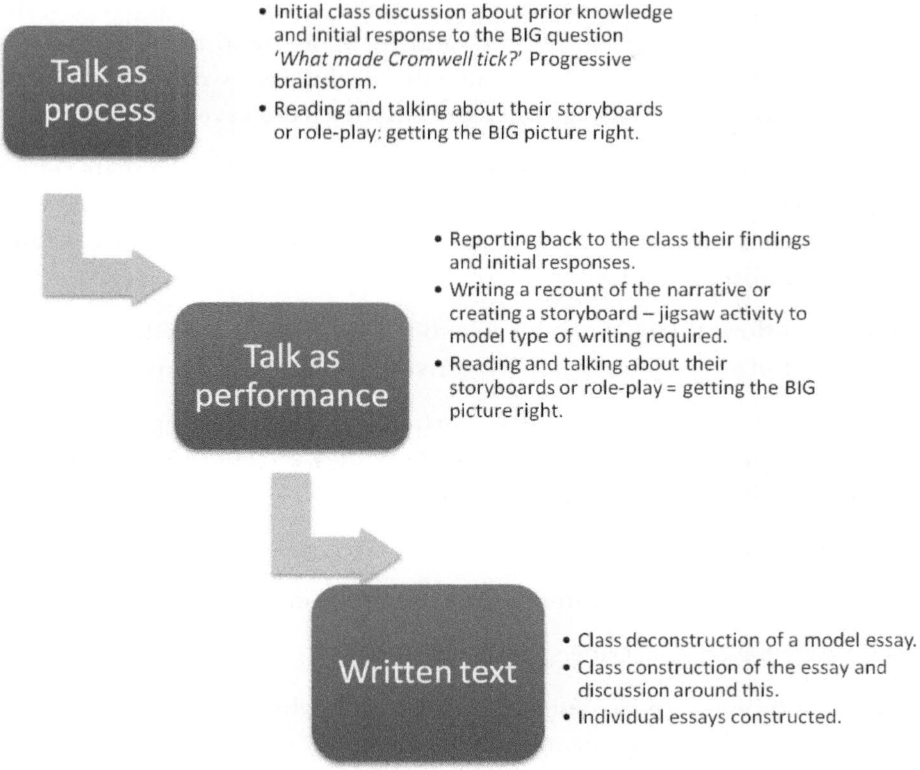

Talk as process
- Initial class discussion about prior knowledge and initial response to the BIG question *'What made Cromwell tick?'* Progressive brainstorm.
- Reading and talking about their storyboards or role-play: getting the BIG picture right.

Talk as performance
- Reporting back to the class their findings and initial responses.
- Writing a recount of the narrative or creating a storyboard – jigsaw activity to model type of writing required.
- Reading and talking about their storyboards or role-play = getting the BIG picture right.

Written text
- Class deconstruction of a model essay.
- Class construction of the essay and discussion around this.
- Individual essays constructed.

Figure 3.7   Using the Mode Continuum to scaffold language progression in History

Why is writing difficult?[19]

We said earlier that the most effective questions in a lesson are those that place the teacher and student on the same intellectual plane, thereby making the teacher's problem the student's problem, and allowing the teacher to model the ways of thinking and learning behaviours the students will need to answer the question. The same principle is true of setting up writing tasks in the classroom; the teacher must see the task through the eyes of the learner.

This begins with understanding all the ways in which students find writing difficult. When writing, students have to be able to operate at different levels of language to create texts which adhere to the conventions of formal written academic language. Some of these levels are:

- **spelling**: accurate spelling of all common words, and all but the most difficult academic/specialized words.

- **vocabulary**: students have to be able to use subject-specific language and terminology. This requires them to i) understand the underlying concepts this language is used to express and ii) understand how it expresses it. They also have to use general academic vocabulary – words which are fairly specific to school language but can be used across several subjects.

- **grammar and sentencing**: students have to be able to formulate sentences grammatically correctly and to use some grammatical structures which tend to characterize formal academic writing, for example passive sentences and subordinate clauses.

- **punctuation**: they have to be able to use key punctuation features: capital letters, full stops, question marks, inverted commas, colons, etc.

- **thinking processes**: this is all important. Academic writing makes thinking visible. Students have to be able to show they are engaging in the kinds of thinking processes which the writing requires:

  - they have to give reasons;

  - they have to give opinions and support them;

  - they have to describe specific processes.

- **text**: they have to use all the conventions which formal school writing employs to show organization in a text:

  - headings

  - sub-headings

  - numbering

  - bulleting

  - paragraphs

  - devices which show organization within paragraphs, e.g. topic sentences.

- **formality**: students have to develop a formal written style. Common features of formal academic writing are those mentioned above, e.g. passives, academic vocabulary, subordination, clear signalling of textual organization. Similarly they have to learn to under-use features of informal writing and speech, e.g. personalization (use of *I, we*), also informal vocabulary.

Again, it is not the sole job of the English Department to take on the above list. Students will make rapid progress in the quality of their writing if all teachers are making the features of good writing explicit, and all are giving them feedback on their literacy. A common marking shorthand in a school, where all teachers mark using the same symbols, will help with this. There is an example from Ark Academy below. What will help even more is if all teachers understand the Mode Continuum, and how to drip feed the characteristics of academic writing to students as they move through the Fertile Question.

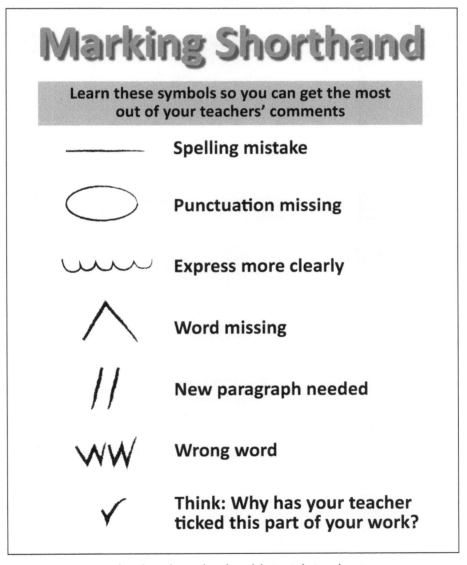

Figure 3.8 An example of marking shorthand from Ark Academy

Stage 2: Teaching and Learning cycle for academic language acquisition[20]

One way to help develop your students into confident writers is to use the Teaching and Learning cycle outlined below as a guideline. It helps students get to grips with how writing happens from beginning to end. It sets out four distinct phases and then looks at what these phases look like in practice. This cycle tends to take place during the third part of the Mode Continuum moving into academic writing following the rules of the genre.

Building in language acquisition to a Fertile Question

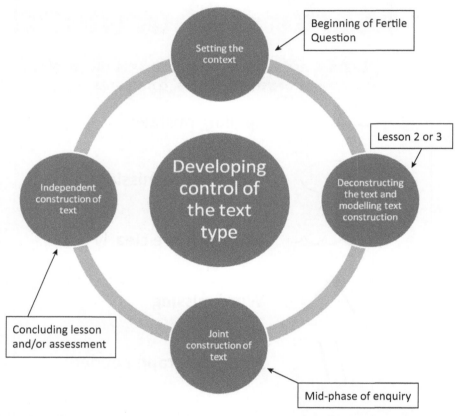

Figure 3.9 The Teaching and Learning cycle for academic language acquisition

The phases of this cycle:[21]

Setting the context:

i. finding out what students already know about the topic;

ii. engaging students with the topic;

iii. establishing the purpose and audience for the text they are going to create.

Deconstruction and modelling:

i.   examining the structure and purposes of the text, identifying key features and rules;

ii. looking at the language choices of the author and the types of language experts use;

iii. modelling the text constructions process and choices – structures, purposes and features.

Joint construction:

i.   working alongside students to jointly produce a draft text;

ii. drawing on shared understandings about the topic and the text;

iii. pupils providing feedback to one another before working independently – peer review of the drafts using the success criteria to provide provocative feedback to one another. (See assessment section for further detail on this process.)

Independent construction:

i.   supporting students to produce their own texts;

ii. providing explicit developmental feedback.

Stage 3: The writing process boiled down

The cycle above represents the four phases a student goes through in moving from first being introduced to a topic to being able to write at length about it. It is quite mechanistic, focusing on the technical features of the text, and does not necessarily involve any disciplinary perspective. The cycle is all about the process of writing rather than a reflection of how writers in different disciplines write.

To that end the four phases above have been boiled down into a more coherent 'flow' that takes the learner from beginning to end of the process but includes content as well as context. The process outlined below is easy to embed across a Fertile Question. Individual lessons then look at one or more of the phases and progression is planned for across lessons and made explicit in longer-term plans. This is where we come back to the ideas in the curriculum section of *planning backwards.* By looking at the writing requirements of Year 11 or Year 13 it is then possible to map this back to Year 7 and look at how writing progression needs to be structured across five or seven years.

The writing process[22]		
Before the writing takes place	**During the writing**	**After the writing has been done**
Exploring ideas: • talk and discussion • playing the story • role-play • retelling • drawing • mapping.	*Shaping for purpose and audience:* • shared writing • response and editing partners • talking about process • reading own writing aloud • commenting on each other's work • sharing ideas • collaborative writing • writing conferences.	*Evaluating and valuing:* • talking about the process as a writer: student–teacher; student–student. Polishing: • support for spelling • rewriting for a purpose • celebrating achievement • publishing • book-making • performing the writing for others to enjoy.

Stage 4: Building writing into Fertile Questions

From looking at the three stages above it should be clear when and how to build writing into Fertile Questions. In order to make the planning clearer there are some points about the kind of writing tasks you can include in lessons. This is not a full list just some examples to get you thinking.

i. Most students need forms of support to help them write. There is a repertoire of task types which you can use for this. They give support at different levels of language:[23]

- word

- sentence

- text

ii. The most useful types are:

- word lists

- substitution tables

- sentence starters

- writing frames

- tables

- visuals

iii. Writing support tasks give support at different levels of language.

- word lists: support at the word level;

- substitution tables: support at the word and sentence level;

- sentence starters: support at the sentence level;

- writing frames: support at the sentence and text level;

- tables: support varies according to the form of support chosen;

- visuals: support varies according to the form of support chosen.

iv. These tasks will be useful to all learners, but may be of particular benefit to English as an Additional Language (EAL) learners. These students often need support at the sentence level – they may find it hard to construct a sentence grammatically correctly. Note that a substitution table, for example, does not allow you to make grammatical mistakes – which helps the EAL learner focus wholly on the thinking behind the topic. Word lists do not help learners who need support with constructing sentences, whereas sentence starters do. You need to think about your own class, their specific writing needs, and gauge the support accordingly.

TRAINING ACTIVITY

Examples of writing tasks

Look at the examples of writing tasks below and discuss the pros and cons of each method.

Example 1: Word lists

Geography: Task – write about the water cycle using this list:

sun	warm	water
condense	drops	turn into
water vapour	fall	groundwater
rise	wind	soak into
clouds	run along	droplets
seep through	rain	pass through
hail	evaporate	sleet
take up	leaves	blow
roots	form	rock
cycle	flow	

Example 2: Substitution tables

Science: Task – write about an ecosystem using this substitution table:

A caterpillar	eat(s)	caterpillars
A wood mouse	feed(s) on	wood mice
A fox	break(s) down	foxes
Funghi	is/are eaten by	funghi
Bacteria		bacteria
Earthworms		earthworms
Insects		insects

Example 3: Writing frames

Science: Task – write about the extinction of the dinosaurs

Gradualist theory	
The gradualist hypothesis says…	Mammals / numbers / land / diversity / marine / decline
The reason for the extinction was…	Climate / fall / change / sea level / cool / dinosaurs / marine / mammals
Asteroid impact theory	
The impact hypothesis suggests…	asteroid / Cretaceous
The evidence for this is that…	Clay / deposit / Cretaceous / iridium / rare / common / meteorites

Planning questions for guided writing

When you come to write your Fertile Questions, the list below may help you to craft the best writing tasks:

Before your students start writing:

i. What learning are you trying to demonstrate with this writing?

ii. Are you going to prepare students for the writing or use the activity as a way of testing understanding?

iii. Are you clear about the role the writing task will play?

iv. How much emphasis is on the writing and how much is on the thinking displayed within the writing?

v. Who is going to read the piece of writing and what difference will that make?

vi. What is the purpose behind this type of text?

vii. What do they need to know about the features of the type of writing you want them to do?

viii. In what sequence will you structure the writing process across the Fertile Question?

ix. Have they encountered this type of writing before? If so, make connections to it.

x. Is this a concluding activity for a Fertile Question or part of the process of solving the problem?

During the writing:

i. How much structure do your students need during the process?

ii. What opportunities are there for peer review?

iii. How much time will be dedicated to deconstructing the genre?

iv. Are the criteria for the piece of writing clear?

v. Are there exemplars of the desired standard you can deconstruct with students?

vi. What particular stylistic features will be new to the students?

vii. How many drafts will they be writing?

After the writing:

i.   How will you know your teaching has been successful?

ii. What are you going to do with the piece of writing?

iii. How will you use this new learning to inform and deepen the learning in the next Fertile Question?

Thinking about your writing as you are writing: What is the conversation between the author and the reader?

Below is probably the best demonstration we have ever come across for enabling students to get to grips with the idea that the reader (mainly examiner) of their work is engaged in a continuous conversation with them. We wish we had been intelligent enough to create the diagram ourselves but it is absolute dynamite.

Talking to your examiner[24]

Examiner	*So what are you trying to tell me?*	
Writer	This is the point I want to make, the idea I want you to see.	
Part of the Paragraph		i. **Topic sentence**
Examiner	*Ah, I see. Tell me more.*	
Writer	Let me explain….	
Part of the Paragraph		ii. **Explain the focus of the paragraph**
Examiner	*I see. What evidence do you base this on?*	
Writer	Here is my evidence.	

Part of the Paragraph		iii. Show your evidence
Examiner	*I see. How does this connect with the point you are making?*	
Writer	Like this. I think that this evidence supports my point by...	
Part of the Paragraph		iv. Explain how your evidence supports your main point
Examiner	*Fair enough. So where does this leave us?*	
Writer	I have shown that the point I have made is a solid one and it makes you think that the next thing we should be thinking about is...	
Part of the Paragraph		v. Conclude by making links back to the question and forward to the next paragraph
Examiner	*What is the next thing then?*	

...and you move on to the main point in the topic sentence of the next paragraph.

Stage 5: Developing independence in your students[25]

Scaffolds and writing frames are only helpful if the eventual outcome is that they are removed and the students become independent. GCSE and A-Level exams will offer minimal scaffolding of students' written responses (at least on the higher tiers) so the sooner students feel comfortable writing without this crutch, the better.

i. Any piece of writing, if it consists of an organized series of thoughts, i.e. more than one sentence, requires planning. Confident writers are experienced in planning their writing; it is the only way to make the eventual outcome structured and organized. Two common planning methods are:

(a) Write a series of headings and to make notes under each heading. Headings may be numbered, points and sub-points either numbered, bulleted or indented. This form allows you to show an order in the points you make.

(b) Draw a spider diagram. Main nodes are the key points; sub-nodes are points to make under each key point. Plans will be drafted and redrafted until they look right. Students do not have to write full sentences within their notes – key words will do.

ii.   Another characteristic of independent writers is that they are experienced at drafting and redrafting their work. Students should get in the habit of creating a first draft and then revising it. They need guidance when they revise: what should they check? A set of criteria for success is crucial.

iii. Students can also get help in revising by asking another person to read it – a peer or a teacher. Students need practice in revising peers' work and should use clear criteria for this.

iv. They then need to revise and write a final draft.

The checklist below is a useful guide in helping move students towards independent writing.

Planning	Drafting	Finalising
• Purpose	• Write 1st draft	• Individual write a final draft
• Core knowledge and ideas	• Self-assess against criteria	• Discuss the writing process
• Stylistic features	• Peer review and feedback	• Display/use the writing for a purpose
• Intended audience	• Group re-drafting/ working on the difficult parts	
• Deconstruct a model		

Figure 3.10   Moving towards independent writing

Student discussion questions for guided writing[26]

Below is a similar list to the version for teachers above, but this one is for students. We have borrowed this material, which may be of use, from the Centre for Literacy in Primary Education.

Before writing

i.   What learning are you trying to demonstrate in this writing?

ii.   Are you clear about the task?

iii. Who is going to read this and what difference will that make?

iv.   What is the purpose behind this type of text?

v.   What do you know about the features of this type of writing?

vi.   What would be the best way to plan this?

vii. How best can you organize the ideas you have?

viii. What might be the best way to start?

ix.   How might you conclude the piece?

During writing

i.   What sentence are you thinking of writing next? Let's reread what you have written and see if the new sentence will sound right.

ii.   How do you want your reader to react at this point?

iii. Would changing anything improve the effect on the reader?

iv.   Do you need to add anything?

v.   Could you use fewer words?

vi.   Have you varied your sentences enough? How do your sentences start? Do they vary in length? Are they linked in different ways?

vii. Do your paragraphs hang together well?

viii. Does your evidence match your explanations?

ix.   Does your punctuation help to make your meaning clear?

After writing

    i.   Does what you have written match the task and fulfil the success criteria?

    ii. Does the opening lead the reader in?

    iii. Are your paragraphs in the best order?

    iv. Are your paragraphs linked effectively?

    v.   Does each paragraph make sense? Have you used topic sentences? Are sentences linked?

    vi. Have you used spelling strategies to make a best guess of any spellings you are unsure of? Have you checked your spellings?

    vii. Does your use of punctuation help the reader to understand your meaning?

Conclusion: Two case studies on language acquisition and progress

We will now look at two case studies that relate to the ideas in this chapter. They both share real experiences of the process of implementing this approach in schools. They form the concluding ideas to this part of the book as they sum up the key ideas and principles and look at converting them into classroom practice.

Case study 3: Ark and morning reading – adapted from a case study first published in *Ark Academy case studies 2012*

Nurturing a love of reading: All teachers are reading teachers at Ark Academy
Sheila Ball | Assistant Principal | Ark Academy

Introduction

At Ark Academy, all teachers are teachers of reading. Our school day starts with a 20 minute reading lesson for every student. Because every teacher has a reading group, class sizes are small; an average of 12 students per group.

And these reading lessons are not about silent reading, or 'Drop Everything and Read', or other common approaches. In schools like ours, which have significant numbers of students who start Year 7 as poor readers, one of the worst things you can do is just have *more* reading. Telling students who lack confidence in reading to all read their books in silence during form time, and disciplining them when they do not, is not a reading lesson.

We take another approach, which starts with training all staff how to teach reading. It is a different skill, and one unfamiliar to most secondary teachers. Training on how to teach reading forms part of our staff induction to the academy.

During their morning reading sessions, teachers then *explicitly teach students reading skills*: they develop vocabulary; teach them how to read aloud with expression; how to skim, scan and summarize; how to question a text and predict where it is heading, and much more. Our reading programme is a major priority for the school, and something we invest in heavily. In this case study I will explain how the programme works, and try to assess the impact it has had.

Background

At Ark Academy we will never have a 'Literacy Coordinator', who runs around sticking up posters of connectives, corralling Heads of Department to build 'literacy skills' into their schemes of work. The need for students to be literate, to have the vocabulary to explain complicated ideas, and to be able to construct extended written responses, is *absolutely fundamental* to secondary education. It must be fully integrated into how we teach each individual subject, and not an 'initiative' which is bolted on.

Teaching a subject means teaching the language of the subject.[27] We believe at Ark Academy that all learning takes place through dialogue – and dialogue requires language. This does not mean students do not learn on an individual, independent basis. But when you are reading a text book or solving an equation you are having a dialogue, of sorts, with yourself, and it is through this dialogue that understanding is developed. So mastering language and being a confident reader is key – not just to a successful education, but to a full and happy life:

> Adolescents entering the adult world in the 21st century will read and write more than at any other time in human history. They will need advanced levels of literacy to perform their jobs, run their households, act as citizens, and conduct their personal lives. They will need literacy to cope with the flood of information they will find everywhere they turn. They will need literacy to feed their imaginations so they can create the world of the future. In a complex and sometimes even dangerous world, their ability to read can be crucial.[28]

Or put a different way:

> 'Finding ways to engage pupils in reading may be one of the most effective ways to leverage social change.'[29]

Elements of our approach

Based on our own experience, and what we had seen in other schools, we were convinced that starting every day with a 20 minute reading lesson was the way forward for our new school. Our thinking can be grouped into three areas:

- For us morning reading was not about 'instructing' students how to read; instead we wanted students to learn to read for pleasure. This needed more time and resources. If students read for pleasure they will direct their own reading, and become life-long readers; if they read because they are made to, they may develop the skill but not the desire to read, and will stop reading when they leave us.[30] Reading is not just about academics, but also expanding general knowledge, promoting a better understanding of other cultures, becoming a good citizen and gaining a greater insight into human nature and decision making.[31]

- From an academic perspective, students who are confident readers, who enjoy texts and have a wide vocabulary, are much more effective and motivated learners generally. A great morning reading programme ripples out into the teaching of all subjects.

- Reading is key to our 'catch-up' strategy. Looking forward, we want the majority of our students to gain five or more good GCSEs in the EBacc subjects (this was our stated aim before this government's policy). These subjects have a heavy literacy focus, and if students who have average to low attainment on entry are going to cope with GCSE when they get there, they need to improve their reading skills in Year 7, and quickly.

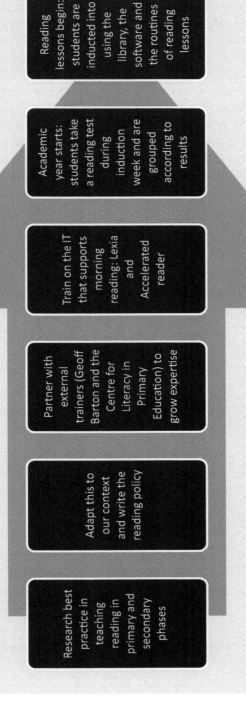

Figure 3.11 The process followed in order to develop a high quality reading programme

So our timetable had, in total, 1 hour 40 minutes of reading each week – more time than was given to some subjects. In order to get the most out of this time we needed to research and develop a high quality approach (codified in our Morning Reading Policy), train on it, then implement it in our lessons. The figure opposite shows the process.

High quality training of teachers was essential. They needed to be inspired to teach outside of their comfort zones. The Centre for Literacy in Primary Education (CLPE) led a full day with all our founder teachers. Many of us found it had a transformational effect on not just our reading teaching, but on our general classroom practice. The CLPE teach strategies for encouraging positive attitudes to reading, such as exploring images and literacy circles.[19] They also ask teachers to reflect on their own identities as readers, and their childhood attitudes to reading. Teachers worked in small groups discussing questions like: *Can you remember the first time you read? As a child where did you read? When did you read?* Conversations with colleagues revealed that we all had very different reading habits. Staff gained a heightened awareness of their identities as readers, particularly useful for reading teachers who were not from English or the humanities.

To make the most of this training, we made the decision to suspend IT based reading activities during morning reading for the first term. This gave teachers the space to implement the ideas they had had in training and share with students their passion for reading. During this first term reading lessons were highly interactive; group reading, drama and art based activities were common. This helped morning reading to get off to a flying start, and for our reading culture to start to bed in.

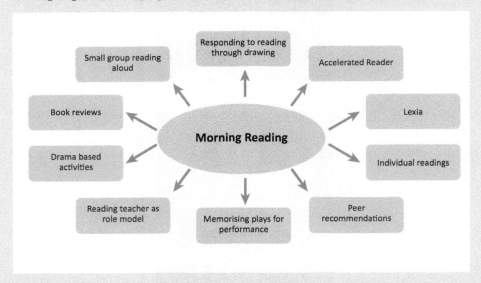

Figure 3.12   Different reading activities from the morning reading programme

Conclusion

A clear rationale, careful training, and a structured approach – these were the building blocks on our morning reading programme. Teachers owned the planning of their reading groups, and were guided by the reading handbook. Reading sessions blended activities from the diagram below, according to the individual teacher's style and the group's needs. We believe the impact on our school has been significant: both in terms of students' attainment and in their enjoyment of school.

'To read is to fly: it is to soar to a point of vantage which gives a view over wide terrains of history, human variety, ideas, shared experience and the fruits of many inquiries.'(A.C. Grayling)

Case study 4: 'Language for All.' The Learning Schools Trust and embedding a coherent approach to language acquisition across 4 Academies

This case study briefly outlines the way one Academy Trust wanted to embed the approach to language acquisition outlined above across all of their academies. This involved writing a trust-specific training handbook, training all staff on it and building in the outcomes from the training to existing systems and processes. **This case study is both looking at the leadership of embedding a trust-wide approach and on what the approach looked like 'on the ground' and how it evolved to fit the ethos of LST.** The approach was managed by John Baumber, CEO and Education Director at LST and written and delivered by Oli Knight, Vanguard Education.

The important point is that the principles of the approach outlined in this book were met whilst at the same time the programme was built around the existing and Trust-specific approaches to teaching and learning that were already in place. This case study does not explain what the specific strategies were but looks at how they were embedded.

1. Who are the Learning Schools Trust?

The Learning Schools Trust (LST) is the non-profit, charitable organisation that operates the Kunskapsskolan-sponsored academies in England. LST´s Academies are non-fee paying, not faith-based, non-selective and strive to offer its students the widest range of possible qualifications, based on the English National Curriculum and incorporating Kunskapsskolan´s unique personalised learning model.

2. What is their learning concept?

The LST model has a number of key elements that work together to provide a personalised learning experience for each student: (Taken from the LST handbook)

(a) Personalised Learning

Our aim is to embed personalised learning and thinking skills within the Academy. This means developing the competence and confidence of every student by actively engaging them, stretching them and developing their skills so that they can take forward their own learning. Students are only given the amount of freedom to manage their own time that they are mature enough to handle.

(b) Goals

Everyone is different and has their own goals in life. A tutor works with the student and their parents/ carers to understand these and to set ambitious, yet realistic, goals for their time in the school, the coming year and term. We recognise that students in

Year 7 may not yet have clear goals. Tutors work with these students, and with older students with low aspirations, to develop their ambitions during their time in the Academy.

(c) One-to-One Tutorial

Every student has a personal tutor who they meet on a one-to-one basis each week for between 15 and 20 minutes. The tutor receives reports on the student´s progress from other teachers to build a rounded picture. During the weekly tutorial they work with the student to review and reflect on progress toward their goals, define new goals for the coming week, identify priorities and agree learning strategies that they will pursue to achieve their goals. Personal tutors have both an academic and a pastoral role. They would be responsible for identifying additional support needs for students. For example this might be through extra learning support or via a wider range of external services.

(d) Personal Timetable and the Logbook

Each student has a personal timetable based on their needs, goals and learning strategies. The timetable is made up of goals and learning strategies. The timetable is made up of interactive lessons, lectures, workshops, group work and private study time. The timetable for the coming week is recorded in a logbook along with the new goals and strategies for the week. The logbook is also used to record teacher comments and for communication between school and home.

(e) ICT

Information on courses, assessment, learning resources are all made available through a web site that can be accessed from home as well as at school. Progress tracking —We aim to give parents/carers a continuous view of their child´s progress, so that, as well as in their termly meetings with tutors, they would be able to assess online records of their child´s progress in all subjects, including teacher and tutor comments, at any time. Paper copies of student achievements and progress would continue to be freely available to parents/carers and students, since online access is not universally available or convenient for all families.

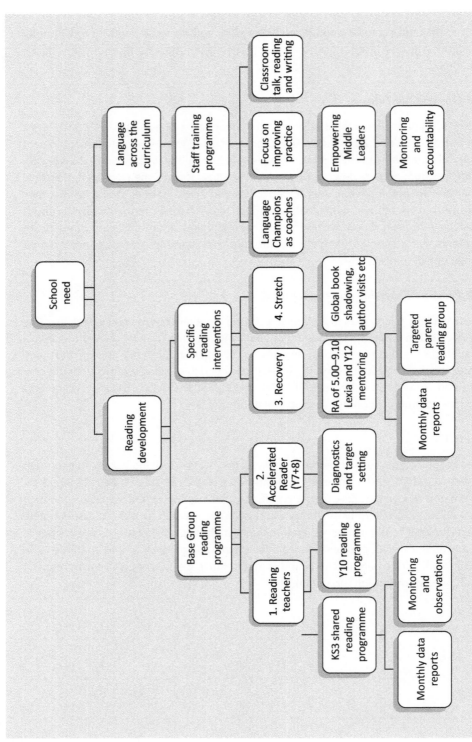

Figure 3.13 Language for All Programme: 2012/13

© 2014, Creating Outstanding Classrooms, Oliver Knight and David Benson, Routledge

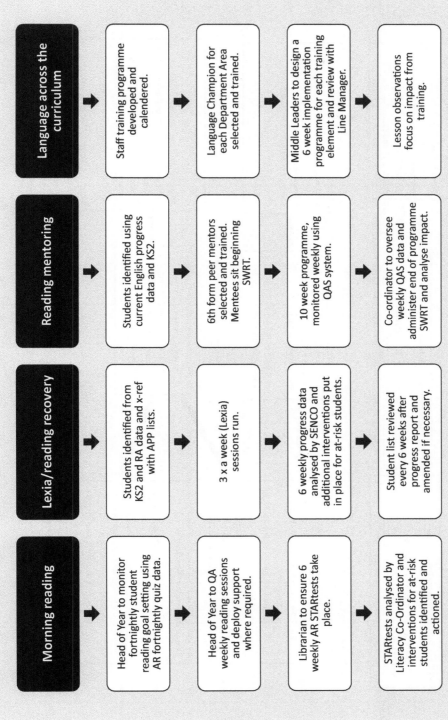

Figure 3.14 Learning Schools Trust – Monitoring and evaluating impact of Language for All

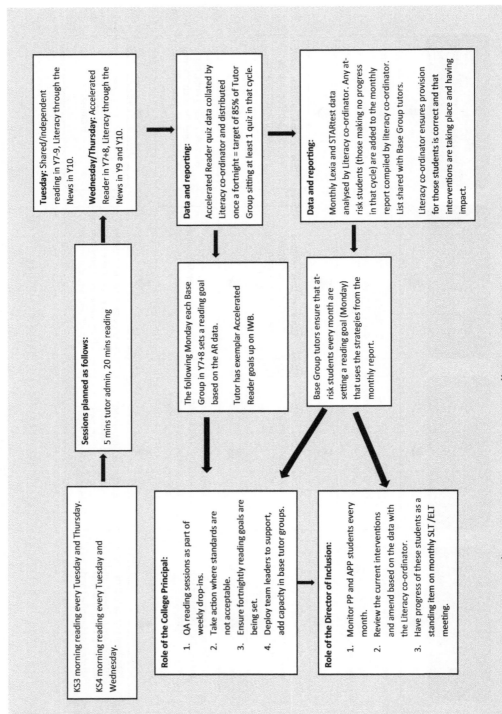

KS3 morning reading every Tuesday and Thursday.

KS4 morning reading every Tuesday and Wednesday.

Sessions planned as follows:

5 mins tutor admin, 20 mins reading

Tuesday: Shared/independent reading in Y7-9, Literacy through the News in Y10.

Wednesday/Thursday: Accelerated Reader in Y7+8, Literacy through the News in Y9 and Y10.

Role of the College Principal:

1. QA reading sessions as part of weekly drop-ins.
2. Take action where standards are not acceptable.
3. Ensure fortnightly reading goals are being set.
4. Deploy team leaders to support, add capacity in base tutor groups.

Role of the Director of Inclusion:

1. Monitor PP and APP students every month.
2. Review the current interventions and amend based on the data with the Literacy co-ordinator.
3. Have progress of these students as a standing item on monthly SLT /ELT meeting.

The following Monday each Base Group in Y7+8 sets a reading goal based on the AR data.

Tutor has exemplar Accelerated Reader goals up on IWB.

Base Group tutors ensure that at-risk students every month are setting a reading goal (Monday) that uses the strategies from the monthly report.

Data and reporting:

Accelerated Reader quiz data collated by Literacy co-ordinator and distributed once a fortnight = target of 85% of Tutor Group sitting at least 1 quiz in that cycle.

Data and reporting:

Monthly Lexia and STARtest data analysed by Literacy co-ordinator. Any at-risk students (those making no progress in that cycle) are added to the monthly report compiled by literacy co-ordinator. List shared with Base Group tutors.

Literacy co-ordinator ensures provision for those students is correct and that interventions are taking place and having impact.

Figure 3.15 Monitoring reading programme – ensuring excellence at KS3

Language for All action plan

Strand 1: Reading recovery and BG (tutor time) reading programme:

Year group	Phase 1: Assess and Design	Phase 2: Implement and evaluate	Phase 3: Sustainability.	Next steps as of 24/03/13.
Year 7	i Collect and analyse Y7 reading data and collate with other (KS2) data – OK NOV 12 ii Create an initial action plan and share with ALT to be agreed – OK NOV 12 iii Identify students in Y7 that require extra challenge and extra access – OK NOV 12 iv Identify core staff to deliver the sessions – OK DEC 12 v Design a reading mentoring programme with Y12 – OK JAN 13 vi Dates set for data check points highlight student progress in reading age – OK JAN 13	i Y7 Train BGTs on 3 strategies for running shared reading in BG time – OK NOV 12 ii Design and train BGTs on an 11 session shared reading programme around the book 'Way Home.' OK JAN 13 iii Use Lexia to run targeted additional support for students in Y7 that require it – OK JAN 13 iv Every student who arrived at L3 or below to have an appropriate intervention running for them – OK+DOI JAN 13 v Establish Accelerated Reader as an independent reading tool and set fortnightly data targets – OK FEB 13 vi Distribute a clear plan for tutors on reading for the year so tutors know what they should be doing each week and what the outcomes should be – OK FEB 13 vii Tutors to be trained on how to interpret the Accelerated Reader data and help students set fortnightly reading goals OK MARCH 13.	i Ensure that all students in Y7 in their College are consistently setting fortnightly reading targets – COLLEGE PRINCIPALS FROM 18/3/13 ii Reading sessions to be consistently Quality Assured – COLLEGE PRINCIPALS MARCH 13 ONWARDS iii Need to x-ref the list of Pupil Premium and Literacy catch-up premium (Those arriving at NCL3 or lower in Y7) with reading age and then next to each student what additional support they are receiving and what the data check-in points are to ensure the support matches their needs and that we can show progress over time – DIRECTOR OF INCLUSION MARCH 13 iv Lexia needs to be dovetailed with SEN/Access provision as there are a lot of useful teacher resources that can be used with individuals and classes – JK+SENCO APRIL 13	i OK+DOI to ensure all PP and PP+ are on the correct programme. Reviewed 24/04/14. ii College Principals to continue to QA shared reading and intervene where necessary. iii Senco to ensure Lexia dovetails with other access provision and supports classroom strategies. iv Principal to build BG reading into Performance management systems to ensure consistency and accountability. v College Principals to continue to monitor quality of fortnightly reading goals. vi College Principals to continue to ensure reading takes place on same days each week. vii JK to establish a parent reading group with a clear focus. viii JK to ensure Lexia is used at home by targeted students with support from Sadia Lodhi. ix Lexia additional time is monitored for attendance and impact. JK

Year group	Phase 1: Assess and Design	Phase 2: Implement and evaluate	Phase 3: Sustainability.	Next steps as of 24/03/13.
		viii Students consistently set a reading goal once a fortnight based on the reading data from the Librarian – COLLEGE PRINCIPALS FROM 18/3/13 ix Textnow reading mentoring being linked to school EAL need. 9 KS3 students selected and matched to a 6th form mentor. OK+ KT April 13. x Set days each week need to be sacrosanct for reading and not other activities – COLLEGE PRINCIPALS JAN 13 xi Y7 students sit NFER NGRTB as summative test point – ALT JULY 13	v Reading needs to be built into Line Management/Performance Management systems so all BGTs talk with their Line Managers about reading and student progress half-termly using the published reading data – PRINCIPAL APRIL 13 vi Lexia has a range of individual interventions that sit behind it – these need to be used so that every fortnight a Lexia report is produced that highlights struggling students and what additional support they need. This should then be used to inform their goal setting and the use of Lexia at home and in the holidays – OK/JK APRIL 13 vii Parent group established – getting dads into reading – JK MARCH 13 viii Lexia additional time built into the week for at risk students – OK+PD APRIL 13. ix Build model for next year into Academy Activity Plan – ALT JUNE 13	x Ensure Lexia fortnightly reports are produced and analysis sent to BGTs to inform reading goals. xi Follow-up on Text Now and ensure starts on time.

Year 8	i Create an initial action plan and share with ALT to be agreed – OK AS ABOVE ii Identify core staff to deliver the sessions – OK AS ABOVE	i BGTs trained on 3 strategies and have been given 5 short stories to choose from to use the strategies with OK JAN 13 ii Design and deliver a structured reading programme for Y8 – JK JAN 13.	i Reading sessions to be consistently Quality Assured – COLLEGE PRINCIPALS MARCH 13 ONWARDS	i College Principals to continue to ensure that the same day each week is set aside for reading. ii College Principals to continue to QA the reading sessions and intervene where necessary.
	iii Dates set for data check points highlight student progress in reading age. (6 weekly) – OK AS ABOVE	iii Distribute a clear plan for tutors on reading for the year so tutors know what they should be doing each week and what the outcomes should be – JK JAN 13 iv Set days each week need to be sacrosanct for reading and not other activities – COLLEGE PRINCIPALS JAN 13	ii Reading needs to be built into Line Management/Performance Management systems so all BGTs talk with their Line Managers about reading and student progress half-termly using the published reading data – PRINCIPAL APRIL 13 iii Build model for next year into Academy Activity Plan – ALT JUNE 13	iii Principal to build reading into Performance management systems to ensure consistency and accountability.
Year 9	i Create an initial action plan and share with ALT to be agreed – OK AS ABOVE ii Identify core staff to deliver the sessions – OK AS ABOVE iii Dates set for data check points highlight student progress in reading age. (6 weekly) -OK AS ABOVE	i BGTs trained on 3 strategies and have been given 5 short stories to choose from to use the strategies with – OK JAN 13 ii Deliver training to Y9 on the News Programme – OK April 13. iii Distribute a clear plan for tutors on reading for the year so tutors know what they should be doing each week and what the outcomes should be – JK JAN 13 iv Train tutors on the weekly news literacy programme – OK MARCH 13	i Reading sessions to be consistently Quality Assured – COLLEGE PRINCIPAL MARCH 13 ONWARDS ii Reading needs to be built into Line Management/Performance Management systems so all BGTs talk with their Line Managers about reading and student progress half-termly using the published reading data – PRINCIPAL APRIL 13 iii Build model for next year into Academy Activity Plan – ALT+ PRINCIPAL JUNE 13.	i College Principals to continue to ensure that the same day each week is set aside for reading. ii College Principals to continue to QA the reading sessions and intervene where necessary. iii Principal to build reading into Performance management systems to ensure consistency and accountability.

Year group	Phase 1: Assess and Design	Phase 2: Implement and evaluate	Phase 3: Sustainability.	Next steps as of 24/03/13.
		v Launch a weekly news session focussing on talk and the GCSE English requirements – OK+ COLLEGE PRINCIPALS MARCH 13 vi Set days each week need to be sacrosanct for reading and not other activities – COLLEGE PRINCIPALS MARCH 13		
Year 10	i Create an initial action plan and share with ALT to be agreed – OK NOV 12 ii Identify core staff to deliver the sessions – OK NOV 12	i Train tutors on the weekly news literacy programme – OK MARCH 13 ii Launch the weekly news session focussing on talk and the GCSE English requirements – COLLEGE PRINCIPAL MARCH 13 iii Set days each week need to be sacrosanct for reading and not other activities – COLLEGE PRINCIPAL MARCH 13	i Reading sessions to be consistently Quality Assured – COLLEGE PRINCIPAL MARCH 13 ONWARDS ii Reading needs to be built into Line Management/Performance Management systems so all BGTs talk with their Line Managers about reading and student progress half-termly using the published reading data – PRINCIPAL APRIL 13 iii Build model for next year into Academy Activity Plan. Academy to identify at Senior and Middle leadership levels who is responsible for what and how it will be evaluated – ALT JUNE 13	i College Principal to continue to QA the News programme and intervene where necessary. ii Principal to build reading into Performance management systems to ensure consistency and accountability.

© 2014, Creating Outstanding Classrooms, Oliver Knight and David Benson, Routledge

Strand 2 – Developing language across the curriculum

Phase 1: Assess and Design	Phase 2: Implement and evaluate	Phase 3: Sustainability	Next steps as of March 13
i Design the language training programme so all staff develop the skills to develop literacy throughout the curriculum – OK NOV 12. ii Allocate Language Champions as figureheads for each Programme Area and train them on use of the developmental observation proforma so they can observe the strategies and action and provide developmental feedback – ALT+OK NOV 12	i Train all staff on 10 strategies for immediate use to move from monologic to dialogic talk – OK NOV 12 ii Train all staff on reciprocal reading and reciprocal teaching – OK DEC 12 iii Train all staff on using key words and connectives to get students to develop more formal talk registers – OK FEB 12 iv Train all staff on 5 strategies for enabling students to engage with longer texts in the classroom – OK FEB 12	i Middle Leaders to take ownership of the training – PRINCIPAL + ELT JAN 13 ii Middle Leaders to ensure consistency across all of their classrooms in terms of use of the selected strategies – ELT JAN 13 iii Middle Leaders to engage with feedback from Language Champions and use it in their department action plans – ELT JAN 13 iv Middle Leaders to have a shared script – how the strategies have raised achievement in their area and what they are doing next – ALT LINE MANAGEMENT FEB 13 ONWARDS	i All Middle Leaders to take ownership of the language programme through Line Management conversations. Language targets to become part of the annual Programme Area review and Line Management questions. ii Middle Leaders to create a script focussing on how the strategies have raised achievement in their area. iii

Phase 1: Assess and Design	Phase 2: Implement and evaluate	Phase 3: Sustainability	Next steps as of March 13
iii Design a process for monitoring of uptake of training and Language Champion observations – OK DEC 12.

iv System designed to capture what each Programme Area is focussing on after each training session and gather feedback from observations – OK DEC 12. | v Train all staff on how to help students plan for writing – OK APRIL 13 – Changed as focus still needed on embedding the 7 non-negotiables so training on 29/4/13 now on re-visiting these and designing a 6 week action plan.

vi Train all staff on how to enable students to monitor the quality of their own writing – OK MAY 13. | v Link the language training to Performance Management – 6 weekly review of student progress and impact of new strategies. What are they doing and how do they know it is working – PRINCIPAL APRIL 13.

vi Ensure Quality Assurance of lessons takes place and build into literacy to existing observation structures – ALT JAN 13 ONWARDS

vii Review the impact of Year 1 - Programme Areas to have evaluated impact of Language for All on teacher practices and student progress – ALT+ELT JUNE 13

viii Design and calendar the programme for Year 2 – ALT JULY 13 | iv Middle Leaders to store and analyse observation data on their department and know where they are know and what needs to happen next.

v ALT to build in literacy to their lesson observation framework and BLINKs. |

Twice weekly shared reading programme in Base Group time. **October 12 to December 12** teacher led. **January 13 onwards**, building in Accelerated Reader.

Reading Age 5.00–7.00. (23 students)
- Lexia Foundation (20 mins a day, 5 days a week.)

Reading Age 7.02–9.03. (21 students)
- Lexia strategies for older readers. (20 mins a day, 5 days a week.)

Reading Age 9.05–9.07. (9 students)
- TextNow reading programme. (20 mins a day, 5 days a week for 10 weeks)

Reading Age 9.10 +
- Accelerated Reader with fortnightly diagnostic reporting.
- Twice weekly shared reading.

Reading Age 14.03 + (Includes FSM RA 13.02+) **(26 students)**
- Author visits
- Video conferencing with other LST schools and global club
- Monthly Parent group.

Extra Access

Chronological Reading Age

Extra Challenge

Testing Regime and data points: Monthly testing and reporting – half-termly changes to provision registers.

Figure 3.16 Year 7 exemplar Intervention Pathway – reading

Roles and Accountability

Shared reading session:

- Using the strategies outlined below – to engage students and empower Base Group Tutors.

Accelerated Reader session:

- Students reading their own book and sitting a quiz on it.

- Base Group tutors using the fortnightly diagnostic feedback to have 1:1 discussions with struggling students during this time.

Key Roles:

1. **Literacy co-ordinator:**
   - Responsible for managing the provision.
   - Responsible for ensuring consistency and quality assurance.

2. **Base Group Tutor:**
   - Responsible for planning and delivering the shared reading activities during the first 9 weeks of this programme.
   - Responsible for ensuring Monday target setting includes a reading (AR) target each week from 25/02/13 onwards.
   - Responsible for their classes participation in AR and engaging with the diagnostic feedback.
   - Responsible for getting key info back to parents – successes and lack of effort.

3. **Librarian:**
   - Responsible for providing Base Group Tutors with the fortnightly colour-coded diagnostic feedback every other Tuesday for the Thursday session.
   - Responsible for ensuring there are sufficient class book for the Tuesday session.
   - Responsible for ensuring all students are on the AR system and have sat the Star Test.

- Responsible for managing the feedback into the Academy rewards system

- Responsible for ensuring parents have engaged with AR and have signed up for the weekly parental emails the system can provide.

4. **College Leader:**

- Responsible for ensuring their Base Groups tutors are actively engaged with the sessions.

- Responsible for ensuring all Base Groups make suitable progress through Accelerated Reader.

- Responsible for sharing reading successes in morning briefings and end of term celebrations/assemblies.

TRAINING ACTIVITY

Building language progression into your Fertile Questions

As outlined at the beginning of this chapter – the most effective way of using the research and examples in this chapter is to take two or three Fertile Questions you have already planned and build in this new learning to those plans.

You may want to design a series of lessons around dialogic talk or moving from talk to writing. The most effective way to do this is to follow the format below:

i.   Pick a Fertile Question.

ii. Decide what aspect of language you are going to work on – talk, reading, writing.

iii. Plan the lessons with that as the primary focus – it is really important when building in new learning to your planning to really shine the spotlight on the thinking – it must be at the forefront of your mind during the planning phase. As you get more familiar with the ideas and processes it will become easier to plan at multiple levels concurrently.

iv. Teach the lesson(s) and either get a colleague to observe you or video the lesson(s).

v.   Review the learning and progress that took place and use this feedback to amend your planning.

vi. Rewrite the plans for the Fertile Question.

This approach is outlined in more detail in Chapter 5, section 3; modelling life-long learning.

Notes

1   Wolf, M. (2008) *Proust and the squid: The story and science of the reading brain*: Harper Perennial; Reprint edition.
2   Michael Smith and Jeffrey D. Wilhelm (2006) *Going with the flow. How to engage boys (and girls) in their literacy learning*: Heinemann.
3   Wolf, M. (2008) *Proust and the squid: The story and science of the reading brain*: Harper Perennial; Reprint edition.
4   Moore, D.W., Bean, T.W., Birdyshaw, D. and Rycik, J. (1999) *Adolescent literacy: A position statement*: International Reading Association, p. 3.
5   LINC materials, now out of print.
6   The model used is adapted from *Strategies for Reading* (1997): NEALS.
7   Palinscar, A. and Brown, A. (1984) 'Reciprocal teaching of comprehension fostering and comprehension monitoring activities', *Cognition and Instruction*, I (2) 117–175.
8   Palinscar, A. and Brown, A. (1984) 'Reciprocal teaching of comprehension fostering and comprehension monitoring activities', *Cognition and Instruction*, I (2) 168.
9   The State of South Australia, Department of Education and Children's Services, (2006).
10   Gibbons, P. (2002) *Scaffolding language, scaffolding learning*: Heinemann.
11   Wallace, C. (2010) Institute of Education.
12   Alexander, R. (2004) 'Towards dialogic teaching: Rethinking classroom talk': Dialogos UK.
13   For any teacher who is looking for such a list, try Chapter 4 and Chapter 7 of Gibbons, P. (2009) *English learners academic literacy and thinking*: Heinemann.
14   Mercer, N. (2000) *Words and minds: How we use language to think together*: Routledge.
15   Wallace, C. (2010) Institute of Education.
16   Adapted from Wallace, C. (2010) Institute of Education.
17   The State of South Australia, Department of Education and Children's Services, (2006).
18   Polias, J. (2006) *Teaching ESL in the mainstream*: Government of South Australia.
19   Clegg, J. (2004) 'Tasks for language support'. Unpublished.
20   The State of South Australia, Department of Education and Children's Services, (2006).
21   The State of South Australia, Department of Education and Children's Services, (2006).
22   Centre for Literacy in Primary Education (2010).
23   Clegg, J. (2010) Institute of Education.
24   Williams, K. (2003) *Essential writing skills 1: Developing writing*: The Oxford Centre for Staff Development.
25   Adapted from Clegg, J. IOE (2010).
26   CLPE (2010). Whilst the CLPE primarily focuses on Primary School issues, their expertise and research-based approaches are of considerable value to *all* teachers. We have used them and their ideas to train teachers from EYFS to KS5.
27   Ark Academy Teaching and Learning Policy.
28   International Reading Association (Moore et al., 1999, p. 3)

29 OECD (2002).

30 Distinctions between reading instruction and reading for pleasure from The United Kingdom Literacy Association. 2007–08 Executive Summary.

31 National Literacy Trust (2006).

32 See *Ark Academy Reading Handbook* – www.arkacademy.org

33 Dickinson, D. and Smith, M. (1994) 'Long-term effects of preschool teachers' book readings on low-income children's vocabulary and story comprehension': *Reading Research Quarterly*, 29, 104–122.

34 'Removing barriers to literacy' Ofsted, January 2011.

4

Assessment models – what do we value and are we assessing it?

4

Assessment models

What do we value and are we assessing it?

This part of the handbook sets out the policies and procedures for assessment at whole-school level. Assessment is a general term, covering a range of issues. We separate assessment into two main sections:

- **Formative assessments:** the assessment strategies we use *during a Fertile Question.* (Although the Performance of Understanding at the end of a Fertile Question is also formative in that the information it provides the teacher and students helps clarify where to go next ('Review Week' planning).)

- **Summative assessments:** the assessment strategies we use *at the end of a Fertile Question and end of year exams.*

There is of course scope to mix the two, but it is helpful to separate them out when explaining the overall approach.

Below are some key definitions:

- **Formative assessment** is concerned with how judgements about the quality of student responses – performances, pieces or words – can be used to shape and improve the student's competence and performance.

- **Summative assessment** is concerned with summing up or summarizing the achievement status of a student and is geared towards reporting at the end of a Fertile Question, academic year or Key Stage.

- **Feedback** is usually defined in terms of information about how successfully something has been or is being done. Feedback takes place from teacher to pupil, from pupil to teacher, from pupil to pupil and from teacher to parent.

Formative assessment models

Formative assessment and Fertile Questions go hand in hand. It is impossible for students to develop disciplinary perspectives without having constant and meaningful feedback from an expert in that discipline. However, too often the feedback a student receives is retrospective and of limited value. The approach below is the simplest yet most effective way of generating learner autonomy through powerful feedback.

What does this mean?

Assessment is one of the most powerful educational tools for promoting effective learning. But it must be used in the right way. There is no evidence that increasing the amount of testing will enhance learning. Instead the focus needs to be on helping teachers use assessment, as part of teaching and learning, in ways that will raise pupils' achievement (Assessment for Learning, 'Beyond the Black Box': ARG 1999).

This is all well and good but what does this look like in practice? Many books have been written about assessment, feedback and Assessment for Learning. This chapter is concerned simply with enabling teachers to use assessment to help students understand what they are trying to do and devise strategies to get better at it. This can all be boiled down to three key processes:

i.   establishing where the learners are in their learning;

ii.   establishing where they are going;

iii. working out how to get there.

Running alongside this approach is the idea that there appear to be two types of formative assessment and teachers need to be able to move between the two:

i.   **Convergent formative assessment:** aims to discover *if* the learner knows, understands or can do a pre-determined thing.

ii.   **Divergent formative assessment:** aims to discover *what* the learner knows, understands or can do.

The table on the next page outlines the differences between the two. For the purposes of this approach there is no hierarchy between them, just the idea that you need to be aware of the two forms and what practice looks like within them. As students move through a Fertile Question the type of formative assessment will change. At times the feedback will be focused on what the learner is currently doing and at other times the feedback will be focused on how far the learner can do what you want them to be able to do.

Convergent and divergent formative assessment[1]

Convergent formative assessment	Divergent formative assessment
Assessment which starts from the aim to discover *if* the learner knows, understands or can do a pre-determined thing. This is characterized by:	Assessment which starts from the aim to discover *what* the learner knows, understands or can do. This is characterized by:
i. precise planning by the teacher and an intention to stick to it; ii. recording via check lists and can-do statements; iii. closed or pseudo-open teacher questioning and tasks; iv. a focus on contrasting errors with correct responses; v. authoritative, judgemental or quantitative feedback; vi. feedback focused on performance and the successful completion of the task in hand; vii. formative assessment focused on communicating criteria usually closely related to those used in summative assessment; viii. involvement of the learners as recipients of assessments; ix. an analysis of the interaction of learners and the curriculum from the point of view of the curriculum; x. may conform to either a behaviourist or a constructivist view of education; xi. an intention to teach or assess the next pre-determined thing in a linear progression; xii. an interaction usually embedded within an Initiation-Response-Feedback (IRF) sequence; xiii. a view of assessment as accomplished mainly by the teacher.	i. flexible planning or complex planning which incorporates alternatives; ii. open forms of recording (narrative, quotations, etc); iii. primarily open tasks with questioning by teachers and learners directed at 'helping' rather than testing; iv. a focus on miscues – aspects of learners' work which yield insights into their current understanding – and on prompting metacognition; v. exploratory, provisional or provocative feedback aimed at prompting further engagement from the learner; vi. discussion prompting reflection on the task and its context with a view to constructing understanding of future situations in which new knowledge might be applied; vii. formative assessment focused on a holistic view of criteria, the learners' understandings of them and how they fit into wider notions of knowledge and competence; viii. involvement of the learners as initiators of assessments as well as recipients; ix. an analysis of the interaction of learners and the curriculum from the point of view of both learners and the curriculum; x. conforms to a socio-cultural view of education with an acknowledgement of the importance of the context for the assessment; xi. an intention to teach in the zone of proximal development; xii. part of an ongoing dialogue between and amongst learners and teachers where learners initiate as well as respond, ask questions as well as reply; xiii. a view of assessment as a collaboration between and amongst teachers and students.

Providing feedback and ensuring progression

So, feedback is a key element in formative assessment and effective feedback is crucial in improving attainment. As we have already seen the feedback we give students is closely connected to both the views we hold of them as learners and the views they hold of themselves. Therefore effective feedback is concerned solely with gap closure and not with making fixed judgements about their ability. 'Feedback is information about the gap between the current level of understanding/task completion and the desired level which is used to alter the gap in some way.'[2] Nothing else!

This type of feedback is designed for two main audiences:[3]

i.   **Teachers** use feedback to make planning decisions with respect to readiness to sit an assessment, diagnosis of misconceptions or knowledge gaps and the remediation required before moving on.

ii. **Students** use feedback to monitor the strengths and weaknesses of their performances, so that aspects associated with success or high quality can be recognized and reinforced, and unsatisfactory aspects modified or improved.

Again, as we saw with the Growth Mindset, we as teachers must be acutely aware of how we are giving feedback if it is to have the desired effect. This is easiest to achieve if the following three conditions are met to ensure that all feedback is focused on performance:[4]

i.   For students to be able to improve they must be able to monitor the quality of their own work during actual production.

ii. This requires that students possess an appreciation of what high quality work is and how their piece compares.

iii. Students need to develop a store of tactics or moves which can be drawn upon to modify their own work.

It is not acceptable to simply place some ticks in a book once every two weeks and then write 'well done' at the end. Nor is it acceptable to use grades and levels in isolation and without providing the student with the opportunity to reflect on their work against the explicit criteria with which they have been graded. Teaching that does not build in opportunities for the acquisition of evaluative expertise (a student comparing their work to that of an expert) before a final assessment is deficient.

Feedback should be a continuous part of the lesson and Fertile Question and departments need to devise their own systems to allow pupils to capture this feedback and for teachers to capture and use the feedback from students during and at the end of each lesson. *What were pupils saying or doing that will impact on the planning for the next lesson?*

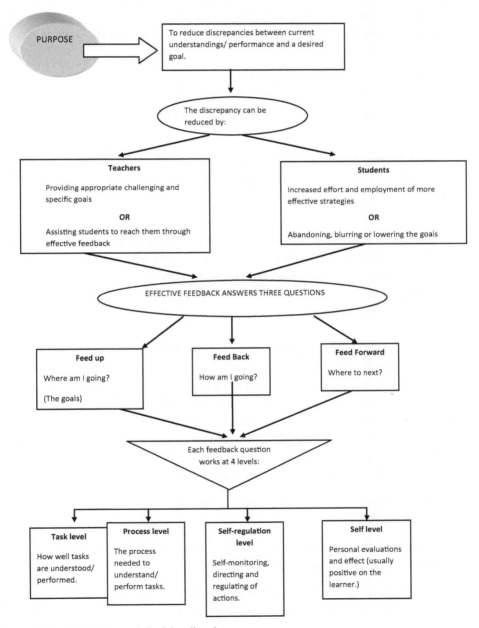

Figure 4.1 Hattie's model of feedback

How feedback works at the four levels above in Hattie's model:

i.   **Task level:** this level of feedback may include directions to acquire more, different or correct information. 'You need to focus more on...'

ii. **Process level:** this level of feedback is aimed at the learning processes required for understanding or completing the task. 'You need to edit this piece of writing using the descriptors you have so the reader can follow your central argument.'

iii. **Self-regulation level:** this level of feedback can include greater skill in self-evaluation. 'You already know the key features of a paragraph. Read back through your first paragraph and check to see if it follows the same format.'

iv. **Self level:** Feedback directed to the learner – rarely has an impact on learning. This is feedback at ego level. 'Well done, you have tried really hard in this essay.'

> Feedback is not 'the answer' to effective teaching and learning; rather it is but one powerful answer. With inefficient learners or learners at the acquisition (not proficiency) stage, it is better for a teacher to provide elaborations through instruction than to provide feedback on poorly understood concepts.[5]

As Hattie says, feedback can only build on something; it is of little use when there is no initial learning or surface information. Feedback is what happens second and is one of the most powerful influences on learning.

The model by Hattie gives a high-level overview of assessment strategies that can run through a whole Fertile Question; it is not designed to work lesson to lesson. With that in mind it is useful to look at the three most important things every teacher needs to do to allow for progress and understanding to take place. These are the three conditions outlined earlier:

i.   Students must be able to monitor the quality of their own work during actual production.

ii. Students must possess an appreciation of what high quality work is and how their piece compares.

iii. Students must develop a store of tactics or moves which can be drawn upon to modify their own work in order to meet the desired standard.

How is this achieved?[6]

This section is the 'business end' of the approach to formative assessment. It relies heavily on the work of Sadler and follows a simple approach to ensuring that every student in every classroom knows *what they are trying to achieve, what success looks like* and *what they can do to improve their current level of achievement in order to reach that standard.* Nothing else is required and answering these questions helps students navigate their way through a Fertile Question.

Allowing students to develop a concept of the standard being aimed for

There are two main approaches to highlighting standards to students and removing the mystery of what constitutes an outstanding performance. All students need to be aware of what the Performance of Understanding at the end of a Fertile Question will look like and should not be playing 'guess what is in the teacher's head'. The two things students need are:

i. descriptive statements

ii. exemplars.

Descriptive statements may be used to specify key qualities being looked for in a certain task or performance. For example the National Curriculum level descriptors (or an adapted, student friendly version of these) or success criteria which are co-constructed by teacher and students. There are obvious limitations in relying on descriptive statements, in that it can lead to a reductive approach of teaching to the criteria. But the reality is that every performance has criteria against which it will be judged and every student should be made aware of these criteria before they start drafting their response.

Exemplars are chosen to illustrate what distinguishes high and low quality responses. Students need several exemplars to precisely learn that there are different ways in which work of the desired standard can find expression. Unless students can come to realize that there are many ways of writing, talking, making, etc. which are regarded as excellent – three A* essays on the same question which, whilst different from each other, share certain qualities and structural features – they will not grasp fully the concept of quality.

Providing students with experience of comparing their work with the standard being aimed for

As Sadler aptly points out:

> when students rely solely on a teacher's written comments it relies too heavily on the willingness and time of the teacher and the ability of the student to interpret and act on the comments. Therefore feedback against criteria is only effective when the student has concrete examples of things that possess the criteria/properties in question. (Sadler 1989)

For these reasons much teacher marking can be said to have little impact on student progress and is probably little more than a school-led PR exercise for parents.

In other words, students must not only compare their own work against the success criteria, but they must have opportunities to compare many examples of outstanding work and deficient work, using the criteria to guide them, in order to understand the key differences in structure and content. This is vital for students to develop an independent and deep understanding of the desired standard. Students must have opportunities built into their drafting and redrafting to compare their work to examples of the standard being aimed for in order that they can generate strategies to self-regulate.

Knowledge of criteria has to be taught through experience of using the criteria to judge quality – they must understand and then apply the knowledge. This involves pupils being engaged in evaluating work against criteria and amending it – either individually or in groups. Through this process, the student also:

> Unconsciously picks up the rules of the art (writing a poem or experiment report), including those which are not explicitly known to the master (teacher)....Connoisseurship...can be communicated only by example, not by precept.[7]

Enabling students to develop strategies for gap closure in order to reach the desired standard

Traditionally students have relied on their teachers to tell them how to improve. If a student's only exposure to evaluative and editorial activity is as it is received from the teacher, it will only have limited impact. Although this is changing, as the case study below will highlight, many of the strategies teachers currently deploy to 'facilitate' student engagement with the learning process are still reliant on teacher creation and teacher sanction.

Therefore, if we are to generate meaningful autonomy, *students need to be taught a pool of strategies to help them bring their own performance closer to the desired goal* and students need to be sufficiently independent to know when to deploy what strategy. The most readily available material for students to work on for evaluative and remedial experience is that of fellow students. Sadler outlines four key reasons why working on a fellow student's draft and finished work is more valuable than on a teacher-prepared version.

Engaging in evaluative and corrective activity on each other's work has the advantage for students that:

i.   The work is of the same type and addresses the same task.

ii. Students experience a broad range of strategies employed by their peers and exposure to these expands their own repertoire.

iii. Other students' attempts normally cover a wide range of imperfections.

iv. Students are less defensive of other students' work than of their own.

Students develop their pool of strategies by learning to revise and refine their own work in cooperation with the teacher, and by editing and helping other students to improve theirs.

> Students who become conscious of what they are doing by explaining their decisions to others also learn new strategies for solving writing problems. And because students should become progressively more independent and self-confident as writers, they need to evaluate each other's work and their own frequently, a practice which teaches constructive criticism, close-reading and rewriting.[8]

The case study below outlines the reflective process one teacher went through in trying to plan Fertile Questions around the five principles outlined at the beginning of this book. As well as grappling with how to create independent learners, the author also sets out his thinking about how to plan for assessment that enables progress in thinking to be seen and demonstrated. The case study was written for an academic audience and is quite out of character with the rest of the book. However we have chosen to include it in full because it maps out very clearly an approach to assessment and then an evaluation of that approach.

Read the case study and then reflect on it using the training activity questions that follow.

Case study 5: 'Create something interesting to show that you have learnt something': Building and assessing learner autonomy within the Key Stage 3 History classroom

This article first appeared in *Teaching History* 131, June 2008: The Historical Association. It was written by Oli Knight and edited by C. Counsell.

Assessment is an ideological battleground, fought over by educational theorists, government advisers and classroom practitioners. Positions range from a desire to use assessment to maintain the status quo and churn out *Homo Sovieticus* to the goal of constructing a new type of learner, a *Homines Novi,* constructed through autonomy and self-regulation. But the debates in educational circles have complex fault-lines; it is not a simple dichotomy of extremes. It seems that those in government strategy or management circles imagine that they are doing one thing whilst actually doing another. Anyone who has been through a recent Ofsted inspection will be aware of the drive to get pupils to set and monitor their own targets and to be involved in the assessment process. It is easy to dress that up in the language of autonomy. My experience from several schools, however, is that it leads to a reductive, teacher-led approach that focuses on the 'critical steps' that a pupil might need to make to 'reach' the next level descriptor instead of developing pupil autonomy or 'deep' learning about the structure of a subject.[1] Thus, not only is assessment a disputed practice, but the attachment of quite different meanings to particular terms often masks or distorts the lines of debate. Thus the dispute is not always visible, lurking as it does under an imagined consensus around Assessment for Learning (AfL).[2]

The value and meaning that a teacher attaches to the word 'assessment' and its attendant processes will always be derived from the conceptual framework within which it is placed. Any analysis of the word must be seen as being a part of the values, assumptions and theoretical framework of the practitioner. James argues that as our understanding of learning changes so then, in turn, must our conceptualization and development of assessment practices. When learning was largely seen as being a private and individual affair, classical test theory was dominant. Our understanding of learning has moved on, however. Where learning is now seen as an interactive event and the role of language in constructing learning is taking on greater importance, our assessment practices shift in order to recognize the importance of the processes involved in acquiring and constructing knowledge.[3] If learning is a socially constructed activity, this will have implications for assessment.

My initial understanding of AfL saw assessment as formative: I treated the shortcomings which assessment revealed as influences on the next stage in the learning flow. My implementation of AfL was originally a simple application of procedures in the classroom, a formulaic process working within the framework of a summative, national examination structure – what Marshall and Drummond would label as the 'letter' of AfL.[4] My experience echoes Stobart's concern that teachers sometimes implement strategies without understanding why they might lead to effective learning. AfL, when viewed through the lens of a social-constructivist theorization of learning, would transcend simple procedures and become a process that emphasizes learners becoming self-regulated and autonomous. A social-constructivist perspective might suggest that this can best be developed through self-assessment and classroom dialogue.[5]

Thus there is a distinction between seeing AfL as a series of *procedures* and seeing AfL as a *process*. Much AfL in schools has become procedure-led. In many instances it has even turned into a series of tick-sheets to enable school senior managers to complete their Ofsted 'Self-Evaluation Form'. For me as a teacher, AfL – when constructed within a socio-cultural framework of learning – ought to become a powerful means of developing real learner autonomy and transcending the ever-shifting requirements of the education system.

My view of learning

My view of learning is symbiotic with my theorization of assessment. I see learning as a knowledge-building process that is part of doing things with others. In other words, meaning is constructed through collaboration and interdependence.[6] Thus knowledge itself is constructed just as the conceptual and theoretical frameworks that create the basis of our practice are themselves constructed. For me, it is helpful to see AfL itself within this framework. AfL could be seen as part of a polythetic framework of disputed and competing ideologies revolving around a central issue of pupil autonomy.

Whilst working on my Masters, I found myself exploring these issues in my own classroom and grappling with trying to move from seeing myself as knowledge-giver to 'learning facilitator' – an expression with which I am not entirely happy but one which helped me to think about my role and how I might go about shifting the teacher–pupil relationship. This also helped me to think again about the nature of historical knowledge and my aims for pupils studying History. How could I help pupils *really to see* the constructed and contested nature of historical knowledge? That historical knowledge is constructed and contested has been central to History curriculum demands and to teacher debate and practice for many years, but if I was honest there was still a long way to go for it to become a deep reality in my classroom.[7]

Assessment practices can change the relationship in the classroom whereby pupil and teacher work collaboratively to improve progress. Black argues that for formative assessment to be successful it must meet certain conditions. These are that it is criterion-referenced and not normative and that it must be tuned to the needs of each individual pupil. Blame should be avoided and praise is most helpful when it is used sparingly and linked with objective advice about specific performance.[8] This stance, however, is only of limited value. I feel that it runs counter to the central aim of pupil autonomy and does not fit within the social-constructivist framework of learning outlined above.

My main critique of Black is that in his framework, successful assessment practices are still, at root, a teacher-dominated affair.

The weakness of reliance on criterion-referenced assessment is that feedback is related to criteria compliance. This seems to result in the procedure-driven approach common in many schools – for example, the target sheet in the back of their book outlining exactly what pupils need to do to 'move up' one level, sometimes even including phrases they should use and tiny procedures they should follow related to sub-levels and slices of levels. As Cottingham argues, chasing non-existent sub-levels can, at best, be a mere proxy for pupil thinking and for growing confidence with subject complexity and, at worst, a grave distortion of it.[9]

Thus, although much of Black's work sought to show the dangers of measurement at the expense of learning, this emphasis on pupils moving consciously through a minutely structured pre-determined map can only undermine the original intention. Paradoxically, therefore, I would argue that Black's construction of assessment is actually misaligned with his desire to allow each pupil to flourish. For Torrance, this reliance on criterion-referenced assessment removes the challenge of learning and reduces the quality and validity of outcomes achieved.[10]

The relationship between assessment and learning

How, then, could I construct assessment practices to best secure progression for learners that fits with the view of learning outlined above? First, it is important to note the relationship between assessment practice and the way pupils learn. Thus the validity of an assessment practice might be measured by how far it aligns with the theory of learning that a curriculum is designed around. A danger exists when teachers use a model of assessment borrowed from elsewhere (usually from national, external examinations or prescribed assessment frameworks) that does not fit in with their theory of learning and their curriculum model.[11] One might argue that in History, for example, assessment practices have to be able to reflect pupils' growing understanding of second-order concepts which characterize progression within History as an academic discipline. James argues that too many types of assessment fail to take account of the way the subject domain is structured, the key concepts or 'big ideas' associated with it and the methods and processes that characterize practice in the field. Without this type of construct validity, assessments become valueless.

Therefore, for assessments to have value and meaning it is important that social-psychological, sociological and epistemological dimensions be taken into consideration, dimensions not only of the classroom environment but of the nature of the subject's structure. In other words, it is necessary for teachers to have a view about the kinds of learning that are most valuable for their students and an understanding of how these relate to the epistemology of the subject discipline or subject practice that pupils are engaging with. Teachers can then choose and develop approaches to teaching and assessment accordingly.[12]

In the History community we have plenty of models of this already being explored. For example, Burnham and Brown, two Heads of History in contrasting schools, in their argument against using the National Curriculum Level Descriptions as markers for progress, nonetheless have a well-developed view about how pupils might advance in thinking about history and in historical consciousness. It is a view related to the epistemology of History and its second-order and substantive concepts specified in the National Curriculum (such as evidence, interpretation and forms of historical reasoning) and one that stays faithful to the original guidance of SCAA and QCA in 1995 – that the Level Descriptions could never and should never be used to chart small increments in progress and were certainly not designed for assessing individual pieces of work. Burnham and Brown tie their understanding of the epistemology of the subject to a range of flexible processes, taking place over a long period of time, which can be monitored and developed without rigid tying of every stage to performance indicators. Such rigidity, they argue, distorts and detracts from pupils' historical learning as it cannot capture the riches of history as a practice let alone the 'messy' and diverse ways in which diverse pupils necessarily encounter it. For pupils to deepen their grasp of difficult matters such as causal reasoning or evidential thinking, they need to experiment with new concepts and take risks with new understandings. If being assessed regularly in a linear, predictive way, *true* progress would show up as apparent dips and troughs in performance as pupils' experiments will go wrong, their ideas may temporarily break down and their thinking can only be forged through reflection on challenging exploration and experiment. Evidence of some forward, linear march, Burnham and Brown argue, rigidly sought in the name of 'progress', will quickly become a mask for no progress.

A governing flaw in Black and Wiliam's argument

Black and Wiliam place emphasis on this notion of appropriate goals as discernible stages in mapping out future progress and whilst this is intended to be emancipatory, I would argue that it has an inbuilt flaw and that it has led to the very reductionism we now see in so many school assessment/monitoring policies. Black and Wiliam argue that the main feature of effective assessment is to realize that the learner's task is to close the gap between the present state of understanding and the learning goal, and that self-assessment is essential if the learner is to be able to do this.

The teacher's role, for Black and Wiliam, is to communicate appropriate goals and to promote self-assessment as students work towards them. In this process, feedback in the classroom should operate both from teacher to student and from students to the teacher. This feedback has to be based upon a teacher's understanding of Vygotsky's theory of the Zone of Proximal Development and constitutes a sophisticated level of differentiation at individual level.[13]

On one level this links into the work of Torrance and Pryor who argue that for feedback to be effective it must not be teacher-dominated with a focus on pre-determined objectives. They argue that for formative assessment to be effective it should essentially be focused on the pupil experience. In other words it must involve pupils reflecting on what they have achieved and how they have achieved it.[14]

I feel, however, that for Black and Wiliam, pupil autonomy is still taking place within an aggregative, summative framework where learning goals are connected to externally set objectives. For Black and Wiliam it would appear that the process of formative assessment is still largely teacher controlled, with teachers providing feedback to pupils on how well they have achieved particular objectives at a particular point in hand and what else they might need to do in order to improve. For all their emphasis on pupil involvement, pupil sharing of goals, peer-assessment and so forth, Black and Wiliam's structure remains set by teachers and controlled by teachers. Thus the now all-too-common micro-management of assessment by many Senior Leadership Teams (SLTs): requiring teachers to link every aspect of every lesson to some prescribed goal or stage was perhaps an inevitable result of Black and Wiliam's assumptions concerning the need for a 'map' setting out a pupils' way ahead. Once this became tied to externally set objectives, the current distortions of AfL were inevitable.

For me, a more powerful construct would be to take the view that formative assessment should be focused on pupil experience, moving beyond political concerns for accountability and focusing on educational concerns for learning.[15] Black and Wiliam would appear to be working with a reductionist perspective in that the metanarrative of their theorization is the political compliance of education.

Achievement objectives versus expressive objectives

There is much research that points to the limitations of instructional objectives and the fact that the notion of raising achievement might not be best characterized in terms of achievement objectives. I argued above that assessment through teacher-defined objectives can lead to a limited construction of knowledge. Neither excellence nor pupil autonomy are likely to come from the measurement of performance against externally set objectives. But what is a teacher to do if all goals and objectives are problematic?

How can any sort of learning journey or validity be posited, discerned or valued? One answer is to reconceptualize the idea of 'objectives'.

Elliott offers an interesting way forward here. Elliott argues that, even where there is an intention in the curriculum to foster thinking and reasoning, any *externally constructed* learning objectives will lead to pupils viewing learning as knowledge transmission and the curriculum as fact. Elliott argues that excellence is unlikely to conform to predictable outcomes but is likely to transcend prescription and be demonstrated through imagination and creativity. Instead, teachers should be encouraged to use 'expressive objectives'. An expressive objective identifies a situation in which pupils are to work, a problem with which they are to cope, a task with which they are to engage. In other words, it is an invitation to explore, evocative rather than prescriptive. It encourages pupils to challenge their preconception that what is worth knowing can be reduced to objective statements and the idea that progression is linear and aggregative. Expressive objectives are far more likely to lead to self-efficacy and higher motivation. In other words, a move away from instructional objectives is more likely to lead to self-monitoring, self-evaluation and goal setting. Learning can be seen as renewal and as working towards a central goal – that of pupil autonomy. This move away from instructional objectives leads to what Dann describes as self-efficacy in that the more capable pupils believe themselves to be, the higher the goals they set for themselves.[16]

All this could be seen to fit into a polythetic framework of AfL as it is working towards pupil autonomy but consciously selecting different themes of competing learning ideologies to meet the long-term central aim.

Self-assessment – lip-service or reality?

This brings us to the learner's role in the assessment process in terms of creating meaningful self-assessment rather than simply getting pupils to mark their own work! The importance of metacognition as a tool for assessment is highlighted in Sarig's work on academic literacy. Sarig sees academic literacy as the creative and reflective manipulation of knowledge and the learners' reflection on the act of manipulation is central to progression.[17] Hacker expands this notion: a definition of metacognition should include at least these notions: knowledge of one's own knowledge, processes and cognitive and affective states; and the ability to consciously and deliberately monitor and regulate one's knowledge, processes, and cognitive and affective states.[18] A nascent example of this kind of self-regulation being fostered in the History classroom might be Burnham's work on pupils generating their own enquiry questions and building their own criteria for *historical* questions. She uses their reflection on the wording of their own enquiry questions as a way of enabling pupils to develop and demonstrate higher-order understandings with the second-order concepts. Pupils are encouraged to test the meaning and historical power of their questions. The whole class later works on a Scheme of Work (SoW) substantially framed by their own questions.[19]

This focus on deliberately monitoring and regulating one's own knowledge and processes links in well with the language dimension of progression in History where students in History classrooms are often taught to experiment with language, such as different ways of expressing the same point to construe different meanings, different modes of analysis or different ways of showing narrative significance within an account.[20] Since the History-literacy revolution of the 1990s when many History educationalists began making the History-literacy relationship more explicit, many new theorists have arisen amongst History teachers. A clear example is the work of James Woodcock, where he sets out ways of breaking out of traditional preparation for causation examination answers by enabling pupils to experiment with a wide range of formulations for expressing causal thinking. His pupils find themselves making subtle choices between similar words and judging their explanatory power within a causation context.[21]

In my experience, pupils do need to be explicitly taught disciplinary concepts – such as causation and evidence – which allow them both to manipulate the substantive content and to see how academic historians do the same. This approach also allows learners to reflect upon this manipulation and to arrive at the idea that history is a form, not a body, of knowledge. Such an approach is connected to a disciplinary perspective of historical progression, in that the language pupils use enables them to develop and play with more and less powerful ideas about the past. The implications of all this for a successful assessment philosophy are complex. If we are to do justice to these different layers of thinking and meta-thinking, then at the very least one might suggest that feedback on multiple levels is necessary.

Crucially, the student must somehow be centrally involved in these feedback processes. As Donovan and Bransford point out, there is a difference between responding to feedback that someone else provides and actively seeking feedback in order to assess one's current level of thinking and understanding.[22]

Inside the Black Abyss

Now that I have tentatively set out a framework for critically appraising and using AfL and how it might be applied within the History subject domain, I will attempt to evaluate my recent practice in the light of this framework. The example I have selected is a series of Year 8 History lessons designed around the central premise *'Create something interesting to show you have learnt something'*.[23] As in so much current History teaching practice, the lessons were built around a social-constructivist theory of learning whereby learning is viewed as being a social activity and knowledge is seen as being created and constructed through interaction and experimentation rather than as being a given entity that is merely found and passed on. Many examples of such an overt, co-constructed and experimental approach can be found in *Teaching History* and at History teacher conferences such as the Historical Association's London History Forum.[24] Where I chose to innovate, however, was in bringing my *assessment* practices in line with this social-constructivist framework.

This was a unit of work on mid-seventeenth century conflict that would take place over six lessons. The end product was presented simply as: *Create something interesting to show you have learnt something*. Pupils would work in small groups and be given *carte blanche* to create something that I could *'see, read or hear that proves they have answered the enquiry question'*.[25]

There was scope to expand the number of lessons rather than rush the creative process and limit reflection time. In the first lesson, pupils were given an overview of the new topic by watching a recording of their Head of Year being interviewed in character as Charles I.

The video was paused at strategic places and issues discussed and built upon. Questioning was not used as testing listening but as a dialogue to expand and build upon the initial ideas put forward.

Pupils discussed the Fertile Question *'Why were brothers fighting brothers in 1642?'* This was used as a recap from the previous lesson but also as a chance for pupils to see *how* Fertile Questions are constructed. They then had a go at creating their own. This is similar to the work of Burnham amongst others, but in my lesson sequence the construction of enquiry questions was to start the process of enquiry pursuit amongst the pupils rather than to form the basis of later whole-class investigation.[26]

In the following lesson pupils were introduced to the overview and rationale of the project and given the temporal and conceptual frameworks. They read a pack of information and related it to the video from Lesson 1 – building on the ideas put forward as the start of the lesson. Through whole-class discussion the class created success criteria for their assessment piece. I then allowed pupils to select their own groups. This was part of building autonomy and would also form part of the post-activity reflection process. The rest of the lesson was spent brainstorming ideas with a feedback at the end.

Pupils then spent the next three lessons independently constructing their end products. They had to draw up a time-plan, allocate tasks and roles, create a resources list and create a draft outline. They then worked for three lessons in small groups, sourcing what they needed or asking me for help finding it. The end of each lesson was a referral back to the success criteria that they had constructed in Lesson 2.

This relative autonomy – relative because they were still working within a defined substantive and conceptual framework created by me – had a huge impact on motivation and led to pupils designing assessment pieces that I would never have thought of. The range was extensive – from a Trisha style chat show of two sisters arguing about Charles and Parliament through to a recorded movie. This could be seen as communal constructivism as they were not only creating an end product for themselves but directly helping pupils in subsequent years through creating resources to be used by teacher and pupils.

Pupils then presented their assessment pieces and were assessed by the rest of the class against the criteria that they had devised. The use of 'provocative feedback' was encouraged rather than 'prescriptive feedback'.[27] Provocative feedback is the idea that pupils pose questions to probe more deeply into the underlying processes of construction rather than describing or critiquing at surface level – a trap that many teachers also fall into. The key teacher feedback comes in the form not of testing their knowledge of the Civil War – which was assessed through two of the success criteria – but in enabling pupils to reflect upon the processes involved and their ability to relate it to other learning situations.

Evaluating my practice

How far does my experiment fit into the polythetic framework surrounding AfL that I explored earlier? The first point that arises in critiquing this AfL opportunity is the limitation of my learning journey for the pupils when compared to the structural matrix designed by Pryor and Crossouard (see earlier on in this chapter).[28] For me, where divergent formative assessment is most successful is when it is connected to the ideas put forward by Hacker.[29] In other words, divergent formative assessment only achieves its desired end of learner autonomy if pupils are consciously reflecting on this process, otherwise it remains in the realm of convergent formative assessment as it fails to develop pupil autonomy and remains procedural. Pryor and Crossouard see learning as a wider process of becoming, of constructing identity and ways of being. For them, learning and identity are inseparable. My Year 8 journey failed to address this meta-social as well as meta-cognitive progression in that despite creating a socio-cultural model of formative assessment it failed to fully scale the mountain.

Convergent and divergent formative assessment[9]

Convergent formative assessment	Divergent formative assessment
Assessment which starts from the aim to discover *if* the learner knows, understands or can do a pre-determined thing. This is characterized by:	Assessment which starts from the aim to discover *what* the learner knows, understands or can do. This is characterized by:
i. precise planning by the teacher and an intention to stick to it; ii. recording via check lists and can-do statements; iii. closed or pseudo-open teacher questioning and tasks; iv. a focus on contrasting errors with correct responses; v. authoritative, judgemental or quantitative feedback;	i. flexible planning or complex planning which incorporates alternatives; ii. open forms of recording (narrative, quotations, etc); iii. primarily open tasks with questioning by teachers and learners directed at 'helping' rather than testing; iv. a focus on miscues – aspects of learners' work which yield insights into their current understanding – and on prompting metacognition;

vi. feedback focused on performance and the successful completion of the task in hand;	v. exploratory, provisional or provocative feedback aimed at prompting further engagement from the learner;
vii. formative assessment focused on communicating criteria usually closely related to those used in summative assessment;	vi. discussion prompting reflection on the task and its context with a view to constructing understanding of future situations in which new knowledge might be applied;
viii. involvement of the learners as recipients of assessments;	vii. formative assessment focused on a holistic view of criteria, the learners' understandings of them and how they fit into wider notions of knowledge and competence;
ix. an analysis of the interaction of learners and the curriculum from the point of view of the curriculum;	viii. involvement of the learners as initiators of assessments as well as recipients;
x. may conform to either a behaviourist or a constructivist view of education;	ix. an analysis of the interaction of learners and the curriculum from the point of view of both learners and the curriculum;
xi. an intention to teach or assess the next pre-determined thing in a linear progression;	x. conforms to a socio-cultural view of education with an acknowledgement of the importance of the context for the assessment;
xii. an interaction usually embedded within An Initiation-Response-Feedback (IRF) sequence.	xi. an intention to teach in the zone of proximal development;
xiii. a view of assessment as accomplished mainly by the teacher.	xii. part of an ongoing dialogue between and amongst learners and teachers where learners initiate as well as respond, ask questions as well as reply;
	xiii. a view of assessment as a collaboration between and amongst teachers and students.

Despite there being negotiation of task and quality criteria, there was not a full reflection process and the task still took place within a goal-orientated educational framework and so failed to move pupils to see learning as indeterminate and prospective. The task design and final product were limited in their conception as they existed within a summative educational framework and so failed to create space for recognizing difference. Pupils still saw some ways of thinking and being as having greater gravitas than others.[30] Despite using the processes described in their matrix and meeting Stobart's criteria,[31] the learning situations failed to fully develop divergent formative assessment. It hit an impasse in terms of failing to move beyond the political metanarrative highlighted in my critique of Black.

However, despite not fully realizing the aspirations of Pryor and Crossouard, the Year 8 example could be seen to fit with Serafini's paradigm of 'assessment as inquiry'. The task enabled pupils and teacher to make a 'paradigm shift' in that the pupils were meaningfully involved in the assessment process. This enabled pupils to assess their progress through negotiating the success criteria for the activity.[32] However, for Serafini, classroom rubrics designed with student and teacher input are an excellent vehicle for negotiation and involvement in the assessment process. Students and teachers come together to 'unpack' their values and beliefs about education in order to expose these to discussion and negotiation. It is this process of negotiation that is of primary importance, not necessarily the actual outcomes that are created. In the Year 8 classroom this 'negotiating process' took a back-seat as the creation of the presentations took primacy.

Therefore, whilst the activities may have been 'assessment as inquiry', it could be said that they failed to fully develop pupil autonomy as the negotiating was still deemed less important than the more tangible final activity creations.

It is this dilemma of where to place AfL activities along a continuum from full autonomy, through more modified forms of autonomy, to purely prescriptive procedure, and the subconscious creation of a hierarchy that this entails, that leads me into a more troubled analysis of my experiment. The context of my experiment is my hypothesis that AfL, in its essential principles, is built on an underlying pedagogic principle that foregrounds the promotion of pupil autonomy.[33] For Marshall and Drummond, for example, the implementation of AfL in the classroom becomes more than the application of certain procedures and revolves around the realization of certain principles of Teaching and Learning.

These two 'styles' are labelled *letter* and *spirit* by Marshall and Drummond – the *spirit* fostering the future goal of pupil autonomy whereby knowledge is built through conversation and uncertainty, the *letter* being procedural and formulaic, working within the short-term goal of summative progress.

Marshall and Drummond would probably label my lessons as demonstrating the *spirit* of AfL because pupils were involved in framing their own notion of quality, negotiating and refining these within groups, applying these principles to a piece of work, then using this understanding to reassess their own work in light of judgements about quality. Exchanges between pupils and between teacher and pupil were all understood in terms of refinement of the central aim: understanding what constitutes quality or a good answer. On the other hand, it is possible to argue that these lessons were still *lettery* in that they took place within an aggregative, national summative framework. So, although it is more *spirit* than the English lesson that Marshall and Drummond cite in their article, its long-term goal of learner autonomy is still only autonomy within the externally set, criterion-referenced framework of a teacher-led classroom.

What I mean by this is that whilst my pupils negotiated their own criteria and final product, I still felt that their own 'assessment careers' held their reflection back.[34] The pupils are so used to seeing assessment as a tool for measurement and the curriculum as something to be swallowed up that they failed to see the long-term validity of this experience differently and, whilst I have not yet seen the long-term effects, I imagine that their views of assessment and knowledge will change little. So whilst, on the surface, one could argue that in my lessons pupils did become 'eager constructors of knowledge',[35] this construction was still too reliant on the external criteria that run through all of their curriculum experiences to really move pupils beyond seeing learning as a means to an end.

I may be being too critical of myself here and Marshall and Drummond might argue that the activities did create what Eckert describes as 'communities of practice' in that learning became the primary vehicle for engagement with others.

However, the empowerment that this generated was not framed within the context of lifelong learning, but instead took place within a culture of short-term goals that always keep examinations in view, thus failing to transcend the political metanarrative that so inhibited the work of Black. My view is that this glass ceiling inhibits the rising of pupil autonomy above the confines of the current educational context. Even researchers sometimes do not seem conscious of its existence within their theoretical stance and of the influence it exerts on their findings.

Perhaps a more powerful conceptualization of AfL is that suggested by Hargreaves.[36] He sees AfL as meaning *teachers* learning about children's learning and children taking some control of their own learning and assessment. Again, one could argue that my lessons were somewhat aligned with this conceptualization as learners were collaboratively building knowledge as members of the whole knowledge-constructing community. That said, the overall emphasis was on performance as pupils applied their learning to previous work in order to raise their performance in subsequent summative assessments.

Towards a conceptualization of AfL

In conclusion I want tentatively to conceptualize AfL as a polythetic framework of disputed and competing ideologies revolving around a central core of pupil autonomy. This is perhaps one way of resolving the latent tensions of constructing assessment and learning processes. This idea would seem to fit with both the views of Torrance and Sfard. For Sfard, the 'metaphorical pluralism' of seeing learning as *both* acquisition *and* participation and the need not to exclusively rely on one metaphor fit with the idea of *choosing* activities or processes that take pupils on a journey towards autonomy. This is supported by Torrance, Pryor and Crossouard who argue that if the huge potential of divergent formative assessment is to be tapped, then teachers would need to be able to move between the convergent and divergent. This seeming paradox is perhaps best summed up as follows:

> As researchers, we seem doomed to living in a reality constructed from a variety of metaphors. We have to accept the fact that the metaphors we use whilst theorizing may be good enough to fit small areas, but none of them suffice to cover the entire field. In other words, we must learn to satisfy ourselves with only local sense-making. A realistic thinker knows he or she has to give up the hope that the little patches of coherence will eventually combine into a consistent global theory.[37]

Thus the knowledgeable teacher needs to be able to *move between* all these competing ideas and concepts of AfL, deploying different stances that best fit with their shifting knowledge of the learners, whilst the whole time working towards the long-term goal of learner autonomy – an autonomy that transcends the political metanarrative of the subordination of education to politics.

References

1. Parts of the History education community in England are already vocal in their criticism of the abuse of Level Descriptions by senior managers. Burnham and Brown (2004) argue that the use of Level Descriptions can 'neither predict nor reward' true gains in curiosity, conceptual thinking, knowledge or analytic skill. Burnham, S. and Brown, G. (2004) 'Assessment without Level Descriptions' *Teaching History 115, Assessment Without Levels Edition.*
2. Black, P. and Wiliam, D. (1998) *Inside the black box*: King's College.
3. James, M. (2006) 'Assessment, teaching and theories of learning' in Gardner, J. (ed.) *Assessment, teaching and theories of learning*: Sage.
4. Marshall, B. and Drummond, M.J. (2006) 'How teachers engage with AfL: Lessons from the classroom' *Research Papers in Education*, 21, 2.
5. Stobart, G. (2008) 'Reasons to be cheerful: AfL' in Stobart, G. (2008) *The uses and abuses of assessment*: Sage.
6. Watkins, C. (2003) 'Learning: a sense-makers guide': ATL.
7. Arthur, J. and Phillips, R. (2000) *Issues in History teaching*: Routledge.
8. Black, P. (2003) *Testing: Friend or foe? The theory and practice of assessment and testing*: Routledge.
9. Cottingham, M. (2004) 'Dr Black Box or How I learned to stop worrying and love assessment', *Teaching History 115, Assessment Without Levels Edition.*
10. Torrance, H. (2007) 'Assessment as learning? How the use of explicit learning objectives, assessment criteria and feedback in post-secondary education and training can come to dominate learning', *Assessment in Education, 14, 3.*
11. James, M. (2006) 'Assessment, teaching and theories of learning' in Gardner, J. (ed.) *Assessment and learning*: Sage.
12. James, M. (2006) 'Assessment, teaching and theories of learning' in Gardner, J. (ed.) *Assessment and learning*: Sage, 49.
13. Black, P. and Wiliam, D. (1998) *Inside the black box*: King's College.
14. Pryor, J. and Torrance, H. (1998) *Investigating formative assessment: Teaching, learning and assessment in the classroom*: OUP.

15. Pryor, J. and Torrance, H. (1998) *Investigating formative assessment: Teaching, learning and assessment in the classroom*: OUP.

16. Dann, R. (2002) *Promoting assessment as learning: Improving the learning process*: Routledge Falmer.

17. Sarig, G. (1996) 'Academic literacy as ways of getting-to-know: What can be assessed?' in Birenbaum, M. and Dochy, F., *Alternatives in assessment of achievements, learning processes and prior knowledge*: KAP.

18. Hacker (1998) cited in Dann, R. (2002) *Promoting assessment as learning: Improving the learning process*: Routledge Falmer.

19. Burnham, S. (2007) 'Getting Year 7 to set their own questions about the Islamic Empire, 600–1600', *Teaching History 128, Beyond the Exam Edition*.

20. E.g. Counsell (2004) *Building the lesson around the text: History and literacy in Year 7*: Hodder Murray.

21. Woodcock, J. (2005) 'Does the linguistic release the conceptual? Helping Year 10 to improve their causal reasoning', *Teaching History, 119, Language Edition*.

22. Donovan, S. and Bransford, J. (2005) *How students learn*: National Academies Press

23. Holmes, B., Tangney, B., FitzGibbon, A., Savage, T. and Mehan, S. (2006) 'Communal constructivism: Students constructing learning *for* as well as *with* others': Centre for Research in IT Education, Trinity College.

24. See for example, work on helping pupils to make their own meaning out of history: Harris, R. and Rea, A. (2006) 'Making history meaningful', *Teaching History, 125, Significance Edition* or work in strengthening pupils' sense of their own agency in the construction of argument: Fordham, M. (2007) 'Slaying dragons and sorcerers in Year 12: in search of historical argument', *Teaching History, 129, Disciplined Minds Edition*.

25. Riley, M. (2000) 'Into the Key Stage 3 history garden: Choosing and planting your enquiry questions', *Teaching History, 99, Curriculum Planning Edition*.

26. Burnham, S. (2007) 'Getting Year 7 to set their own questions about the Islamic Empire, 600–1600', *Teaching History 128, Beyond the Exam Edition*.

27. Hargreaves, D. (2005) 'AfL? Thinking outside the (black) box', *Cambridge Journal of Education, 35, 2, 213–224*.

28. Pryor and Crossouard (2008) 'A socio-cultural theorisation of formative assessment', *Oxford Review of Education, 34 (1), 1–20*.

29. Hacker (1998) cited in Dann, R. (2002) *Promoting assessment as learning: Improving the learning process*: Routledge Falmer.

30. Pryor and Crossouard (2008) 'A socio-cultural theorisation of formative assessment', *Oxford Review of Education, 34 (1), 1–20*.

31. Stobart, G. (2008) 'Reasons to be cheerful: AfL' in Stobart, G. (2008) *The uses and abuses of assessment*: Sage.

32. Serafini, F. (2001) 'Three paradigms of assessment: Measurement, procedure and enquiry' *The Reading Teacher, 54, 4, 384–393*.

33. Marshall, B. and Drummond, M.J. (2006) 'How teachers engage with AfL: Lessons from the classroom', *Research Papers in Education, 21, 2*.

34. Ecclestone, K. and Pryor, J. (2003) 'Learning careers or assessment careers? The impact of assessment systems on learning', *British Educational Research Journal, 29, 4, 471–489*.

35. Eckert, P. 'The school as a community of engaged learners', *Wingspread Journal, 9, 3, 4–6*.

36. Hargreaves, D. (2005) 'AfL? Thinking outside the (black) box', *Cambridge Journal of Education 35, 2, 213–224*.

37. Sfard, A. (1998) 'On two metaphors for learning and the dangers of choosing just one', *Educational Researcher, 27, 2, 4–13*.

TRAINING ACTIVITY

Building in meaningful assessment to Fertile Questions: Lessons from an Outstanding History Department

Thinking about Oli's approach:

- What problems did Oli encounter in his initial planning stages?

- How did he overcome these?

- How did Oli build his Fertile Question around the five principles outlined at the beginning of this book?

- What can you take from this case study to help you in your own planning?

Summing up the approach to formative assessment outlined in this chapter:

The approach we take is based on the three key principles of effective assessment and feedback:

i.   Students must be able to monitor the quality of their own work during actual production.

ii. Students must possess an appreciation of what high quality work is and how their piece compares.

iii. Students must develop a store of tactics or moves which can be drawn upon to modify their own work in order to meet the desired standard.

There are so many hints, tips and off-the-shelf approaches to assessment and AfL that it may seem pointless to cover formative assessment here. However, the approach above is designed to develop real and meaningful learner autonomy – or in the words of Marshall and Drummond – follow the *spirit* rather than the *letter* of AfL.

This approach has to be actively built into the journey through the Fertile Question and maps perfectly onto the approach to language acquisition. Namely, that as students move along the continuum from speaking about the problem/question in everyday language through to writing/performing in academic language, they receive feedback at the various stages. This feedback is focused solely on the success criteria for the eventual Performance of Understanding and in helping students to generate their own pool of strategies and resources for gap closure. Therefore, on one level, the route through a Fertile Question should be seen as one long drafting and redrafting exercise.

Summative assessment models

There is no school system in the world that does not make summative judgements about students' performance in different subjects, and report these judgements to staff, parents, external bodies and the students themselves. However, summative data on attainment and progress can be fraught with difficulties, and can potentially contradict aspects of the whole-school model. Two potential tensions are:

Assessment must be viewed as an ongoing dialogue. It should emphasize the student as a developing individual, and explicitly reinforce aspects of the Learner Profile.	Vs	It is necessary to make summative judgements about students' attainment and share these with teachers, students and parents. These judgements can, if handled poorly, encourage excessive comparison between students and become de-motivating.
The assessment regime should be driven by individual departments, who are the only teachers expert enough to design, deliver, mark and moderate assessments in their subjects. SLT can provide a framework for expert assessment – but cannot lead it themselves.	Vs	Schools are subject to increasing accountability and rising floor targets, and school leaders must be continuously aware of how students' outcomes compare to national benchmarks. There is a need for tight control on target setting and interventions from the top.

This section suggests some approaches that could reconcile these tensions. Schools are data rich places, and this will be even truer in the future. So why has data got such a bad name with so many teachers? Why do teachers so often view data as a management tool, or a bureaucratic exercise? The best schools encourage teachers and Middle Leaders to embrace the data. They must learn to love it! This can only be achieved if teachers and subject leads:

- feel the data has integrity – they trust it, and know where it has come from;

- are trained how best to use it, and Line Management supports this process;

- are consulted over target setting – do not just tell teachers everyone is getting an A* or else!

- the data is used to stimulate discussion and target resources, not as a blunt performance management tool.

In short, our approach is to use data to support what is happening in teachers' classrooms and to improve Teaching and Learning. The worst thing is to have data for data's sake, or data as a stick to beat teachers with. Done effectively, rigorous tracking of student performance can support the process of classroom teaching, not frustrate or corrupt it. Data can, and should, help teachers teach.

Definitions of terms

Before we go further it may be helpful to define some of the terminology we use around data and tracking, and where some of our assumptions come from. Being clear and sharing the rationale behind your approach to data and target setting is key to gaining support from teachers.

Students' attainment is, generally speaking, measured in National Curriculum Levels in Key Stages 1, 2 and 3, GCSE grades in Key Stage 4 and A-Level grades in Key Stage 5. This is, of course, not always the case, but where other measures are used (e.g. BTECs), or indeed if National Curriculum Levels are replaced in the next few years, all the principles of effective tracking outlined below can be easily reapplied to whatever new metrics are being employed. A student will always have a starting point each year (a baseline) and an end point they need to get to (a target).

To allow target setting to be more precise many schools break each grade/level into sub-grades/sub-levels.

For example:

Level 5	5a	High Level 5	}	3 sub-levels for each level
	5b	Middle Level 5		
	5c	Low Level 5		

Grade C	C1	High C	}	3 sub-grades for each grade
	C2	Middle C		
	C3	Low C		

Where do students' baselines come from?

Any system for setting targets is flawed unless the target is relative to an accurate baseline grade for the student. Also unless baselines are in place it will be impossible to measure progress.

Calculating baselines can be complicated, and there is significant variety in the methods schools use. A summary of some different practices is below:

Phase	Where the baselines comes from
Key Stage 1	Teacher assessment. A conversion from the end of reception level.
Key Stage 2	End of Key Stage 1 level – often a SATs style test moderated by a teacher assessment.
Key Stage 3	For English and Maths: • Year 6 SATs results; • the school's own 'baseline test*'; • a commercially purchased test – for example CATs or MIDYIS; • a combination of all of the above. For other subjects: • Some schools copy the baseline from English or Maths into other subjects (for example, Science might take the Maths base, History the English one, Geography might take an average of the two). • Alternatively, a baseline test can be administered by each department. This would be essential in a fresh start subject such as French or Spanish (where students' baselines will be low if they have never studied before – Level 1 or 2), or in a subject like PE, where there is no necessary correlation in attainment with Maths or English.
Key Stage 4	For all subjects: • convert their End of Key Stage 3 National Curriculum level to Key Stage 4 GCSE using a baseline conversion table (there is an example below); • a Key Stage 4 baseline assessment in the first term of Year 10; • have students undertake a YELLIS test to establish Key Stage 4 baseline and predict Key Stage 4 attainment; • any combination of the above, where the different approaches are used to moderate each other to arrive at an accurate Key Stage 4 base and target.
Key Stage 5	For all subjects: • convert their GCSE result in the subject to an A-Level baseline (a bit of a shot in the dark?); • a Key Stage 5 baseline assessment in the first term of Year 12; • an ALIS test to establish Key Stage 5 base and predict their final A-Level grade; • any combination of the above where the different measures moderate each other.

*schools should note that RAISEOnline and Ofsted will analyse the cohort's eventual results against their Year 6 SATs scores. This means deviating from them by using an in-house baseline test is risky (although clearly does have other advantages). If a student starts Year 7 with an English baseline of 5B, and a History baseline of 3B, their History target will be too low. So, baselines in foundation subjects should be informed by, if not identical to, Key Stage 2 SATs results.

This table only describes how to arrive at Key Stage baselines. Schools should also give students a year baseline and a year target at the beginning of each academic year. Year targets are obviously informed by Key Stage targets (they feed forward to them), but tracking from year to year is more meaningful for students than simply talking about where they need to get in the Key Stage. This is particularly true of Key Stages 2 and 3 (the longer ones). Imagine telling a Year 7 with a baseline of 4C that her end of Year 9 target is 7C – it would seem very far off! Much better to say to her that by the end of the year she should get to 5C (meaning she would still be on track for her 7C in Year 9). Year targets also increase teacher accountability, as students may have several teachers in each Key Stage but only one each year.

One problem with setting GCSE and A-Level baselines is students often start very low. Giving a student a very low baseline at the start of Year 10 ('You are now on an F grade') can be de-motivating, although this can be avoided by careful presentation of the baselines and targets to parents and students. A message of 'of course you're starting at a low grade, it's because these GCSE courses are challenging, but over the year you will start to climb through the grades with hard work, etc.' can work. Alternatively some schools deliberately do not talk about the Key Stage 4 baseline much, and instead talk about a student's distance from their target ('your target for Year 10 is X, and based on your last assessment you are four sub-levels away at the moment').

Converting an End of Key Stage 3 National Curriculum level to Key Stage 4 GCSE baseline[10]

NC levels	GCSE	BTEC	DIDA	OCR
	A*1	Di*1		Di1
	A*2	Di*2		Di2
	A*3	Di*3		Di3
	A1	Di1	Di1	Me1
	A2	Di2	Di2	Me2
	A3	Di3	Di3	Me3
8a	B1	Me1	Me1	Cr1

8b	B2	Me2	Me2	Cr2
8c	B3	Me3	Me3	Cr3
7a	C1	Pa1	Pa1	Pa1
7b	C2	Pa2	Pa2	Pa2
7c	C3	Pa3	Pa3	Pa3
6a	D1	WT	WT	WT
6b	D2	WT	WT	WT
6c	D3	WT	WT	WT
5a	E1	WT	WT	WT
5b	E2	WT	WT	WT
5c	E3	WT	WT	WT
4a	F1	WT	WT	WT
4b	F2	WT	WT	WT
4c	F3	WT	WT	WT
3a	G1	WT	WT	WT
3b	G2	WT	WT	WT
3c	G3	WT	WT	WT
<3	<G	U	U	U

Progress and attainment expectations

Outstanding schools will have a highly developed approach to setting student targets. They will analyse the attainment profile of each intake, set targets above national expectations, and track students' progress towards these. Targets are of course specific to the school's context and students' attainment on entry; this makes it difficult to talk here about what you should be aiming for in terms of final outcomes. However we can offer some methodology. One approach to setting your targets could be:

Example of setting Year 7 targets

Stage 1	• Have a top-line figure in mind for both progress and attainment. For example you might want 90 per cent of students to make two sub-levels or more of progress, and 90 per cent of students to finish the year on 4A or above (clearly these two targets are interrelated).
	• These top-line goals cannot be plucked from thin air. They should be informed by:
	  ○ how your school has achieved in the past;
	  ○ the students' KS2 SATs results;
	  ○ borough and national expectations;
	  ○ some schools employ other predictions – for example Fisher Family Trust data.

Stage 2	• Now you have some parameters in place which are suitably challenging, you can start to go through each student and set their target. This should be done with the Heads of Department – they need to be consulted so they have ownership of the targets. In the above case most students will be set a target of two sub-levels, but some may be three (for example students who are starting in Year 7 below Level 4, or students who have been identified as Gifted and Talented in that subject).
Stage 3	• Once you have set the targets with the Head of Department on a case by case basis, you can finalize the top-line figure. It may be that it has shifted slightly (for example perhaps 94 per cent are now targeted for two sub-levels or more).
Stage 4	• Share targets with staff, students and parents, so everyone is aware where they need to be by the end of the year.

Planning, planning and more planning

Having the right targets is, of course, just the jumping off point for this process. The real work is in designing and implementing your whole-school plan to achieve them. Writing School Improvement Plans is not covered in detail in this handbook, but it is good practice to start whatever plan you write with a summary of the targets. Here is an example from Key Stage 3 in Ark Academy:

Year	Subject	Progress targets	Attainment targets	National expectations*		ARK Network minimum requirements	
		sub-levels	% at grade	sub-levels	grade	sub-levels	grade
9	English	76% @ 2 sub-levels +	77% @ 6C+	1.3	5C/5B	2	5B
	Maths	81% @ 2 sub-levels +	77% @ 6C+	1.3	5C/5B	2	6C
	Science	84% @ 2 sub-levels +	65% @ 6C+	1.3	5C/5B	2	5B
8	English	99% @ 2 sub-levels +	83% @ 5B+	1.3	4A/5C	2	4A
	Maths	97% @ 2 sub-levels +	77% @ 5B+	1.3	4A/5C	2	5B
	Science	90% @ 2 sub-levels +	60% @ 5B+	1.3	4A/5C	2	4A
7	English	75% @ 3 sub-levels +	85% @ 4A+	1.3	4B	2	4C
	Maths	75% @ 3 sub-levels +	85% @ 4A+	1.3	4B	2	4A
	Science	75% @ 3 sub-levels +	75% @ 4A+	1.3	4B	2	4C

*Benchmarking against national expectations

Knowing how you are doing relative to other schools is a key part of your own self-evaluation, and will help enormously with any external inspections. Being able to tell the story of your data, and give a full account of your school's performance (the good and the bad), is a characteristic of effective leadership. As such it is important to fully engage with the guidance for Ofsted inspectors on making judgements about progress and attainment. Working from the same rubric as Ofsted will make sure you do not have radically different impressions of what is happening, and will help an inspection team to have confidence in your judgements.

Useful guidance is available from Ofsted's website (look for the guidance for inspectors section) but we have picked out here some data we have used in the past to make judgements about students' performance in Key Stage 3.

Rather than talk in terms of levels, Ofsted inspectors refer to Average Point Scores (APS). APS is a way of combining a student's results in national tests (for example KS2 SATs or GCSEs) into an average score. The scores are also averaged at year group level – giving an APS for the whole cohort.

For your own calculations you will want to convert APS back to levels (because these are what teachers and students understand). This is easily done using the conversion table below.

Ofsted inspectors use national statistics for APS to categorize attainment and progress in schools into Outstanding, Good, Satisfactory and Inadequate. For example in Key Stage 3:

● Outstanding progress is four APS per year (approximately two sub-levels);

● Very high attainment is an APS of 36/7 at the end of Year 9 (approximately 5A).

Ofsted look at a school's results relative to borough and national averages. If the school has a statistical significance of plus 1 it will be judged to have high attainment and good progress; plus 2 is very high attainment and outstanding progress.

● Average attainment at the end of KS1: 15.5 APS | 2C/2B;

● Average attainment at the end of KS2: 27.5 APS |4C/4B;

● Average attainment at the end of KS3: 34.1 APS | 5C/5B.[11]

Level to APS conversion chart for Key Stage

APS	NC Level
3	WC
4	
5	WB
6	
7	WA
8	
9	1C
10	
11	1B
12	
13	1A
14	
15	2C
16	
17	2B
18	
19	2A
20	
21	3C
22	
23	3B
24	
25	3A
26	
27	4C
28	
29	4B

APS	NC Level
30	
31	4A
32	
33	5C
34	
35	5B
36	
37	5A
38	
39	6C
40	
41	6B
42	
43	6A
44	
45	7C
46	
47	7B
48	
49	7A
50	
51	8C
52	
53	8B
54	
55	8A

Principles of effective target setting – a summary

This is a whistle-stop tour of baseline and target setting, but hopefully includes some useful pointers. In summary:

- Get the Key Stage baselines right (or as close to right as you can). This is best achieved by reviewing and improving the methodology each year.

- Use these baselines to set challenging targets, above national expectations, but do not impose these targets on department leaders – they will know the students and the assessment regime best so can personalize the targets to the individual child. Give teachers a degree of control over the target setting process, within clear parameters, then interrogate what they have done – this is better than setting the targets for them.

- Track from Year Base to Year Target, as well as Key Stage Base to Key Stage Target. Revise targets (generally upwards) as students move through the Key Stage based on their recent attainment.

- Benchmark against national comparisons and be ready to explain the data to external stakeholders in language they can understand.

Clean, clear and simple – how to share data with students, parents and teachers

One reason data can sometimes be rejected or ignored by teachers is because it is presented in horribly complicated forms. Data managers and Senior Leaders in schools may be highly skilled in excel, but if they do not have an ability to communicate clearly and present simply then they will not reap the full reward of their analysis. One person in charge of data sitting in an office with boxes full of indecipherable spreadsheets is not what you are looking for.

Take a very common example of a teacher engaging with school data: an occasion where they look up their class list on a school's database. What data should they see? We would argue that in terms of attainment the datasheet should show:

- year baseline;

- 'working at' grade (their level/grade on their most recent assessment);

- year target.

And leave it at that. Excessive columns are not helpful. Clearly teachers should be able to call up other data – for example their results from previous assessments/modules and their Key Stage baselines and targets, but the basic template should show just base, working at and target.

Also when teachers need to view this data they should do it online through the central system. A lot of schools currently share data through spreadsheets which are sent out to departments, usually at the beginning of the year. The problem with this approach is that when something changes – a student comes on or off roll, or a target is revised – it will not be automatically updated on the individual departments' spreadsheets. It is much better to have one central system through which teachers can view attainment and progress data for their classes simply and easily.

Datasheets should also have contextual information which can inform teachers' planning and assist them to target specific groups. For example:

- gender

- reading age

- FSM

- EAL

- SEN

- G&T.

So if you can get your system to look something like the table below, rather than show a forest of columns, you will be a long way towards getting teachers to engage with the data. It may seem that we are labouring the point about data presentation, but it is absolutely vital to teachers buying in.

Example datasheet:

Name	Gender	Year Base	Working at December	End of Year Target	Reading Age	FSM	EAL	SEN	G&T
Student A	M	5C	5C	5A	12.6	Y			
Student B	F	5B	5A	6C	12.8	Y			Y

Parent reports

Exactly the same principles apply to reporting to parents and students themselves: do not baffle them with columns and numbers that are not strictly necessary. What is the real objective of the parent report? To tell parents where their child needs to get to, and where they are in relation to that point. An example from Ark Academy is below:

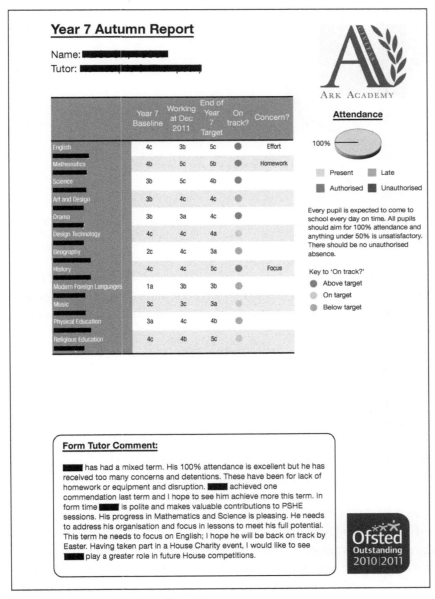

Year 7 Autumn Report

Name: ▮▮▮▮▮▮▮▮▮▮▮▮
Tutor: ▮▮▮▮▮▮▮▮▮▮▮▮▮▮▮

	Year 7 Baseline	Working at Dec 2011	End of Year 7 Target	On track?	Concern?
English	4c	3b	5c	●	Effort
Mathematics	4b	5c	5b	●	Homework
Science	3b	5c	4b	●	
Art and Design	3b	4c	4c	◐	
Drama	3b	3a	4c	●	
Design Technology	4c	4c	4a	◐	
Geography	2c	4c	3a	●	
History	4c	4c	5c	●	Focus
Modern Foreign Languages	1a	3b	3b	◐	
Music	3c	3c	3a	◐	
Physical Education	3a	4c	4b	●	
Religious Education	4c	4b	5c	◐	

ARK ACADEMY

Attendance

100%

Present   Late
Authorised   Unauthorised

Every pupil is expected to come to school every day on time. All pupils should aim for 100% attendance and anything under 50% is unsatisfactory. There should be no unauthorised absence.

Key to 'On track?'
● Above target
○ On target
◐ Below target

Form Tutor Comment:

▮▮▮ has had a mixed term. His 100% attendance is excellent but he has received too many concerns and detentions. These have been for lack of homework or equipment and disruption. ▮▮▮ achieved one commendation last term and I hope to see him achieve more this term. In form time ▮▮▮ is polite and makes valuable contributions to PSHE sessions. His progress in Mathematics and Science is pleasing. He needs to address his organisation and focus in lessons to meet his full potential. This term he needs to focus on English; I hope he will be back on track by Easter. Having taken part in a House Charity event, I would like to see ▮▮▮ play a greater role in future House competitions.

Ofsted
Outstanding
2010|2011

Figure 4.2 An example Ark Academy parent report

Principles of data use in schools: Never the tail wagging the dog

Figure 4.3 The tail wagging the dog!

The data in any school is there to support one purpose – Teaching and Learning. Never let the necessities and pressures of your data system restrict what is happening in the classroom or in the curriculum – the tail should never wag the dog, always the other way around.

The biggest potential tension between data and Teaching and Learning comes with decisions about the curriculum and assessments. We have set out in this book the belief that the curriculum should be built around rigorous academic subjects, and should challenge students to engage with the big, complicated, grown-up ideas and principles in those subjects at an early age.

You cannot on the one hand encourage curriculum leaders to inject challenge and maturity into their SoWs, and on the other demand that students' results will always increase term by term. Student progress does not come in a straight line; some assessments will be harder than others. Many consider Pure Maths modules to be harder than Statistics, or an essay on *King Lear* to be more difficult than a persuasive letter to the Headteacher. A challenging assessment, where the students experience some degree of failure, is a good thing: it shows that the assessments are not excessively predictable, that the full range of subject topics is being covered, and that the tests are actually identifying elements of deep understanding.

This does, however, mean that there needs to be an understanding of the assessment regime at all levels of the school. If the Year 9 Autumn Term science test is on a particularly hard topic (say, balancing chemical equations), then students' levels are likely to go down. This is not necessarily a problem, as long as the SLT and anyone else looking at the data understand it in context, and the students' end of year performance, when they are assessed on the entire year's work, hits the progress and attainment targets the school has set.

A linked point is about what data the teachers are entering at each assessment point. If we are asking teachers to enter a current attainment level for each student at the end of each term, where does that level come from? Is it, as suggested above, the student's result in a specific test? Or is it a teacher assessment of the student's overall performance in the subject at that point, where they look at test results and a series of other indicators?

We would say the first method is far superior. It might mean that students' attainment does not steadily increase each term (because it is following the varying difficulty in the cycle of assessments) but this can be tolerated. The problem with the teacher assessed 'overall' level is that the tail is beginning to wag the dog: now the teacher needs to mark the Autumn Term test, enter the result, and then enter a second, overall, teacher assessed level, which is less robust (because it does not come directly from an assessment, but from an impression of the student's performance based on this assessment, other assessments, classwork, homework, how they have been working in recent lessons, etc.). You have increased the work for the teachers, all because you need to satisfy your demand for a graph that is heading in the right direction. But the reality is that some topics are harder than others, students do better or worse on different tests, and students, parents, teachers and governors are intelligent enough to understand this.

So, in our model the in-year results (October half-term, Christmas, February half-term and so on) will move around, and as such should be used principally as a means to generate a discussion, at department and Line Management level, about what the data is telling us. The discussion can focus on how students performed on that particular topic, who needs intervention, how we can revise the SoW for next time and so on. In-year assessments should not be used to make overall judgements about student performance, because they are not a measure of their understanding of the overall subject. It is the end of year examination result, which should always be a test of the whole year's work, that will allow you to see how much progress the student has made overall, and whether each student has achieved their target.

The real benefit of regular assessment is the department's response to the students' results. You want teachers to eagerly receive the data, to mine it and then plan based on what it tells them. There is a possible list of department responses to data cycle below. But you will only achieve this level of response if the departments support the assessment regime; if they feel a strong degree of ownership over it. This can be achieved if i) they are allowed to test what they want, when they want it, according to the curriculum decisions they have made as subject specialists, as spelt out earlier in the book, and ii) the rationale behind the setting of students' baselines and targets has been explained to them, and they have been consulted about this process.

Possible department responses to a set of assessment data:

- What lessons came from marking and moderation? Use these findings to plan 'Review Week' lessons (see below for an explanation of Review Week).

- As a department team, collaboratively review the SoW: what areas were covered well; what ideas/concepts did they not understand? What can we change for next year? (Quickly note this before you are on to the next one).

- Make any changes to pupil groupings that the results suggest. Should students move up or down? Are some groups too big or small?

- Redeploy teaching assistants based on where need is greatest.

- Teachers need to adjust seating plans.

- Make parental contact. This can come in many forms: reward postcards, positive phone calls, meetings with parents where there is a real concern, etc. One creative idea we saw recently was a department who photocopied the actual assessment scripts of the 20 most underperforming students and sent them home to parents, along with a copy of the success criteria and a covering letter instructing them that their child should redo the assessment over half-term. Nice surprise at the start of the holiday!

- Consider the Fertile Questions ahead – what did we learn from this SoW that can improve the next one?

- How can we ensure students prepare even more thoroughly for the next assessment? Consider revision skills/booklets/Homeworks/displays/assemblies and so on.

Progress does not come in a straight line

The only way you can demonstrate linear progress from assessment point to assessment point is if every test assesses the same skills and concepts. In most cases this will lead to reductive testing that fails to prepare students for the only assessments that count – GCSE and A-Level.

The progress a student makes, or their 'flight path' through the academic year, is a complex assessment and curriculum issue. Teachers and managers need to know that a student's performance (or flight path) is heading in the right direction, but how can you know this when the flight paths are:

- subject specific

- curriculum specific

- year specific

- class specific (for example top sets may progress differently to bottom sets)

- student specific?

Flight paths – three examples

Below are examples from three different subjects of how a series of assessments might work across the academic year:

In this example students are assessed three times in the year, once at the end of each term. Each assessment is equally weighted across the three core elements of Music at Key Stage 3 – performing, composing and a listening analysis. The assessments are varied – some will be group performance, some will be individual – but the elements being tested are consistent. But because the same three areas are tested each time, we can reasonably expect progress to move in a straight line, and for students to be a bit closer to their end of year

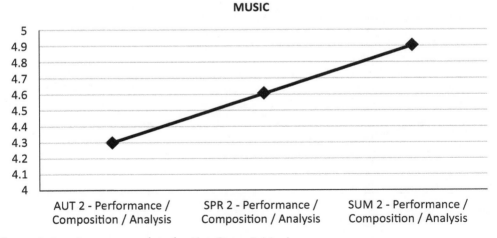

Figure 4.4a   Assessment data for Key Stage 3 Music

target at each assessment point (although inevitably there will be more to it than this – and unpicking any set of results will need to be done in consultation with the Music Department).

A Maths department is likely to run a very different assessment cycle to that of Music. Each half term they would test a new, discrete topic: probability and fractions in Autumn 1, geometry in Autumn 2 and so on. There are of course links between these topics, but one does not necessarily build directly on the other. As such, the student's results should not increase gradually over the year – they should be consistently high. Students need to be achieving their target level on every assessment; if the aim is for you to be 5B by the end of Year 7 then you need to be 5B in probability, and 5B in algebra, and 5B in shapes and space and so on.

A third model might be English. One way to think of English in Key Stage 3 is to divide it into reading and writing (putting speaking and listening to one

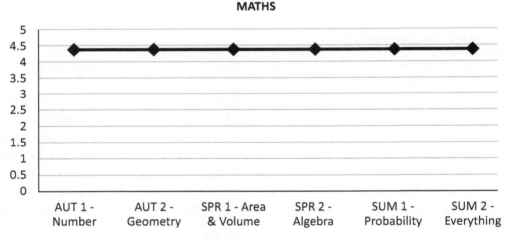

Figure 4.4b   Assessment data for Key Stage 3 Maths

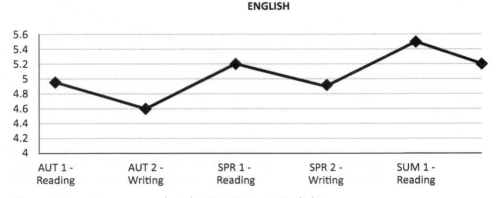

Figure 4.4c   Assessment data for Key Stage 3 English

side for the moment). Reading assessments could be on plays, poems, novels – but they are testing the same concepts: decoding a writer's meaning by examining their language, plots, characters, etc. A writing assessment could be a persuasive letter, a descriptive essay, a short story, a newspaper opinion piece – different genres but with significant overlap (all the technical skills of writing: grammar, punctuation, spelling, paragraphing, style etc).

The different assessments test similar concepts, but some will be harder than others. Students may find persuasive writing easier than discursive writing (because they have practiced it more at primary school). They may find an essay about characterization in a modern novel easier than an essay about language in Shakespeare. We do not want to discourage Heads of English from introducing Shakespeare to students at a young age, so we must be prepared for their reading levels to (potentially) dip the first time they are asked to write an extended written response to a Shakespeare play. So depending on which texts and styles of writing are studied at which point, the data may meander around a bit as it follows the curriculum. This is why the end of year English exam becomes key – it should be a catch-all that tests student's performance across the whole year's work and provides a full picture of their understanding of the subject.

Designing summative assessments

The design of the Performance of Understanding students undertake as the end of the Fertile Question is all important. Curriculum leaders should be expert at designing these assessments. They need to remember that every assessment week that comes and goes in a school is just preparation for the assessment months of GCSEs and A-Level. As such the assessments that round-up each Fertile Question should mirror the demands of these national exams. Heads of Department (and aspiring ones) need training on how to design assessments. They should be avid consumers of examiners' reports and mark national exams at least once in their careers. They should start planning each Fertile Question by considering the outcome first, the Performance of Understanding that students will demonstrate at the end, and then keep this assessment sharply in mind when planning each lesson.

And because assessments must be matched to the curriculum in this way, our view is that external assessments which some schools buy in, that operate as stand-alone tests that do not fit directly with the taught curriculum, are not an effective means of assessment.

The example of Key Stage 3 SATs is useful here. Now they are gone, secondary schools have the opportunity to introduce mature assessments into Key Stage 3; assessments that are essentially junior versions of the tests students will take in Key Stage 4 and 5 assessments. In English, Year 7 students should be studying challenging texts, collecting key quotes, unpicking language, developing an understanding of the author's intentions, and then writing an extended written essay where they deploy these quotes and analyse them. In short – they should be writing GCSE style essays in Year 7. The Key Stage 3 English SATs did not include any extended essays; instead they used short answer questions based on unseen extracts from fiction and non-fiction texts. They were essentially a harder version of the tests students take in Year 6. Unsurprisingly, the Key Stage 3 SATs did not end up helping schools prepare their students for Key Stage 4. Under the SATs assessment regime:

> Assessment had adverse impact on teaching and learning, with specific problems emerging in relation to narrow drilling for the test....teachers have little choice...other than relate learning to past test papers... [Assessments do not] identify those elements of deep learning essential to understanding subjects (and focus only on a narrow range of surface elements).[12]

The experience of independent schools is telling. They have never had to adapt their Key Stage 2 and 3 curricula to accommodate SATs exams. This freedom means they can teach Years 5–9 according to their vision of how the subjects should be taught at that age. And what they seem to do is employ GCSE style assessments (simplified of course, but along the lines) with students long before they actually arrive at GCSE. This level of preparedness certainly helps with their results, and avoids the problem we see in many comprehensives of having to do repeated interventions in Key Stage 4.

Garbage in, garbage out – the importance of moderation

We cannot discuss how schools can collect and analyse attainment data for students at regular intervals without talking about *moderation of assessments*. Robust and accurate moderation procedures for every department are essential. There is very little point in a school reporting that a student has written a C grade essay unless they actually have done; it might sound nice in the short term, but in the long run, if you enter inaccurate data into the system, you will get nothing useful out of it.

After each assessment cycle all departments should moderate their results before they enter any data. At least once a year you should partner with a department from another school, or an LEA or academy network consultant, and have them externally validate your results.

This is not just about ensuring the data has integrity. Done properly, moderation is a developmental process for teachers, as it sharpens their understanding of the assessment criteria and helps identify areas of strength and weakness in students' performance. They can then plan collaboratively where to go next.

The way in which each department moderates their assessments should be decided by the subject leaders, and reviewed through Line Management. Moderation procedures must be thorough, and allow for the finalized data to be entered onto the school's database in time for any reports to be produced. The exact process for moderation will vary between departments. An example from English follows:

English – Autumn Term 1 Assessment: An essay exploring language in Macbeth

School assessment calendar:

Monday 10 October	Autumn 1 assessment week begins (English, Maths, Science)
Monday 17 October	Review Week begins
Wednesday 19 October	All levels on the system

English Department schedule:

Monday 10 Oct	Students complete their assessments under exam conditions.
Tuesday 11 Oct	Teachers bring a sample of three marked scripts (top/middle/bottom) to the department meeting. Scripts are then swapped, and adjustments are made to ensure consistency.
Wednesday 12 Oct	Teachers can now mark the rest of their scripts, taking into account the feedback from the moderation meeting.
Wednesday 19 Oct	Teachers input marks to database in time for the deadline.

Review Week: Exploiting the assessment for the most Teaching and Learning value

Where exactly should the assessment fall in the calendar of each term or half term? The practice in many schools is to teach right up to the last possible moment, administer an assessment, mark it over the holidays, discover that for many students there is a gap between their actual performance and the desired outcome, enter the results, and then begin the next half term with a new topic. What a waste!

A summative assessment represents a rich Teaching and Learning opportunity. Students should pore over their performance, review it against exemplars and the success criteria, understand the deficiencies and start to close the gaps. Assessment is about looking forward not back. An assessment that tells a student they have failed to master aspects of the term's work, but gives them no chance to do anything about it, is essentially useless. We believe that assessments should always take place in the penultimate week of a term or half term, to allow a full week for review.

In a sentence we *teach/test/reteach*.

Much of what has come earlier in this handbook will help you plan effective 'review' lessons. Here are some further points:

- Endless peer or self-marking can lead to vague, meaningless commentary by students on each others' work. If they are just reading their partner's essay and writing 'EBI: More detail' at the bottom it is not a useful exercise. When students do not have a precise understanding of how to improve they fall back on default responses: *'My target is to try harder'* or *'I must do more homework'*. It is better to ask students to correct their own or their partner's work from an exemplar answer (one that shows all the working out, or good planning, or other desired characteristics). Reviewing and amending work against exemplars or criteria – yes. Reviewing for the sake of reviewing – no.

- Start review lessons by restating the 'whole game' of the year, and the whole game of the assessments. Link the assessments to the underlying concepts they are studying, and to the Fertile Questions that have gone before.

- Classroom dialogue is an important part of review; it is how students build their understanding of what they need to do next.

- Review lessons need challenge. Zone in on a specific area; the one just beyond their current level of performance.

- Use Do Nows in Review Week to pick off common errors from the assessments. Once you have seen that a mistake is being repeated by most of the class, it is better to spend time planning a great Do Now that explores this mistake and corrects it, than it is to individually correct each student's script.

- Review Week is a key moment to reinforce the idea of the Growth Mindset. Be wary of labelling in Review Week; students' academic confidence and self-perception can hit rock bottom after assessment, especially if they start to see through the review all the mistakes they made.

- What will help students show resilience and grow in confidence is if they have the opportunity to put what they have learnt in review lessons into practice. Allow students time to rewrite/redo parts of the assessment that they struggled with. Ideally the students themselves will diagnose the most urgent thing they need to redo (based on the understanding they have built up over the review lessons). Do not rush the redoing of work – time spent on this now will help them when they revisit these topics in future.

TRAINING ACTIVITY

Assessment exercises

Exercise 1

What is the single most important reason for having routine assessments in schools? Brainstorm ideas in groups and feedback.

Possible answers:
Promote accountability, motivate students, inform parents, track progress, target interventions, *to help teachers teach.*

Exercise 2

Consider this series of assessments in English. Why have they been ordered in this way? How does this link to the sequence of assessments in your subject?

	Au1 Assessment	Au2 Assessment	Sp1 Assessment	Sp2 Assessment	Su1 Assessment	Su2 Assessment
Y7	How does the author present the characters of X and Y in the novel Z? Concepts: The writer at work – how is meaning conveyed through characters, descriptions, actions, words, etc.? Skills: Using quotes, writing an extended essay.	A letter to your Headteacher persuading them to change something about the school. Concepts: Adapting style and form to audience and purpose. Skills: Writing in a persuasive style. Simple spelling, punctuation, paragraphing.	How does the author create tension through their use of language in the Gothic novel X? Concepts: The writer at work – how is meaning conveyed through figurative language? Skills: Embedding quotes.	A description of a nightmare world. Concepts: Consistently adapting style and form to audience and purpose. Skills: Writing in a descriptive style. Intermediate spelling, punctuation, paragraphing. Different narrative structures.	An essay comparing the structure and form of two love poems. Concepts: The writer at work – how are the poems structured, and what are the effects of those structures on the reader? Skills: Embedded quotes and comparisons between texts.	End of Year Exam: Section A – Reading: Either i) read an extract and analyse the writer's use of character and language, or ii) read a poem and analyse the writer's use of language and structure. Section B – Writing: Either i) a persuasive letter with a specific audience/purpose, or ii) a description of a darkened alleyway.
Y8	Write an article for a national newspaper arguing X, Y or Z. Concepts: Adapting a more mature style and form to a more complex audience and purpose. Skills: Writing in a discursive style. Advanced spelling, punctuation, paragraphing and structure.	How does the playwright use dramatic devices to engage the audience in Act 1 of play X? Concepts: The writer at work – how is meaning conveyed through lighting, stagecraft, dramatic irony. Skills: Embedding quotations skilfully, commenting on dramatic devices.	Write a ballad. Concepts: Adapting a historical style and form to audience and purpose. Skills: Writing in ballad form, use of figurative language.	How does the author create a sense of loneliness and isolation in the opening of novel X? (This has to be pre-1950.) Concepts: The writer at work – how is meaning conveyed through characters, language, structure and historical context? Skills: Embedding quotes skilfully, commenting on historical context.	Write an entertaining short story about family life. Concepts: Convincingly adapting style and form to audience and purpose. Skills: Writing in an entertaining style. Advanced spelling, punctuation, paragraphing, and structure.	End of Year Exam: Section A – Reading: Choose one pre-1950 extract and one modern extract and compare them in terms of the writer's use of language, character, structure and themes. Section B – Writing: Either i) a discursive essay arguing for or against a controversial subject, or ii) an informal take on school life for a student magazine.

Y9					
	Shakespeare: Who is to blame for the murder of King Duncan in *Macbeth*? Concepts: The writer at work – how is meaning conveyed through character, language, dramatic devices, historical context. Skills: Embedding quotations skilfully, commenting on dramatic devices and a text's literary context.	An extended description of an extraordinary moment in someone's life. Concepts: Adapting style and form to audience and purpose with fluency and skill. Skills: Employing a wide range of vocabulary, sentencing, paragraphing and structure for effect.	Modern poetry: Compare how the poets explore identity and belonging in four poems. Concepts: Alternative interpretations and detailed cross references on the writer at work – how is meaning conveyed through language and structure. Skills: Embedding quotations skilfully, detailed cross reference.	Imitate the style of Edgar Allen Poe in your own thrilling story. Concepts: Adapting to a more complicated style and form. Writing in a convincing, confident style. Skills: Imitating an established writer's style. Employing a wide range of vocabulary, sentencing, paragraphing and structure for effect.	Compare how three pre-1914 short stories present the role of women in society. Concepts: Alternative interpretations and detailed cross references on the writer at work – how is meaning conveyed through language, character, structure and historical context? Skills: Embedding quotations skilfully, detailed cross reference, commenting on historical context.	A GCSE Past Paper: Section A – Reading: A comparison of two poems (students choose from a range of questions/poems). Section B – Writing: Students choose from a selection of questions covering different styles writing to persuade, argue, discuss, describe, etc.

Task

Map your own assessments for a specific year group in the way we have above.

These assessments have been planned as a clear sequence – The key point here is to look at how the core concepts are mapped out across KS3 with the students encountering concepts and engaging with them at a deeper and deeper level across the 3 years. In Y7 for example the concepts are the same each time – we keep coming back to them but the cognitive complexity is escalated = increasing the size of the domain in which the learner is operating.

   BUT – the first time we're looking at character in a modern novel, the next time its language in a gothic novel – the focus and the text are getting increasingly hard. In writing – persuasive writing is very familiar to them from KS2, descriptive is harder (more creative). The exam is, importantly, a catch-all, measuring their understanding of the whole years work – and as such forms a very useful baseline for the following year.

Conclusion:

The approach to assessment design as outlined in this chapter is concerned both with how we plan to allow the learner to play a central role in the journey but also how we design summative assessments that provide authentic evidence of student understanding.

To sum up, the key points of this part of the approach are:

- Formative assessment practices can be boiled down to three key processes:

  ○ Establishing where the learners are in their learning;

  ○ Establishing where they are going;

  ○ Working out how to get there.

- This practice is most powerful when the learner is involved. In order to do this three things are required:

  ○ Students must be able to monitor the quality of their own work during actual production;

  ○ Students must possess an appreciation of what high quality work is and how their piece compares;

  ○ Students must develop a store of tactics or moves which can be drawn upon to modify their own work in order to meet the desired standard.

- Summative assessments must be sequenced in order to demonstrate a progression in understanding. This means that learners must revisit previous concepts as well as surface content and teachers must plan for this over time.

- The design of the Performance of Understanding (summative assessment) students undertake as the end of the Fertile Question is all important. Curriculum leaders should be expert at designing these assessments. They need to remember that every assessment week that comes and goes in a school is just preparation for the assessment months of GCSEs and A-Level.

- Robust and accurate moderation procedures for every department are essential. There is very little point in a school reporting that a student has written a C grade essay unless they actually have done; it might sound nice in the short term, but in the long run, if you enter inaccurate data into the system, you will get nothing useful out of it.

- A summative assessment represents a rich Teaching and Learning opportunity. Students should pore over their performance, review it against exemplars and the success criteria, understand the deficiencies and start to close the gaps.

- Assessment is about looking forward not back. An assessment that tells a student they have failed to master aspects of the term's work, but gives them no chance to do anything about it, is essentially useless. We believe that assessments should always take place in the penultimate week of a term or half term, to allow a full week for review.

Notes

1   Pryor, J. and Crossouard, B. (2008) 'A socio-cultural theorisation of formative assessment', *Oxford Review of Education*, 34 (1), 1–20.
2   Ramaprasad, A. (1983) 'On the definition of feedback' *Behavioural Science*, 28, 4–13.
3   Ramaprasad, A. (1983) 'On the definition of feedback' *Behavioural Science*, 28, 4–13.
4   Sadler, D.R. (1989) 'Formative assessment and the design of instructional systems' *Instructional Science*, 18, 119–144.
5   Hattie, J. (2009) *Visible Learning*: Routledge.
6   Sadler, D.R. (1989) 'Formative assessment and the design of instructional systems' *Instructional Science*, 18, 119–144.
7   Polanyi, M. (1962) *Personal knowledge: Towards a post-critical philosophy*: Routledge.
8   Lindemann, E. (1982) *A rhetoric for writing teachers*: OUP.
9   Pryor, J. and Crossouard, B. (2008) 'A socio-cultural theorisation of formative assessment', *Oxford Review of Education*, 34 (1), 1–20.
10 ARK Schools Assessment Policy.
11 Ofsted – Interpreting Key Stage 1 to 3 Average Point Scores.
12 Oates, T (Chair of NC Review) (2010) *Could do better: Using international comparisons to refine the National Curriculum in England*: Cambridge Assessment.

5

Leadership – the framework for creating the culture

5

Leadership
The framework for creating the culture

What is the focus of this chapter?

This chapter is divided up into four sections:

- Section 1 looks at leadership as a cultural statement.

- Section 2 looks at using data to drive a whole-school dialogue around learning.

- Section 3 looks at modelling lifelong learning.

- Section 4 looks at using Line Management systems to maintain the focus on learning.

There are numerous reference books and training courses on school leadership and this handbook would become too unwieldy if it was to outline every aspect of outstanding school leadership. Instead, the focus of this chapter is on the elements of leadership that have a real and vital impact on learning and classroom culture; the elements that link directly to the whole-school model. So, whilst it is possible, and probably correct, to argue that *all* aspects of leadership dictate the culture and ethos of a school, the ideas below are those that are most pertinent to embedding the approach of this handbook.

A key point here is that if you believe that the main focus of any school should be the quality of the classroom teaching, and that all else ripples out from six great lessons a day, and that the best way to achieve this is by having teachers who are reflective, consider themselves as developing, and view teaching as a craft to be endlessly refined, *then the Senior Leadership of the school must live those values.* You cannot be a member of the Senior Leadership Team (SLT), and definitely not the person in charge of Teaching and Learning, if you are not open to being observed and taking feedback; if you do not follow the Teaching and Learning policy closely; if you do not prioritize your lesson planning and get the very best results. Sometimes we hear Deputy Headteachers say that their teaching is 'suffering' now they are in senior managerial roles; clearly as school leaders our time is squeezed, but do not lose sight of the main thing, or underestimate how closely the rest of the staff are watching your practice. Ultimately, where you go, others are sure to follow – if your teaching slips and you vocalize this, then the teaching throughout the school will slip.

Section 1: Leadership as a cultural statement

What is the culture we are trying to create?

We are not going to attempt a full exploration of school leadership here. We will offer two quotes though which have helped us in the past.

- 'Leadership is the art of getting someone else to do something you want done because he wants to do it.'(Dwight D. Eisenhower)

- 'Leadership describes the way that individuals are wrestling with really complicated, complex problems that don't have simple answers.' (Keith Grint, Professor of Leadership at Warwick University)

The culture we are creating can be defined as:

- 'Students who, over an extended period of time, are treated as if they are intelligent actually become so. If they are taught demanding content, and are expected to explain and find connections as well as memorise and repeat, they learn more and more quickly. They [come to] think of themselves as learners. They are able to bounce back in the face of short term failure.'(Lauren Resnick)

- 'Student results improve most when teachers become learners, and students become their own teacher.' (Hattie, J.)

'The quality of an education system cannot exceed the quality of its teachers. The best systems get the right people to become teachers, and then develop these people into effective instructors (the only way to improve outcomes is to improve instruction).'(McKinsey and Company 2002)[1]

Outstanding school leadership can be summed up then as follows:

> Outstanding schools insist on excellence in the quality of classroom teaching, and have systems in place which mean that leaders know the strengths and weaknesses of all the teaching staff. They operate an evidence-based approach to what is happening in classrooms. If staff teach less than very well, arrangements are in place to offer support. At the same time, outstanding schools have a relaxed collegiate culture in which teaching and classroom management ideas are shared unselfishly and problems acknowledged without fear of blame.[2]

Section 2: Using data to drive a whole-school dialogue around learning

Over the years schools have become flooded with data and pretty graphs measuring every facet of school life. The key thing with data though is to be able to use it and to understand how it can improve the quality of teaching and therefore the life chances of the pupils at your school. This section is concerned solely with the way student data can – and needs to be – used by every teacher to understand the students they teach, know what they can do and where the focus needs to be placed to ensure they all make progress.

In order to achieve this, this section is written as an extended training activity.

EXTENDED TRAINING ACTIVITY

Data analysis and the ability to act on what you find is a key part of being an outstanding teacher. This responsibility or skill set does not rest solely with the Head of Department. All teachers at all levels need to be able to forensically examine data and use the findings to improve their teaching and curriculum provision.

Crucially, this analysis is only fully effective if it is done frequently (termly) and the evidence used to alter teaching and/or curriculum structure immediately. We will come back to this idea more when we look at what makes an outstanding department.

In its simplest guise an outstanding department is a department full of outstanding teachers and one of the things outstanding teachers do well is scrutinize data and act on their findings.

This training activity is an extended session that will allow all teachers from the Headteacher down to analyse data, carry out a review of performance and create an action plan for sustained improvement. The activity looks at GCSE exam analysis as an example of using data to drive improvement. It is important to mention at this point that national summative examination analysis is not the only data analysis that should take place but is a useful case study as the data is standardized.

GCSE data case studies[3]

Below you will find two sets of data for GCSE exams sat by students attending a complex urban school. Although achievement is high, there is still underachievement and it needs to be identified and tackled. You will need to look at the data and analyse how each department has performed and what they need to focus on next year in order to continue to improve.

After this you will find an example of the questions you should be asking yourself at the end of each term to ensure your department has a continuous focus on teaching, learning and progress.

Stage 1: Read and analyse the top-line data from the English Department and carry out a review of the department's performance using the headings provided below.

English Language and Literature
A*-C Grades

	2009	2008	2007	2006
English Language	82.4%	82%	83%	80%
English Literature	83.7%	80%	82%	81%

A*-G Grades

	2009	2008	2007	2006
English Language	100%	100%	100%	100%
English Literature	98.9 %	100%	100%	100%

Residual (comparison of how the subject compared to all others in terms of students' attainment)

English Language   : +0.33 (+0.15 in 2008)
English Literature   : −0.11 (+0.16 in 2008)

Breakdown of English grades

	Total Students	A*	A	B	C	A-C	D	E	F	G	U	A*-C %	A*-G %
2009 Lang	204	18	57	53	40	168	30	6	0	0	0	82.40	100
2009 Lit	178	5	43	54	47	149	21	5	1	0	2	83.70	98.90
2008 Lang	181	23	41	44	40	148	18	13	2	0	0	82	100
2008 Lit	180	8	59	52	21	140	27	12	1	0	0	78	100
2007 Lang	194	6	27	45	83	161	29	4	0	0	0	83	100
2007 Lit	193	15	55	62	26	158	24	9	2	0	0	82	100
2006 Lang	187	10	27	68	53	158	19	9	0	1	0	80	100
2006 Lit	197	7	25	59	69	160	31	4	2	0	0	81	100

Percentages achieving at each grade

English Language	A* %	A %	B %	C %	D %	E %	F %	G %	U %
Our school	8.8	28	25.9	19.7	14.7	2.9	0	0	0
National	4.1	11.5	19.5	27.6	20.4	9.6	4.2	1.8	
English Literature									
Our school	2.8	24.2	30.3	26.4	11.8	2.8	0.5	0	1.1
National	5.6	16.8	24.8	26.3	14.6	6.7	2.7	1.1	1.1

Individual teacher predictions (English Language)

	Students achieving as predicted	Students achieving higher than predicted	Students achieving lower than predicted
Teacher 1	15	10	1
Teacher 2	11	8	9
Teacher 3	15	3	1
Teacher 4	11	11	3
Teacher 5	13	4	4
Teacher 6	5	12	2
Teacher 7	16	0	2
Teacher 8	8	0	10
Teacher 9	4	1	12
Teacher 10	5	3	0

Individual teacher predictions (English Literature)

	Students achieving as predicted	Students achieving higher than predicted	Students achieving lower than predicted
Teacher 1	15	1	10
Teacher 2	12	6	10
Teacher 3	11	1	13
Teacher 4	12	8	5
Teacher 5	9	6	6
Teacher 6	10	6	3
Teacher 7	11	0	7
Teacher 8	5	0	7
Teacher 9	3	0	2
Teacher 10	na	na	na

English Language – overall patterns/observations

English Literature – overall patterns/observations

Priorities for next year

Stage 2: Read the Maths Department's analysis then answer the questions

Mathematics Department GCSE examination analysis 2009
Summary of results

	% A*-C	% A*-G
2009	81.4	100
2008	90.1	100
2007	86.7	100
2006	86.3	99.5

The percentage of students achieving grades A*-C in Mathematics has decreased by 8.7 per cent to 81.4 per cent (90.1 per cent in 2008). All students achieved a grade A*-G.

Unfortunately this result was below the department's predictions (88.7 per cent). The departmental residual this year is 0.14 (compared to 0.47 in 2008). It is pleasing that the residual is still positive.

For the second year running, all students entered for the higher tier examinations in Band A achieved grades A*-C. In Band B students from Sets 6, 7 and 8 were entered for the higher tier examinations; all students from Set 6 achieved grades A*-C. In previous years the department policy of entering all students from Sets 1–8 for the higher tier examination had proven successful. This year the absence of coursework has significantly impacted the results for Mathematics. In the past students worked hard on coursework to the extent that they would secure up to 18 per cent of the 20 per cent mark available for coursework. Without this the department had to rely on previous strategies of higher tier entry and using new higher tier resources for revision.

	% A*	% A	%	% C	% D	% E	% F	% G	% U
2009	8.8	18.6	25.5	28.4	11.8	5.9	1	0	0
2008	16	19.9	32	22.1	4.4	4.4	1	0	0
2007	11.7	22.6	28.3	24.1	7.7	4.1	1.5	0	0
2006	9.1	22.3	31.5	23.4	7.6	4.6	1.0	0	0.5
National (female)	*4.5*	*10.7*	*15.4*	*26.2*	*19.1*	*11.3*	*7.0*	*3.9*	*1.9*

Predictions

Using the above mentioned strategies the department was optimistic with the January 2009 predictions. The predictions exceeded the results by 7.3 per cent. The department continue to set challenging targets for all of their students but it must be noted that in addition to lack of coursework, there was a larger cohort of students for 2009. In order to address this, an extra set was created in Band A. The purpose of this was to ensure C/D borderline students would achieve a grade C. This was accomplished but the draw back was that not enough students in Band B from Sets 7 and 8 achieved a grade C. For Band B an extra set was not created but a teacher was allocated for intervention; four students were taken out from the class and given extra attention. Unfortunately, these students did not achieve a C grade.

Name	Aggregate KS3	Expected Grade	Result
1	5	D	D
2	5 2/3	C	D
3	5	D	D
4	5	D	D

It must also be noted that only five students from Band B who were expected to achieve a grade C did not achieve this.

Comparison with national figures (for girls)

Once again, the results are significantly above national figures for all benchmarks. The percentage of students gaining grade A*-C is 24.6 per cent above the national figure (81.4 per cent compared to 56.8 per cent nationally). In addition, the percentage of students gaining A*-A is almost double the national figure (27.4 per cent compared to 15.2 per cent nationally).

Residual

Overall, the department had a residual of 0.14. Disappointingly, this represents a fall on last year's residual of 0.47. Five out of the nine sets maintained positive residuals, including the lower ability sets 6, 7 and 8. A positive residual was demonstrated by 28.3 per cent of the results (compared to 50.8 per cent in 2008), however 36 students had a negative residual. It must be noted that 26 of these 36 students were in Band A of the year group.

Positives in Maths:

Issues in Maths:

Priorities for next year:

Stage 3 – Read the English Department's analysis then answer the questions

English Department exemplar data analysis:
Observations: English Language

- There has been a decrease in the number of students achieving A*s (18 this year and 23 last year).

- As a percentage, 36.8 per cent of entries achieved an A* or A grade (36 per cent).

- Of those pupils entered for the higher tier,53 per cent achieved an A* or A and 90.8 per cent achieved a grade A*-B.

- There has been a pleasing decrease in the number of students achieving a grade E (6 this year and 14 last year).

- Out of a cohort of 204,36 students did not achieve a grade C or above.

- This year we seemed to be less cautious in our tier of entries and 141 students entered the higher tier (this was 119 last year). This figure represents 69 per cent of the cohort.

- Of the 63 students entered for the foundation tier, 28 achieved a grade C.

- Of the students entered for the higher tier, 99.3 per cent achieved a grade A*-C, accounting for one student achieving a grade D. This is disappointing.

- The overall department residual is positive and a pleasing increase from last year.

- Individual residuals differ. All groups apart from Set 8 have positive residuals. Upper band sets have particularly commendable positive residuals.

- An unprecedented number of students (135) achieved at least one grade better in English Language than in English Literature (38 last year).

- In a complete reversal from 2008, only three students achieved better in Literature (27 last year).

- Again, in a reversal to last year, only 55 students achieved the same in both subjects (last year this was 118).

Observations: English Literature

- There has been a decrease in the number of students achieving A* (five this year and eight last year).

- There has been a dip in the number of students achieving A (43 this year and 55 last year).

- A disappointing 27 per cent achieved A* and A (37 per cent last year).

- Of the students entered for the higher tier, 98.6 per cent achieved A*-C.

- A consistent number of Cs were achieved in the foundation tier (12 out of 38). However, as already noted we did not enter all lower band students this year. In 2010, Set 7 and 8 (the bottom two sets) have not studied Literature and therefore will not be entered.

Priorities for next year

- A rigorous analysis of returned scripts is required, particularly the C grades on the foundation tier.

- All department members are to use AQA Enhanced Exam Analysis to do question level analysis to inform teaching for the current Year 11. A definite focus appears to be on improving students' ability to analyse language in non-fiction texts.

- Create a coherent list of students to target for study support and to be tracked and monitored by the HoD – in Sets 6 and 7 – students who have achieved a Level 5 or above in SATs but who have only achieved a grade E or a low D in End of Year 10 exams. Liaise with the Head Teacher and Director of Pupil Progress to establish which students need to achieve a grade C in English and Maths GCSE. These students need a structured intervention programme to be in place throughout the coming year, with regular reviews as to the progress of key groups of pupils.

- Teacher 2 is to support these students through targeted study support, in liaison with the Director of Pupil Progress. English will use the slack in the staff timetable to carry out meaningful intervention.

- Provide extra coaching for weaker students entered for higher tier. Ensure that they have the opportunity to see every past paper so that they are confident of question styles and paper format.

- Devise strategies for better attendance at study support: prizes for best attendance, sweets, fruit.

- Create a rota of Saturday Study Support for the targeted students in the lead up to exams.

- All teachers are to teach new Schemes of Work (SoW) on Reading in Paper 1 and Literature poetry to ensure consistency in approach and provision. The HoD and 2i/c are to monitor and evaluate the teaching of these SoW through walk-throughs and lesson observation.

- Continue improvements in the quality and rigour of teaching poetry in English paper 2. Ensure students are given a formal mock exam in this paper in March of 2010. Ensure that students are able to compare effectively and can comment on technique and not just content.

- Teach AS skills to higher tier pupils to ensure they improve their ability to critically analyse *poetry* texts and increase the number of students achieving A* for Literature. Use AS Literature scripts in lessons.

- The HoD is to continue to track and monitor coursework grades from the start of Year 10, through half term checks. All teachers are to use a coursework cover sheet from the beginning of Year 10. Have regular meetings with Year 11 teachers to ensure that students coursework folders meet *at least* minimum target grades.

- More lower band students are to be entered for the higher tier exam at Christmas to provide practice and evidence of capabilities.

- Continue to improve and advertise the resources available to students on the MLE.

Strengths/positives of this analysis:

Weaknesses/improvements you could make:

What five strategies does every teacher in the English Department need to do next year?

Section 3: Modelling lifelong learning

How can schools model learning?

No one is born an expert teacher and teaching is not a 'calling' or a raison d'être; it is a profession with professional standards and expectations. It should be every teacher's dream to be an expert at their job. Expertise is a hard thing to come by and one lifetime is generally acknowledged to not be enough to develop fully the craft of teaching. There is also, as Hattie so clearly points out, a difference between being an expert and simply being experienced. Doing the same thing for 20 years does not make you an expert on it.

As teachers we are here to model the behaviour, particularly the learning behaviour, which we expect from our pupils. 'In our school everyone is a learner' is the mantra of great schools. We cannot be good educators if we are not curious, keen, resilient and happy learners. We never 'arrive' as teachers; we are always striving to find out more, try new things, refine and improve our lessons. For this reason you must place staff learning and training at the heart of your school.

So, everyone involved in educating others should have a continual focus on educating themselves as well. There is a very clear way to achieve this and that is in using lesson observations as a developmental tool.

Lesson observation as a developmental tool

Observing lessons is perhaps the most powerful tool for improving our craft. One lifetime is not enough to fully master teaching and so by observing and being observed we can accelerate our own progress and therefore the progress of our pupils.

Lesson observation – observing others and being observed yourself – is the best training you can ever have. This is the purpose of lesson observation – to learn from one another. It is not a top-down, performance management tool. It is not about 'checking up' on each other. It is not something schools do to satisfy external interests. Being observed is an entitlement of professional development, not an imposition from senior management. The best schools have an approach to lesson observation schedule which is non-hierarchical; all teachers should be willing to be observed and take feedback.

The following pages look at how to use lesson observation as a whole-school improvement tool and as a tool to sharpen-up departmental practice and keep the focus on learning. It really is a simple approach and one that is hugely effective in raising standards. The key driver for this to be successful though is getting 100 per cent buy-in from all staff – *lesson observation is a training aid.* This is a cultural issue for all schools and means moving way beyond the idea that teachers only need to be observed three times a year – watching, analysing, copying, modifying are all crucial tools for improvement and develop a more reflective profession.

If lesson observation is done properly, then every time you observe or are observed your teaching should improve. The approach outlined below only works if all teachers are trained in how to observe and judge lessons using the Ofsted criteria. In our experience this can be achieved in one day's full INSET which all staff participate in, and then follow-up co-observations to standardize judgements and develop confidence in less experienced staff.

Whole-school improvement through observation:

i. Lesson observations should not be seen as a judgemental or summative activity. The primary role is to enable all teachers to get better, to reflect on current practice and to inform/shape next practice. Imagine what the quality of medical practice would be like if doctors could not learn from observing their more expert peers or learn from sitting in on clinics and surgery. Observing and copying are crucial features of a successful learning community and teachers need to embrace this.

ii. The focus of the lesson observation is not on the teacher but on the pupils – *what are they saying and doing that indicates what their current level of understanding is and how can that be used to inform future planning?* This means planning at both a classroom and whole-school level.

iii. If lesson observation is to become transformative then all schools need to make use of lesson observation rooms – rooms with .cameras and microphones installed in them to allow recording and real-time observations. These are central to developing a consistent approach in all classrooms.

iv. Using lesson observations effectively requires total buy-in and commitment from all teaching staff. It has to be seen as an entitlement to help you get better rather than a summative judgement to put you into a category. It is also crucial that no one sees their role as 'checking up' on someone else. Everyone learns from everyone and regardless of how long you have been in the profession or how good the students think you are; you can always get better – as Hattie clearly points out, there is a distinct difference between expertise and experience and the one does not necessary follow the other.

v. If observation is going to be developmental then there needs to be a weekly lesson observation schedule that is published and shared. This schedule needs to follow the termly or half-termly staff development focus so that teachers are watching each other with that focus. Feedback then informs where each teacher currently is and what they need to do to keep improving. It is not just for the SLT to decide on the schedule but every teacher should have the opportunity both to request who they would like to observe and with what focus and who they would like to come and observe them and with what focus.

vi. As well as individual teachers, all departments should use the lesson observation rooms once every half term. They should follow the format outlined below.

As you can see, effective lesson observation requires a cultural shift, not just within a school but within a profession as a whole. Whilst it is not the purpose of this book to take a political stance, we cannot abide by a system that claims to be interested in education, learning and lifelong development yet fails to apply those principles to itself.

Departmental improvement through observation:

This should be done a minimum of once every half term and should follow the steps below:

i. Departments and teams should jointly plan a lesson that is to be taught by one member of the team.

ii. The rest of the team then all observe the lesson – either via live feed into another room or afterwards on DVD.

iii. The focus of the observation is on pupil progress and each observer completes a separate copy of the observation proforma on page 349.

iv. These lessons are not graded and are not used for any Performance Management activities.

v. The team then gets together afterwards for a 60-minute debrief activity.

vi. The focus of the debrief is not on the procedures of the teacher but on what the students were thinking and doing:

- *Did planning start from what students could currently do?*

- *Was learning 'visible'?*

- *Was progress made in thinking?*

- *Could the students connect their new learning to previous learning?*

- *What student miscues did you pick up on that would need to be addressed in the next lesson?*

- *Were the language demands of the topic catered for?*

- *How was classroom discussion used?*

- *Were the outcomes of the lesson met?*

- *How do you know this? What could you see, hear, read?*

- *What might need to be changed in order to change the way the pupils were thinking?*

- *How would we amend the plan if we were to teach this lesson again?*

- *What would you plan to teach next given the end results of this lesson?*

Talking about lesson observations

As crucial as observing lessons is talking about what was observed afterwards. Earlier on in the book we looked at two different teacher practices that were embedded through observation – mindsets and talking. The most crucial parts of those training activities were the feedback sessions that came afterwards.

The way we give feedback and talk about learning has a real impact on the value of the entire process. To that end the following guidelines are useful.

Before the observation:

- Remember that this is a formative and not a summative process.

- Remember that both parties are there to learn and improve.

- Make sure both parties are fully aware of the focus of the observation – this will be written on the weekly observation schedule.

- Make sure all the required data and info is present: seating plan, student current performance data, lesson plan, context of lesson.

- Do not be late and do not forget to have a lesson observation form with you.

During the observation:

- Remember that this is a formative and not a summative process.

- Remember that both parties are there to learn and improve.

- Do not feel that you have to sit in your seat: move around, talk to pupils, listen to them.

- Even better, join in with the activities.

- Make sure that the focus of the observation is always at the forefront.

- However, do not disrupt the learning – the pupils and teacher should forget you are there. Remove any ego from the situation; you are not there to 'check up' on Teacher ... and the pupils should not think this.

- Do not focus on what the teacher is doing: observe and reflect on what and how the pupils are learning.

After the observation:

- Remember that this is a formative and not a summative process.

- Remember that both parties are there to learn and improve.

- Set a time and place to feedback – not more than 48 hours after the lesson (ideally 24).

- Before the meeting, make sure that the observer has completed all parts of the required observation sheet.

- Before the meeting, make sure that the observee has completed the reflection grid at the bottom of the lesson plan.

During the feedback meeting:

- The observer should start off by asking the following questions:
  - *How do you feel the lesson went?*
  - *What did you feel went well?*
  - *What would you do differently next time?*

- ○ *What student miscues did you pick up on that would need to be addressed in the next lesson?*

- ○ *Were the outcomes of the lesson met?*

- ○ *How do you know this? What could you see, hear, read?*

- ○ *What might need to be changed in order to change the way the pupils were thinking?*

- ○ *What would you plan to teach next given the end results of this lesson?*

- Once the teacher who delivered the lesson has reflected aloud on the lesson and the focus of the observation, the observer can explain their thoughts. These must be focused on the point of the observation though and be developmental.

- If necessary, set a time and place for a follow-up observation and focus. It is wise to set a follow-up observation two weeks after the first observation with the focus being to look at the developmental points discussed and whether they have been applied.

- Be sure to let the staff member in charge of the weekly observation rota know.

Giving good feedback[4]

Giving good feedback can sometimes be a daunting process but it is vital that you are honest, precise and developmental if the observation process is going to have the desired impact.

- **Focus**: Focus on what you see not what you believe, describe it and do not make judgements (e.g 'You raised your voice' not 'You were angry'). Bad feedback is when someone's behaviour has already been interpreted and judged by the person giving the feedback – maybe wrongly. Being objective allows the receiver to receive it, internalize it and learn from it as part of a continuous behavioural learning process.

- **Evidence**: Refer to specific examples in the lesson and have examples. Giving evidence of what has been seen, helps people decide what to do about it.

- **Encourage**: Recognize and praise good performance, be supportive not threatening so think about how your feedback comes across (e.g. 'I need to have a word with you about that lesson you did the other day' versus 'I thought your lesson was great – if you like, I have a few thoughts on making it even better for next time'. The first way sounds ominous, the second starts positively and then offers an opportunity to discuss improvement. People will take criticism better if they have received praise.

- **Developmental**: It is really important that people do learn from feedback because if everything is great they are not developing, therefore it is important to also give people feedback on things they can improve. Always position developmental feedback in a positive way (e.g. 'Your performance would be even better if you did X', 'Your students would make even greater progress if...'

- **Be specific**: Be clear about what you are wanting to talk about, do not beat around the bush, speak plainly and clearly and check whether the individual has understood.

LESSON OBSERVATION SHEET[5]

Teacher:	**Observer:**	**Set:**	**Year:**

Lesson: 1 2 3 4 5 6   **Class & Room**

Number Present
Number on Roll

Focus of Observation:

Date:

Exercise books/ICT/Technology work/Art work   **Checked**   ☐

Quality of the lesson plan:

- Is the plan time phased?

- Are the lesson objectives clear?

- Is the plenary planned to consolidate understanding?

- Is the plan linked to a current assessment of pupils' prior learning?

- Are differentiated approaches evident, so that it consolidates, builds upon and extends learning for all pupils?

Current Academy focus: The talk-based classroom (Half-termly focus and training plan)

i.   **The structure of the activities – are they truly collaborative?**

ii. **The type of language demand the observed activities make:**

iii. **How is the pupils' language extended at each stage of this lesson?**

LESSON OBSERVATION FEEDBACK

Start of the Lesson – connection phase

- *Was it a prompt start – was the DO NOW in place?*

- *Is the seating plan being used?*

- *Are objectives and outcomes clearly defined for pupils and links made to prior learning?*

- *Was the BIG picture re-visited?*

Main body of the Lesson – activation phase

- *Is the conceptual framework clear?*

- *Has the new information to be presented been turned into a problem to be solved?*

- *Is teacher exposition short? Is the input punctuated with questions?*

- *Do students have the language to access the thinking?*

- *Are pupils working on their own or with others?* Focus on what students are *learning*, not what they are doing.

Main body of the Lesson – demonstration phase

- *What variety of tasks are the pupils undertaking?*

- *Are there opportunities for self and peer monitoring?*

- *How are pupils developing/demonstrating their understanding? Is it application or acquisition?*

- *How is this understanding being assessed – by the teacher and by the students?*

Plenary – consolidation phase

- *Does the plenary recall the lesson objectives and reflect on how pupils learnt?*

- *Do the pupils demonstrate understanding?*

- *Are the pupils required to comment upon their learning?*

- *Do pupils reflect/comment on how this learning connects with previous learning?*

LESSON OBSERVATION FEEDBACK

Areas of Strength: WWW – what went well

Areas for development: EBI – even better if

Overall Quality of Learning (progress made in lesson must be commented on)

Whole class, Individuals, G&T, School Action, School Action+, Statemented, EAL

Evaluation of the Quality of Learning

Outstanding	Good	Requires Improvement	Inadequate
1	2	3	4

Please refer to the Ofsted evaluation criteria on the back of this form
Circle your evaluation of the lesson 1-4.

What to do with all the observation data

Again, as with data on student progression, data created from lesson observations is only useful if it can be used to better develop teachers and deepen students' learning. By data we do not mean numbers or grades but observations about current strengths and weaknesses of individual teachers and departments.

So, to make this happen the data should be used in the following ways:

i. **Data should be used to inform the weekly lesson observation rota** – who should observe whom and with what focus? This needs to be far more than just matching up a Grade 1 Outstanding teacher with a Grade 3 Satisfactory, etc. The observation rota must work at a more detailed level and there needs to be a knowledge of the strengths and weaknesses of all teachers – after all we all have strengths and weaknesses and performance is not a secret. See below for an example of the types of information useful in pairing up teachers on the rota.

ii. **Data should be used to evaluate the impact of the half-termly training schedule** – is the training improving progression for students? If not, change it.

iii. **Data should be used to inform what future training needs are** – what do staff need to develop next to help students progress, what training needs to be re-visited?

iv. **Data should be used to help individual teachers** – just as with our students, progress as a teacher is not linear and we do not all get better at the same things at the same time. To this end observation data should be used to help co-construct mentoring or teacher development programmes for individual teachers or groups of teachers that need additional support.

v. **Data should be used to help individual teachers self-reflect** – the lesson observation data should be used to enable a teacher to choose a self-reflection observation in one of the observation rooms. The focus for this observation should be the weaknesses identified in earlier observations. The long-term aim of any observation programme is to create a team of teachers so in tune with their teaching and their students that they are constantly choosing self-reflection to help tweak their practice based on feedback from students and other teachers.

vi. **Data should be used to facilitate effective coaching** – a coaching programme should be established to help further grow this developmental mindset amongst staff. Whilst it is beyond the focus of this book to outline an approach to coaching, it is our belief that the lesson observation data should be used in coaching sessions to help inform reflection and observation foci.

The grids on the following pages outline one way of capturing and making use of all of this data. Look through the grids and then complete the training activity that follows.

Day	Period	Room	Observer 1	Observer 2	Teacher being observed	Focus:	Cover required?
Tuesday	P2 (a)					Pupil progress	N
Tuesday	P.4 (a)					NQT	N
Tuesday	P.4 (a)					Pupil progress	Y
Tuesday	P.5 (a)					Pupil progress	N
Tuesday	P. 6 (b)					Co-observation	N
Wednesday	P.3 (a)					Pupil progress	N
Wednesday	P.3 (b)					Pupil progress	N
Thursday	P.2 (a)					Talk-based classroom	N
Thursday	P. 3(a)					Pupil progress	N
Thursday	P. 4(a)					Talk-based classroom	N
Thursday	P.5 (a)					Pupil progress	N
Friday	P.3 (a)					Pupil progress	N

i. **First 30 minutes**: the main focus in the first 30 minutes is on our activation phase:

- *How is the learning set-up?*

- *Is it teacher-led?*

- *Are students aware of what they are learning and why?*

- *Have connections been made to prior learning?*

ii. **Last 30 minutes**: the main focus in the last 30 minutes is on the demonstration phase:

- *How are pupils demonstrating understanding?*

- *How do you know that progress has been made?*

- *How are pupils connecting the new learning back to the BIG picture/Fertile Question?*

- *Are pupils commenting on how they have learnt?*

STAFF DEVELOPMENT NEEDS (BASED ON A SIX WEEK OBSERVATION CYCLE)
DATE: XXXXXXX

Member of staff	Strengths	Areas to develop
1	• Relationships with students • Revisiting to check for understanding • Clear use of routines • Excellent activation phase – information as a problem to be solved	• Transition between activities • Teacher-led demonstration phase • 100% compliance[6] – some shouting out • Timings at start – instant engagement missing
2	• Use of everyday examples to explain scientific concepts • Connections with prior learning • Dictagloss activity to activate thinking	• Questioning still IRF at times • Demonstration phase – didn't fully assess understanding
3	• Use of Fronter as an independent learning resource • Excellent classroom management – non-invasive	• Modelling using IWB – thinking too abstract at times for students to grasp • Deployment of additional adults as a learning resource
4	• Use of additional adults to assist • Timings tight and clear • 100% compliance visible and non-verbal gestures used and understood	• Timings – don't squeeze the plenary
5	• Links to literacy through debating and real-world science • Connections to prior learning • Pace – relentless focus on knowledge and scientific understanding	• 100% – could be less invasive • Debating – could be more skillfully deployed and peer-assessed
6	• Excellent use of visible compliance • Plans for misconceptions and deals with effectively • Checking for understanding throughout lesson	• Timings – some students lose focus as end of activity drags a little

7	• Relationship with students • Use of resources to engage and enthuse	• Timings – tighter at beginning • Activation phase – too teacher-led • No checking for understanding before moving on – some left behind
8	• Manner and relationship with students • Good use of resources • Lesson planning in chunks to scaffold student thinking	• Pace and timings – need to be tighter • Questioning – too teacher-led – IRF model being used
9	• Use of classroom display to model thinking and drafting process • Good rapport with students • Use of pupils to feedback learning • Pupil evaluation tools to self-assess	• Use of Fronter to support independent learning • More review of pupil work as an ongoing process • Extension work that stretches and challenges • Extra access for some students
10	• Excellent use of students to demonstrate activities and model success • Excellent use of praise	• Some left with nothing to do whilst others finish off work • Deployment of additional adults not explicit enough to have deep impact
11	• Planning – clear connection between different lesson phases • Relentless focus on standards • Great atmosphere and relationships	• Use of visualizer • Develop 100% techniques with students to ensure all students listen
12	• Pace and pitching of tasks • High standards for spoken answers • Resources designed to scaffold progress without taking away the thinking process	• 100% compliance – some calling out, etc. • More paired or group work that is truly collaborative • Model compliance through folded arms, etc.

TRAINING ACTIVITY

Using observation as a developmental tool

Look at the staff strengths and weaknesses on the pages above. Using the weekly observation rota as an example, create a lesson observation rota based on the info above to help improve Teaching and Learning at the school.

You can build the observations into one or two weeks so that it is manageable. If you are feeling really keen you can map out a six week observation programme so that the learning is embedded.

Remember, you need to think about the why as well as the who: who will observe whom, what will the focus be, will there be a follow-up observation two weeks later?

This is really just the start of using observations to improve practice. The outstanding school will grow lesson observation so that it becomes part of their DNA and self and peer review is as common for teachers as it is for students.

Example of how to capture lesson observation data

Observations for: Sum2

Focus 1 >	100%
Focus 2 >	Pupil progress
Focus 3 >	

Totals:

	Current >		Graded>				Year-To-Date	To-Date>		Graded>					
Total >	2	13	1	8	5	0		42	143	9	100	33	10	143	160
% Outstanding >	25%							42%							
% Good or above >	88%							89%							
% Satisfactory or above >	100%							98%							

Initials	Member of staff	Outstanding	Good	Satisfactory	Inadequate	Self-reflection (ungraded)	Mentoring programme	Outstanding	Good	Satisfactory	Inadequate	Self-reflection (ungraded)	Mentoring programme	Total Year-to-Date Has Been observed	Total Year-to-Date Has observe
Grade>		1	2	3	4	S	M	1	2	3	4	S	M	M	M
		1						4	2			3	1	10	13
		1						2	7			3		12	23
			2			1		3	3	1		2		9	24
			1			1		2	4			3		9	14
								4	1			2	1	8	9
								1	3			1		5	11
			1					5	2			2		9	4
									5	1			2	6	6
						1		1	2				1	5	4
									4			1	1	6	3
				1				3				3	1	7	5
										5	2	3	2	12	3
			1						2	2		2		7	10
								1	2	2		2	1	6	6
								2	1					5	5
								5				1		7	3
								2	3					5	2
						1		2	2			2		6	2
								3	2			3		8	4
															6

Termly and annual training: Using observations to embed change

To be fully effective lesson observations should be linked to a termly and annual training plan for all staff – otherwise the observation schedule lacks focus and can drift into a punitive or subjective experience. Teaching does not improve simply by doing more of it, teachers need time and space to reflect on the craft, learn new ways of doing things, try them out, review them, adapt them and create their own ways of doing things.

To facilitate this, there needs to be a clear training plan for the year mapped against clear targets and outcomes. Often school-based training is not mapped out far in advance and linked to the school's overall development plan. Imagine you picked a UK school at random, visited it and asked a member of the SLT, 'What is the focus of your next INSET day?' How many would be able to tell you straight away? And how many would be able to say, 'The focus is X, it links to our overall model of teaching and learning in the following ways, it is part of our school improvement plan, and has been informed by recent findings from the lesson observation schedule'.

The annual training plan has to be part of a longer-term plan otherwise it becomes too *adhoc* and the whole-school model will never be implemented. The termly training plan then focuses on one of the desired outcomes of the annual plan and the lesson observation cycle is used to evaluate the impact of the training on teacher practices – simple.

This has to be non-negotiable – staff training is not an optional extra, it is a core part of being a professional.

Put another way:

Teachers will be crucial in shaping the desirable futures for teaching and learning. This will require conceptualizing teaching as the learning profession in which teachers engage in problem identification, problem solving, analysis and research within the context of the classroom. This learning needs to be focused on:

- Professional needs of the teacher.

- Improved learning opportunities and outcomes for all students.

- School improvement needs and goals of the school.

This requires teachers to learn from, with and on behalf of each other through networked communities of learning, thus building professional knowledge and capacity of individuals, schools and systems.[7]

The starting point for this is to create a school culture that has staff training at its core. Over time this training provision can be teacher-led in all senses of the word, but initial buy-in and successful implementation will be crucial for this change to manifest.

Section 4: Using Line Management systems to maintain the focus on learning

Line Management in schools has many purposes, and we will not attempt to cover them all here. What we are interested in in this section is how Line Management can provide a professional dialogue around teaching, curriculum and assessment that will help reinforce the whole-school approach. We offer possible systems and structures which are a means to this end. It should be noted here that you cannot have an outstanding school without outstanding Middle Leaders – they are the engine room of the school and need clear lines of accountability as well as the freedom to take control. What they do not need is lots of initiatives to run; what they do need is a clear view of the strategic vision and direction of the school and the tools to interpret this and cascade down to their teachers – whilst holding to account both those above and below them.

Guidance for SLTs – Line Management frameworks

You may have a large and changing SLT. The term 'Line Management' will mean different things to them (or perhaps not even mean that much). Providing checklists to help them structure their weekly meetings with curriculum leaders will help them and provide consistency. An example from Ark Academy of a checklist produced for all SLTs and HoDs is below (the document works month by month – we have just included September here).

	Line Manager	Head of Department
Sept	**T&L:** • Discuss lesson plans for the first few weeks – co-planning, differentiation etc. • Induction of new staff into subject specific routines – routines for practical work / discussion / HW etc. • What is obs plan for first 4 weeks? Who is seeing who and why? • Set date for Sept joint learning walk with HoD. • Review any new departmental policies and training – is department time in these first few weeks building on general staff induction in T&L? Is there a consistent message re teaching? • Check new Fronter resources. **Assessment / Curriculum:** • What does analysis of last year's exam results show? Implications for: pupil groupings, Aut 1 SoW, interventions... • Target setting for the New Year? How many making 2 or 3 sub-levels? What % at attainment thresholds? • Share FQs for Autumn term and beyond – can guidance from T&L handbook be of help in refining FQs?	**T&L:** • Lesson planning – get co-planning up and running? Is there consistency between classrooms AND staff owning their own plans? Ensure enough time is being allowed for the creative discussion about lessons. • Use of department's video archive for department training in the first few weeks. • Continue to drip feed ideas to new staff on the four part lesson through co-planning. • Finalising co-teaching deployment. • Lesson observations for the first half term – what is the overarching plan? • Share departmental handbooks, training materials and initial SoW with LM for discussion. • Update Fronter. • The minutiae – ensure all staff have class lists with contextual data, seating plans, access to all resources etc. **Assessment / Curriculum:** • Complete exam analysis and submit to Principal by 10th September. • Review targets for every student in every year – consult with team members & identify any exceptions to general target setting formula. Focus particularly on students who have made unsatisfactory progress in the previous year(s). What is their target, and what are planned interventions for first half term? • Review FQs from previous years through co-planning and adjust / improve.

- Discuss sequence of assessments in each year. What improvements are being made to last year's plans? What are new plans for Y9?

Leadership & Management:
- Set deadline for performance review.
- Do new staff understand probation period? Discuss NQTs – mentors, observations etc – all in place?
- How are other teachers with responsibilities in dept adapting if new to this role? Any implications for coaching?

Behaviour & Ethos:
- Are all staff clear on behaviour systems?
- Department rewards system in place?

Enrichment:
- Review ENR for Autumn term – what is being offered, and what plan is in place for each activity. Check any external providers have been organized.
- Early plans for dept trips? Dates in calendar asap.

- Engage with whole-school assessment calendar and map department assessments across the year – where are crunch points? Raise any issues with assessment lead now.
- Who is producing revision materials for upcoming assessments, and how are they being shared with students? New displays of students work etc?

Leadership & Management:
- Set deadline for performance review.
- Ensure NQT induction meetings are scheduled and NQTs have absorbed handbook.
- Prepare for performance review with LM and gather portfolio materials.
- Book performance reviews with members of your team.
- Do new staff understand probation period?
- How are other teachers with responsibilities in dept adapting? Any implications for coaching?

Behaviour & ethos:
- Communicate expectations for behaviour to new staff and what to do to reward and sanctions. Emphasise 3:1 ratio.
- Has department relocation timetable been written?
- Department rewards system in place? Does it promote learner profile?

Enrichment:
- Write overviews for each ENR activity and book any externals with XXX. Ditto resources.
- Early plans for trips?

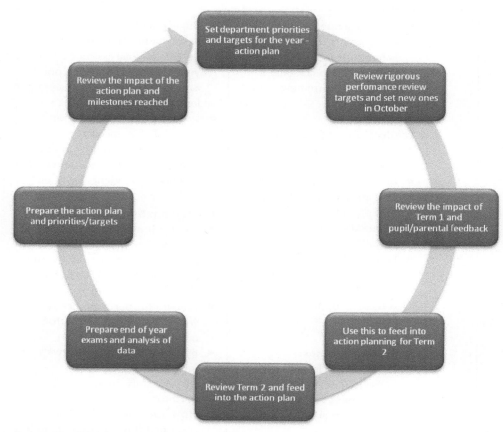

Figure 5.1 The rhythm of an outstanding department

Departmental self-evaluation

SEFs, SIPs and all the rest – schools have many different internal documents that managers write and update each year, evaluating their current practice and planning for the coming 12 months. Our view is that self-evaluation at department level should be focused principally on the quality of teaching (and how to develop it), the curriculum (and how to improve it), and student outcomes (and how to increase them). Asking HoDs to write long documents that are submitted to governors and then ignored for the next 12 months is not the answer – any evaluations and plans they write should be live documents, which are referenced in meetings, read and re-read by teachers. The story of one (successful) school where the Head of RE wrote in his Department Improvement Plan for 12 years straight that he was planning on purchasing a lion and a cage for his office, but was never detected (because nobody ever read the plans), is revealing of some current practice. We have offered below some templates for self-evaluation that may be of help (again these come from Ark Academy documents):

Management questions to probe and clarify

Below are some questions a line manager could use to stimulate useful discussions about teaching, curriculum and assessment with the subject leader as part of their monthly review.

Review of lesson observations carried out:

- What areas of good practice are there to share at academy level?

- How has the department made use of video? Are teachers recording themselves and watching lessons back? Is the department developing an archive of training films for inducting new staff?

- Have lesson observations highlighted any issues and what is being done to address them before the next review?

- Has the department co-planned and then observed a lesson?

- Have members of the department observed outside their own area/ academy?

Review of SoWs and progression maps:

- Is there a three-year and five-year progression map for academic and language progression? Has it been amended since the last review?

- Are pupils aware of the BIG picture of the term/year/Key Stage? (Do they know why they are studying what they are studying and how it all fits together?)

- Have SoWs been reviewed for the term?

- Have SoWs been reviewed for the year?

- How well do SoWs fit together, do they plan for content and language progression?

- Are assessments designed to develop pupils for national exams?

- Are assessments 'university-focused'?

- Do SoWs require amendment to ensure a closer fit with student needs?

- Does student progress data suggest medium-term and/or long-term plans need amending?

Review of student data:

- What is the BIG picture of progress against pupil targets?

- Are all members of the department aware of the progress of individual pupils in their classes?

- Are current tracking spreadsheets up to date?

- Are any groups of pupils underachieving – in individual classes or across the department/area?

  ○ G&T sub-questions:
    - Are G&T pupils on track to make three sub-levels of progress for the year?
    - Are some teachers securing greater G&T progress than others within the department/area?
    - Are there any teacher/department nominations for addition/ removal from G&T/Ghost register?
    - Are there any pupils who require short-term interventions?

  ○ EAL sub-questions:
    - Are EAL pupils on track to make required levels of progress?
    - Are some teachers securing greater EAL progress than others within the department/area?
    - Are there any pupils who require short-term interventions?

  ○ SEN sub-questions:
    - Are students on the Code of Practice on track to make required levels of progress?
    - Are some teachers securing greater SEN progress than others within the department/area?
    - Are teachers engaging with SEN needs and planning accordingly?
    - Are there any pupils who require short-term interventions?

  ○ FSM sub-questions:
    - Are FSM pupils on track to make required levels of progress?

- – Are some teachers securing greater progress than others within the department/area?
- – Are there any pupils who require short-term interventions?

- What interventions are taking place: setting arrangements, homework club, booster classes, etc.?

- What needs to be carried out/amended/built in based on the current termly assessment to ensure greater progression next academic year? For the current cohort as they progress into the next year, what do they need to be taught again in a different way before starting a new content area (the current Year 8 moving up into Year 9); and for a new cohort starting that year next September, how do SoWs need to be changed/re-ordered to ensure greater progression (the current Year 7 becoming Year 8)?

Review of department action plan:

- What should stay?

- What needs to be amended?

- What targets have been met?

- What training needs are there for staff?

- Where will we be by the end of the year?

Review of pupil and/or parent surveys (annual):

- What is going well?

- What needs further attention?

	Current practice that is working well	Priorities for development
The quality of Teaching and Learning:		
Schemes of Work and progression maps: (including opportunities outside the classroom)		
Student progress and target setting: (based on assessment data)		
Current development plan:		
Views of stakeholders		

EXEMPLAR COMPLETED REVIEW: HISTORY DEPARTMENT REVIEW – JANUARY 2011

	Current practice that is working well	Priorities for development
The quality of Teaching and Learning:	<ul><li>Use of the lesson observation room to improve practice.</li><li>Leadership and management of the department.</li><li>Every lesson revolves around a question that relates to the Fertile Question – really helping the students to orientate themselves.</li><li>Whole game of History is explicit and engaging the students.</li></ul>	<ul><li>Use of Fronter to enable students to work independently.</li><li>Use of Thinking and Learning Centre (TLC) to help develop reading in History.</li><li>Some students are still chronologically lost.</li><li>'Walking backwards into tomorrow' – some students not orientated in time and space so losing the conceptual thinking.</li></ul>
Schemes of Work and progression maps: (including opportunities outside the classroom)	<ul><li>Fertile Questions are working well to keep planning tight and focused on core concepts.</li><li>William SoW worked well in terms of key concept of diversity.</li><li>Maiden Castle worked well in terms of engaging students with the discipline of evidential understanding and asking questions like a historian.</li></ul>	<ul><li>William SoW could have been more closely linked to Romans and concept of diversity looked at more closely = continuity across time.</li><li>Use of formative assessment is not as tight as it could be – this can be addressed in the summer term.</li><li>William assessment as an obituary – too many foci meant that the assessment did not link seamlessly to the Fertile Question. Needs to be changed for next year.</li></ul>

	Current practice that is working well	Priorities for development
Student progress and target setting: (based on assessment data)	• Y band making on average two sub-levels of progress and developing their writing. • A Band making slowest amount of progress. • Average progress across one term = 1.75 sub-levels of progress per student against expected rate of 1.0. • SEN students making identical average progress – SA+ students above average for the rest of the cohort – 2.29 sub-levels. • No gender divide or inequality of attainment. • EAL students making above average progress – 2.11 sub-levels.	• A band students making less progress than desired – 7A1 making average of 1.17 sub-levels a term. • G&T only making 1.35 sub-levels progress a term. Although this is above the expected rate of 1.0 it still needs addressing. Is there enough challenge in the current curriculum offer? • Students currently achieving high levels compared to the rest of the cohort need extending. • Standardization of assessments to ensure robust data.
Current development plan:	• SoWs in place and linked to conceptual understandings. • Marking and assessment helps students know where they are and what they need to do next. • Students making progress against core concepts and beginning to think like historians.	• Students still don't write like a historian – many are writing in a very narrative fashion and tell stories rather than analyse. This is partly due to their 'baggage' from primary school and partly due to the History Department not focusing clearly enough on the unique demands of historical writing. • Find a suitable Head of Department for next year!
Views of stakeholders:	N/A	• Use of Fronter to elicit views of students.

MATHEMATICS EVALUATION OF TEACHING AND LEARNING – AUTUMN TERM 2011

	Current practice that is working well	Priorities for development
The quality of Teaching and Learning:	• Co-planning has ensured consistency in teaching of mathematics – e.g. consistent approach to teaching abstract concepts (like algebraic equations) and supported the development and induction of new staff (see lesson observations, video clippings). • Fertile Questions as a pedagogical approach has been embraced by new Maths teaching staff – with real success. Year 7 and 8 curricula are developing real conceptual understanding (see records from visit of Rodborough School in Surrey, lesson observations, student progress data, Maths Schemes of Work, etc.). • Department emphasizes the relevance of Maths in most lessons – high levels of student engagement (evidence in the number of students participating in House Maths competitions e.g. Gelosia off). • Numeracy progress is being addressed in Year 7 and 8 – through the TimesTables Rock Stars and Gelosia Pop Stars programmes. In the most recent unit, we had 89% 4A+ in Year 8 and 72.5% in Year 7 – one indicator of the positive effect of these initiatives. • Real evidence of learning from staff training being embedded in Maths lessons – e.g. 100% techniques are being used across the department in every lesson. • In formal lesson observations, department teaching has been graded: Outstanding: 46% of lessons; Good or better: 39% of lessons; Satisfactory: 15% of lessons.	• Department to share WWW and EBI from a self-video observation – to learn from each other's good practice, to develop as an observer and to encourage teachers to recognize their own strengths and make the most of them. • Year 9 Fertile Questions to be designed and reviewed. • XXX to complete year one of Teaching Leaders programme and to lead on Year 7 Intervention with Maths Challenge clubs in the final term. • XXX to complete ARK Outstanding Teacher Programme. • XXX to complete Prince's Teaching Institute (PTI) NQT Mathematics specific Training Programme. • XXX to run whole school training on questioning; lead a subject development group at PTI Summer School; lead Mathematics teaching professional development sessions for a Study Group School Network and continue facilitating sessions for Teaching Leaders Programme.

	Current practice that is working well	Priorities for development
Schemes of Work and progression maps: (including opportunities outside the classroom)	• We are improving Year 7 Fertile Questions (units of work) created last year (led by XXX) and co-planning Year 8 Fertile Questions (units of work), led by XXX. Our emphasis is still on teaching key mathematical concepts in an engaging and relevant way. In Year 8 we are also considering carefully how we are building on previous learning and integrating more difficult topics that will prepare students for the GCSE examination (e.g. enlargement). • We maintain an informal dialogue in the staff room and during extra planning meetings, during which we talk about how lessons are going, difficulties students are having grasping particular concepts, highlight any issues with whole groups, behaviour/effort issues with key kids. This dialogue allows us to act on any issues before they become an issue – e.g. getting parents in, coming to observe a piece of someone else's lesson to see them teach enlargement from a centre. • Department team time is limited and only allows us time to co-plan current units of work. Any refinement of Schemes of Work or curriculum planning takes place in the evening after school. All department members have worked extremely hard to make this happen this term. • Maths enrichment sessions (support and extension) have been of a consistently high quality. This is evident in the performance in the ARK Maths Challenge competitions (first place in the Year 8 Competition; fourth place in the Year 10 Competition).	• Planning of Year 9 Fertile Questions and units of work. • Pathways – who is doing early entry GCSE, and when, and how does the curriculum need to support this? • Planning of Maths Challenge Tutors programme – a key intervention in the final term of the year. This will involve co-construction of a Scheme of Work and lesson plans with Maths Challenge Tutors in Year 7 and 8. XXX will oversee.

	Current practice that is working well	Priorities for development
Student progress and target setting: (based on assessment data)	• The majority of students in Year 7 (86%) are on or above target to make three sub-levels of progress this year; Students have on average made 1.47 sub-levels of progress in this half term's unit of work. • The majority of Year 7 classes are doing well, however there are some issues with the progress in 7 Turquoise. • In Year 8, students have only made 0.13 sub-levels of progress this half term on average. • There are clear issues with middle groups 2-5 scoring a secure Level 5 (and in the case of Set 2 a Level 6). • However, students whose baseline was a Level 4 or below are doing particularly well – many in the Turquoise/Yellow group.	• All seating plans are being reshuffled to take account of those underperforming in recent assessments. • All LSA/support staff are being made aware of underperforming students – noted on seating plans. • In cases where classes had an average of negative progress/low progress, teachers have phoned home to parents of key students – highlighting behaviour issues, effort/attitude issues, etc. • Students who are more than two sub-levels below their baseline will redo their test over the holidays/in the first week back in order to score an improved mark. If this does not happen, their parents are contacted immediately. • Sustain and develop teaching of independent revision skills, e.g. creation and use of revision cards. • Discuss with XXX how 7MA-TU can be more intensively supported in lessons/when preparing for assessments.
Current development plan:	• XXX/XXX will review progress towards DDP targets in Line Management meetings. • Six month review for XXX by March 2012 by XXX. • NQT termly review (XXX by XXX). • Broadly on track for ambitious attainment targets in Year 7 – (79% 4a+; Average of three sub-levels progress over the year). • Year 8 need to be monitored closely next term. • Department moderation procedures are robust and are also leading to refinements in SoW, revision for assessments/assessments themselves.	• XXX to lead and manage Improvement Initiative to support 'key kids' in Year 7. • Specialism focus – Primary and Secondary to come together to organize cross school events for World Maths Day. • See development for individual staff members above. • Begin process of recruiting new staff. • Department to host the next ARK Hub day for all Mathematics teachers on 20 February.

	Current practice that is working well	Priorities for development

Views of stakeholders:	• The profile of Maths as a specialist subject is high in the school and students – broadly speaking – enjoy their lessons. This is based on:
	   ○ feedback from a questionnaire at the end of last year relating to Fertile Questions (done for case study);
	   ○ student posts on Fronter have been positive and enthusiastic about Maths;
	   ○ numbers entering House Maths competitions – including students and staff;
	   ○ participation on Numbers Day – including students and staff;
	   ○ feedback from Maths Challenge Programmes and team competitions – including comments from ARK Maths teachers.
		• Case study to be published.
		• Discussion on possible case studies for next year.

Olympic planning	• Maths Challenge enrichment – Year 7 and Year 8 have been completing themed activities linked to Olympic events, e.g. boxing, marathon, relay race and swimming. Our Year 8 Maths Challenge competition team participated in the ARK version of this Olympic themed competition and won first place.	• We will be building all of this year's House Maths competitions around Olympic events, starting with this half term's Marathon Timestable Challenge (in the last week of half term). • There will be three further competitions this year that will be Olympic themed. • We will be working with Primary to create World Maths Day activities that have an Olympic theme also.

AN EXAMS ANALYSIS THAT THE HEAD OF DEPARTMENT COULD COMPLETE AT THE START OF EACH YEAR (EXAMPLE FROM YEAR 7)

Attainment targets	Attainment outcomes	Progress targets	Progress outcomes
X% at Level 5+ Y% at Level 4 Z% at Level 3	X% at Level 5+ Y% at Level 4 Z% at Level 3	X% at 3 sub-levels Y% at 2 sub-levels	X% at 3 sub-levels Y% at 2 sub-levels Z% at 1 sub-level or less

Commentary: How did outcomes compare with targets? How many students reached the 4A threshold? How do different teachers' results compare? How did groups/sub-groups of students perform relative to each other (e.g. gender/band/SEN/FSM/EAL/students arriving below L4)? What possible factors have influenced these results?

Plans: What is the department's planned response to the Year 7 results? Discuss interventions, targeted enrichments, pupil groupings, curriculum, teacher deployment, use of co-teachers, parental engagement, revision strategies, target setting for next year, etc.

Key Underachievers: Who are the 10–15 key students in Year 7 who made unsatisfactory progress that the department will be targeting this year?

TRAINING ACTIVITY

Effective self-review

i.   What can you learn from the above about effective self-review?

ii. Use the above ideas to create a cyclical flow-chart that maps out the 'rhythm of the year' for the school in terms of their evaluation and review schedule.

Case study 6: Middle Leaders as the engine room of the school

The case study below is simply the planning framework for how a school might take the ideas and models discussed above and convert them into an annual review policy for all Middle Leaders. There is some repetition from earlier documents as the case study is written as a Middle Leaders toolkit.

Middle Leaders toolkit: Getting to Good and beyond

Aims:

- to enable Middle Leaders to take ownership of their department;
- to provide a clear framework for developing outstanding teaching in every department;
- to provide a clear framework for interpreting the data and using it to plan;
- to hold all teachers to account for student progress and attainment.

Overview:

- the rhythm of the year – what does an Outstanding department do and when?

Part 1: Weekly operations:

- weekly department meetings and agenda items;
- weekly meeting with your Line Manager.

Part 2: Half-termly operations:

- assessment analysis – target setting, monitoring and formative analysis of student assessments.

Part 3: Termly operations:

- evaluating Teaching and Learning and linking it to student data.

Part 4: Annual operations:

- auditing the department and creating an action plan – overall effectiveness of the department, quality of achievement, quality of teaching, quality of the curriculum, quality of leadership and management of the department.

Overview:

The rhythm of the year – what does an outstanding department do and when?

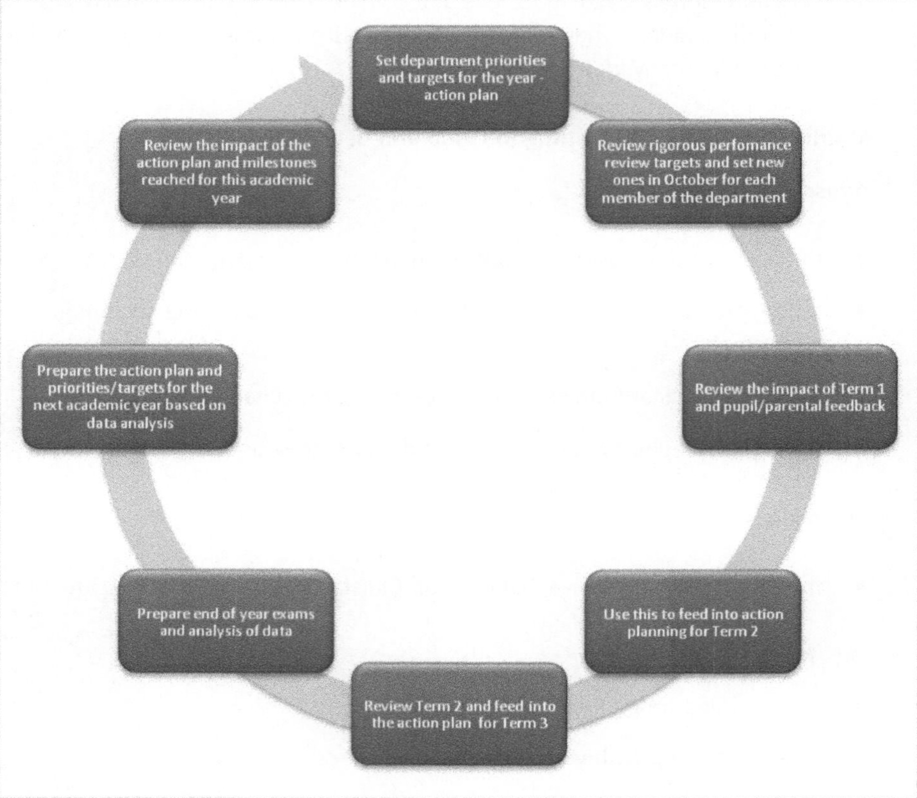

Set department priorities and targets for the year - action plan

Review rigorous perfomance review targets and set new ones in October for each member of the department

Review the impact of Term 1 and pupil/parental feedback

Use this to feed into action planning for Term 2

Review Term 2 and feed into the action plan for Term 3

Prepare end of year exams and analysis of data

Prepare the action plan and priorities/targets for the next academic year based on data analysis

Review the impact of the action plan and milestones reached for this academic year

Figure 5.2   The rhythm of an outstanding department

Part 1: Weekly operations

Weekly department meetings
Department meetings are designed to create space for:

- good practice to be shared;

- student progress to be discussed;

- joint planning to take place;

- reviews of lesson observation data and decisions on new observations;

- action plans for students causing concern;

- new subject knowledge and curriculum innovation to be discussed and reviewed;

- academy strategic items to be disseminated.

Weekly agendas will need to ensure that each of the above points are covered. Line Managers will review weekly agendas and minutes as part of their weekly meetings' schedule.

Weekly meeting with your Line Manager
Weekly Line Management meetings are designed to ensure:

- the department has an unrelenting focus on student achievement;

- the department receives the support it requires;

- the Head of Department shares the agenda for the following Department Meeting with the Line Manager;

- Line Managers can discuss academy strategic planning with Middle Leaders;

- students causing concern are picked up on and interventions put in place swiftly;

- teachers requiring additional support receive this in a timely and targeted fashion.

Weekly agendas will need to ensure that each of the above points are covered.

Part 2: Half-termly operations.

Standardization and moderation of assessments
Every main assessment must be standardized and moderated within each department. Where a department is less than three teachers, external support will be sought to ensure that the data entered onto the tracking system is robust.

Book reviews
Every half term the Head of Department will be required to complete and submit the Academy Evidence Grid on student book analysis with a focus on:

- standards of presentation;

- frequency of marking;

- student responses to marking;

- level of challenge and expectations in the work.

Using data formatively – every assessment cycle
At the end of each six week cycle departments will review student progress against targets: (Example questions below are based on a Spring 1 assessment cycle.)

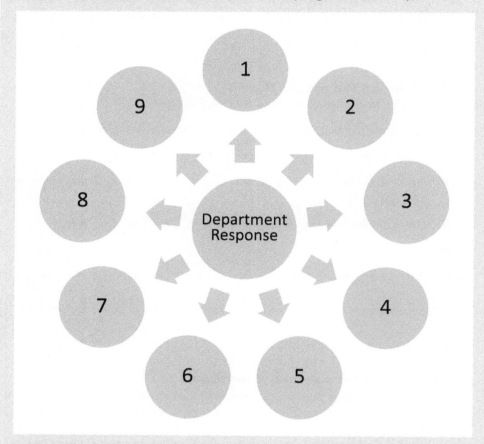

Figure 5.3 Core practices to drive a cycle of continuous improvement

i. Review SoW just gone: what areas of weakness did the assessment show up? How could these areas be better covered next time you teach it? Note EBIs for next year.

ii. Review how students prepared for the assessment: did they take it seriously or could they have revised more thoroughly? What were the homeworks that led up to it? Were exemplars/success criteria shared with students? Were there VLE resources? Who are the key kids not preparing, and how can we improve their performance?

iii. What is the department's strategy to get students revising for Spring 2?

iv. Use the outcomes of assessment to inform this new SoW and lesson planning – what are the biggest gaps in students' understanding and how can we address them through our teaching in Spring 2?

v. Should there be changes to pupil groupings?

vi. Redeployment of Learning Support Assistants (LSAs) and co-teachers to classes that need it most – does the data indicate any need?

vii. Is there a need for parental contact (positive and negative – e.g. reward postcards/ assessments sent home to be redone)?

viii. How can the new ENRs be launched to maximum effect?

ix. Should we introduce review or 'buffer' lessons before Spring 2?

Part 3: Termly operations

Evaluating Teaching and Learning
Subject leaders will carry out a termly review of their department using the questions below.

Review of lesson observations carried out:

- What areas of good practice are there to share at academy level?

- How has the department made use of video? Are teachers recording themselves and watching lessons back? Is the department developing an archive of training films for inducting new staff?

- Have lesson observations highlighted any issues and what is being done to address them before the next review?

- Has the department co-planned and then observed a lesson?

- Have members of the department observed outside their own area/academy?

Review of SoWs and progression maps:

- Is there a three-year and five-year progression map for academic and language progression? Has it been amended since the last review?

- Are pupils aware of the BIG picture of the term/year/Key Stage? (Do they know why they are studying what they are studying and how it all fits together?)

- Have SoWs been reviewed for the term?

- Have SoWs been reviewed for the year?

- How well do SoWs fit together, do they plan for content and language progression?
- Are assessments designed to develop pupils for national exams?
- Are assessments 'university-focused'?
- Do SoWs require amendment to ensure a closer fit with student needs?
- Does student progress data suggest medium-term and/or long-term plans need amending?

Review of student data:

- What is the BIG picture of progress against pupil targets?
- Are all members of the department aware of the progress of individual pupils in their classes?
- Are current tracking spreadsheets up to date?
- Are any groups of pupils underachieving – in individual classes or across the department/area?
  - ○ G&T sub-questions:
    - – Are G&T pupils on track to make three sub-levels of progress for the year?
    - – Are some teachers securing greater G&T progress than others within the department/area?
    - – Are there any teacher/department nominations for addition/removal from G&T/Ghost register?
    - – Are there any pupils who require short-term interventions?
  - ○ EAL sub-questions:
    - – Are EAL pupils on track to make required levels of progress?
    - – Are some teachers securing greater EAL progress than others within the department/area?
    - – Are there any pupils who require short-term interventions?
  - ○ SEN sub-questions:
    - – Are students on the Code of Practice on track to make required levels of progress?

- – Are some teachers securing greater SEN progress than others within the department/area?

- – Are teachers engaging with SEN needs and planning accordingly?

- – Are there any pupils who require short-term interventions?

  o FSM sub-questions:

  - – Are FSM pupils on track to make required levels of progress?

  - – Are some teachers securing greater progress than others within the department/area?

  - – Are there any pupils who require short-term interventions?

- • What interventions are taking place: setting arrangements, homework club, booster classes, etc.?

- • What needs to be carried out/amended/built in based on the current termly assessment to ensure greater progression next academic year? For the current cohort as they progress into the next year, what do they need to be taught again in a different way before starting a new content area (the current Year 8 moving up into Year 9); and for a new cohort starting that year next September, how do SoWs need to be changed/re-ordered to ensure greater progression (the current Year 7 becoming Year 8)?

Review of department action plan:

- • What should stay?

- • What needs to be amended?

- • What targets have been met?

- • What training needs are there for staff?

- • Where will we be by the end of the year?

Review of pupil and/or parent surveys (annual):

- • What is going well?

- • What needs further attention?

To be completed at the end of each termly review prior to the Line Management meeting:

	Current practice that is working well	Priorities for development
The quality of Teaching and Learning:		
Schemes of Work and progression maps: (including opportunities outside the classroom)		
Student progress and target setting: (based on assessment data)		
Current development plan:		
Views of stakeholders		

Exemplar: Mathematics evaluation of Teaching and Learning – Autumn Term

	Current practice that is working well	Priorities for development
The quality of Teaching and Learning:	<ul><li>Co-planning has ensured consistency in teaching of mathematics – e.g. consistent approach to teaching abstract concepts (like algebraic equations) and supported the development and induction of new staff (see lesson observations, video clippings).</li><li>Fertile Questions as a pedagogical approach has been embraced by new Maths teaching staff – with real success. Year 7 and 8 curricula are developing real conceptual understanding (see records from visit of Rodborough School in Surrey, lesson observations, student progress data, Maths Schemes of Work, etc.).</li><li>Department emphasizes the relevance of Maths in most lessons – high levels of student engagement (evidence in the number of students participating in House Maths competitions e.g. Gelosia off).</li><li>Numeracy progress is being addressed in Year 7 and 8 – through the TimesTables Rock Stars and Gelosia Pop Stars programmes. In the most recent unit, we had 89% 4A+ in Year 8 and 72.5% in Year 7 – one indicator of the positive effect of these initiatives.</li><li>Real evidence of learning from staff training being embedded in Maths lessons – e.g. 100% techniques are being used across the department in every lesson.</li></ul>	<ul><li>Department to share WWW and EBI from a self-video observation – to learn from each other's good practice, to develop as an observer and to encourage teachers to recognize their own strengths and make the most of them.</li><li>Year 9 Fertile Questions to be designed and reviewed.</li><li>XXX to complete year one of Teaching Leaders programme and to lead on Year 7 Intervention with Maths Challenge clubs in the final term.</li><li>XXX to complete ARK Outstanding Teacher Programme.</li><li>XXX to complete PTINQT Mathematics specific Training Programme.</li><li>XXX to run whole school training on questioning; lead a subject development group at PTI Summer School; lead Mathematics teaching professional development sessions for a Study Group School Network and continue facilitating sessions for Teaching Leaders Programme.</li></ul>

	Current practice that is working well	Priorities for development
	• In formal lesson observations, department teaching has been graded: Outstanding: 46% of lessons; Good or better: 39% of lessons; Satisfactory: 15% of lessons.	
Schemes of Work and progression maps: (including opportunities outside the classroom)	• We are improving Year 7 Fertile Questions (units of work) created last year (led by XXX) and co-planning Year 8 Fertile Questions (units of work), led by XXX. Our emphasis is still on teaching key mathematical concepts in an engaging and relevant way. In Year 8 we are also considering carefully how we are building on previous learning and integrating more difficult topics that will prepare students for the GCSE examination (e.g. enlargement). • We maintain an informal dialogue in the staff room and during extra planning meetings, during which we talk about how lessons are going, difficulties students are having grasping particular concepts, highlight any issues with whole groups, behaviour/effort issues with key kids. This dialogue allows us to act on any issues before they become an issue e.g. getting parents in, coming to observe a piece of someone else's lesson to see them teach enlargement from a centre.	• Planning of Year 9 Fertile Questions and units of work. • Pathways – who is doing early entry GCSE, and when, and how does the curriculum need to support this? • Planning of Maths Challenge Tutors programme – a key intervention in the final term of the year. This will involve co-construction of a Scheme of Work and lesson plans with Maths Challenge Tutors in Year 7 and 8. XXX will oversee.

	Current practice that is working well	Priorities for development
	• Department team time is limited and only allows us time to co-plan current units of work. Any refinement of Schemes of Work or curriculum planning takes place in the evening after school. All department members have worked extremely hard to make this happen this term. • Maths enrichment sessions (support and extension) have been of a consistently high quality. This is evident in the performance in the ARK Maths Challenge competitions (first place in the Year 8 Competition; fourth place in the Year 10 Competition).	

	Current practice that is working well	Priorities for development
Student progress and target setting: (based on assessment data)	• The majority of students in Year 7 (86%) are on or above target to make three sub-levels of progress this year; Students have on average made 1.47 sub-levels of progress in this half term's unit of work. • The majority of Year 7 classes are doing well, however there are some issues with the progress in 7 Turquoise. • In Year 8, students have only made 0.13 sub-levels of progress this half term on average. • There are clear issues with middle groups 2-5 scoring a secure Level 5 (and in the case of Set 2 a Level 6).	• All seating plans are being reshuffled to take account of those underperforming in recent assessments. • All LSA/support staff are being made aware of underperforming students – noted on seating plans. • In cases where classes had an average of negative progress/ low progress, teachers have phoned home to parents of key students – highlighting behaviour issues, effort/ attitude issues, etc.

	Current practice that is working well	Priorities for development
	• However, students whose baseline was a Level 4 or below are doing particularly well – many in the Turquoise/Yellow group.	• Students who are more than two sub-levels below their baseline will redo their test over the holidays/in the first week back in order to score an improved mark. If this does not happen, their parents are contacted immediately. • Sustain and develop teaching of independent revision skills, e.g. creation and use of revision cards. • Discuss with XXX how 7MA-TU can be more intensively supported in lessons/when preparing for assessments.
Current development plan:	• XXX/XXX will review progress towards DDP targets in Line Management meetings. • Six month review for XXX by March 2012 by XXX. • NQT termly review (XXX by XXX). • Broadly on track for ambitious attainment targets in Year 7 – (79% 4a+; Average of three sub-levels progress over the year). • Year 8 need to be monitored closely next term. • Department moderation procedures are robust and are also leading to refinements in SoW, revision for assessments/assessments themselves.	• XXX to lead and manage Improvement Initiative to support 'key kids' in Year 7. • Specialism focus – Primary and Secondary to come together to organize cross school events for World Maths Day. • See development for individual staff members above. • Begin process of recruiting new staff. • Department to host the next ARK Hub day for all Mathematics teachers on 20 February.

	Current practice that is working well	**Priorities for development**
Views of stakeholders:	• The profile of Maths as a specialist subject is high in the school and students – broadly speaking – enjoy their lessons. This is based on: ○ feedback from a questionnaire at the end of last year relating to Fertile Questions (done for case study); ○ student posts on Fronter have been positive and enthusiastic about Maths; ○ numbers entering House Maths competitions – including students and staff; ○ participation on Numbers Day – including students and staff; ○ feedback from Maths Challenge Programmes and team competitions – including comments from ARK Maths teachers.	• Case study to be published. • Discussion on possible case studies for next year.

Part 4: Annual operations

Annual exams analysis that the Head of Department will complete at the end of each year for each year group to inform DDP (example from Year 7)

Attainment targets	Attainment outcomes	Progress targets	Progress outcomes
X% at Level 5+ Y% at Level 4 Z% at Level 3	X% at Level 5+ Y% at Level 4 Z% at Level 3	X% at 3 sub-levels Y% at 2 sub-levels	X% at 3 sub-levels Y% at 2 sub-levels Z% at 1 sub-level or less
Commentary: • How did outcomes compare with targets? • How many students reached the 4A threshold? • How do different teachers' results compare? • How did groups/sub-groups of students perform relative to each other (e.g. gender/band/SEN/FSM/EAL/students arriving below L4)? • What possible factors have influenced these results?			
Plans: What is the department's planned response to the Year 7 results? Explain: • interventions • targeted enrichments • pupil groupings • curriculum adaptation • teacher deployment • use of additional adults • parental engagement • revision strategies • target setting for next year.			
Key Underachievers: i. Who are the 10–15 key students in Year 7 who made unsatisfactory progress that the department will be targeting this year? ii. What will you do differently for them to ensure they progress?			

Auditing the department and creating an action plan – annual review

An example from English
Grade descriptors – the overall effectiveness of English education provided in the school

Outstanding (1)
English teaching is outstanding and, together with a rich, interesting and relevant English curriculum, contributes to outstanding learning and achievement. Exceptionally, achievement in English may be good and rapidly improving.
Pupils, and particular groups of pupils, have excellent educational experiences in English and these ensure that they are very well-equipped for the next stage of their education, training or employment.
Pupils' high levels of literacy, appropriate to their age, contribute to their outstanding learning and achievement.
Practice in English consistently reflects the highest expectations of staff and the highest aspirations for pupils, including disabled pupils and those with special educational needs. Best practice is spread effectively in a drive for continuous improvement.
The subject makes an outstanding contribution to pupils' spiritual, moral, social and cultural development.
Good (2)
Pupils benefit from English teaching that is at least good and some that is outstanding. This promotes positive attitudes to learning and ensures that pupils' achievement in English is at least good.
Pupils, and particular groups of pupils, have effective educational experiences in English that ensure that they are well prepared for the next stage in their education, training or employment.
Pupils' progress is not held back by an inability to read accurately and fluently.
The school takes effective action as a result of accurate monitoring and evaluation that enables most pupils, including disabled pupils and those with special educational needs, to reach their potential in English.
The subject makes a good contribution to pupils' spiritual, moral, social and cultural development.
Requires improvement (3)
English in the school requires improvement because one or more of the key judgements for achievement; behaviour and safety (in English); the quality of teaching; the curriculum; and the quality of leadership and management of English requires improvement (grade 3).
Inadequate (4)
English in the school is likely to be inadequate if inspectors judge any of the following to be inadequate:
the achievement of pupils in English;
the behaviour and safety of pupils in English;
the quality of teaching in English;
the quality of the curriculum in English;
the quality of the leadership in, and management of English.

Overall effectiveness of the department

Outstanding (1)	Overall effectiveness in your department is likely to be outstanding when:
Good (2)	Overall effectiveness in your department is likely to be good when:
Requires Improvement (3)	Overall effectiveness in your department is likely to be satisfactory when:
Inadequate (4)	Overall effectiveness in your department is likely to be inadequate if any of the following are inadequate:

Developing an Outstanding department

Where is your department now and what needs to happen next? (Use the Ofsted subject-specific guidance to evaluate your current provision.)

Ofsted criteria	What level is your subject area currently at? (Provide clear evidence.)	What needs to change to move forward? (Detail clear actions.)
Achievement		
Quality of teaching		
Quality of the curriculum		
Effectiveness of leadership and management		
Overall effectiveness in the subject		

Use this review to inform the Department Development Plan below.

Using the Department Audit to create an Annual Development Plan

Priority: Achievement All students make outstanding progress and achieve above national expectations.				
Targets	**Actions**	**By whom and when**	**Monitoring and evaluation**	**Resourcing**
% levels progress: for different groups and the cohort as a whole.				
Achievement data: results (outcomes) for different groups and the cohort as a whole.				
Reading: pupils are very keen readers and engage with a variety of texts.				
Writing: pupils' writing shows a high degree of technical accuracy and they write effectively across a range of genres.				

Priority: Quality of teaching Ninety per cent of lessons in the department are graded Good or better.				
Targets	**Actions**	**By whom and when**	**Monitoring and evaluation**	**Resourcing**
Use of ICT engages and deepens understanding.				
Teachers model the reading process.				
Teachers model the writing process.				
Questioning probes understanding and challenges thinking about literature and other texts.				
Clear target setting ensures all students know what they are aiming for.				
Precise marking ensures all students know how they are doing and what they need to do next.				
Teacher feedback supports and challenges all pupils to make precise improvements to their written or oral work.				
Effective use of peer and self-review enables students to set meaningful targets for improvement.				

Priority: Curriculum Curriculum fully meets pupils' needs in reading, writing and wider relevance.				
Targets	**Actions**	**By whom and when**	**Monitoring and evaluation**	**Resourcing**
Literacy is not a barrier to accessing challenging texts.				
Schemes of Work build clearly towards productive outcomes for pupils, involving real audiences and purposes.				
Independent learning and wide reading have a positive impact on achievement.				
ICT used to enable students to analyse and produce a range of texts.				

Priority: Leadership and management High standards and a cycle of continuous improvement ensure all students achieve above expectations.

Targets	Actions	By whom and when	Monitoring and evaluation	Resourcing
Expert subject knowledge is held and developed by every member of the team.				
Joint planning and team teaching ensure best practice is shared.				
Self-evaluation informs continuous planning.				
Clear development plans for all staff enables all students to receive consistently Good and Outstanding lessons.				

Conclusions

The approach to leadership as outlined in this chapter is concerned with how we as Senior Leaders in schools can actually practice what we preach. If leadership is a cultural statement and the way we are as leaders directly influences the extent to which teachers and students buy into the school aims and culture, then we need to be constantly mindful of the culture we create through our actions and statements.

To sum up, the key points of this part of the approach are:

- Senior Leaders in schools must lead the learning – it is absolutely not acceptable for a Senior Leader in a school to say that their teaching is suffering because their spreadsheets need recalibrating.

- Leading on learning does not mean creating action plans and carrying out audits – it means being consistently outstanding, setting the highest standards and maintaining an open house classroom – inviting peer observation and seeking feedback to improve.

- Leading on learning means not expecting others to do what you are unable to – senior teachers should be the most expert teachers in the school, they should constantly reflect on their practice and be engaged in an ongoing professional dialogue with their peers.

- Over the years schools have become flooded with data and pretty graphs measuring every facet of school life. The key thing with data though is to be able to use it and to understand how it can improve the quality of teaching and therefore the life chances of the pupils at your school.

- Student data needs to be used by every teacher to understand the students they teach, know what they can currently do and where the focus needs to be placed to ensure they all make progress.

- Lesson observation is a very powerful tool for improving practice – when planned for.

- Lesson observation should be used to help all teachers reflect on their practice and over time every school should build up a bank of video clips that can be used for training.

- All teachers should be trained in lesson observation, with less expert teachers doing joint observations with their more experienced peers, spending time talking through with them what they saw and what evidence they collected, before having that conversation with the teacher they observed.

- You cannot have an outstanding school without outstanding Middle Leaders – they are the engine room of the school.

- What Middle Leaders do not need is lots of initiatives to run, what they do need is a clear view of the strategic vision and direction of the school and the tools to interpret this and cascade down to their teachers – whilst holding to account both those above and below them.

- Middle Leaders must know how every student in their subject is currently performing as well as know how every teacher in their department is performing.

Notes

1   McKinsey and Company (2002) 'How the best-performing school systems come out on top': McKinsey & Co.
2   CfBT: (2011) 'To the next level: Good schools becoming outstanding': CfBt Education trust.
3   Data from St. Angela's Ursuline School, Newham.
4   These five bullet points were taken and amended from Scott, S. (2003) *Fierce conversations*: Piatkus.
5   Adapted from St. Angela's Ursuline School and Ark Academy.
6   100% Compliance is an idea from Doug Lemov (2010) *Teach like a champion*: Jossey-Bass.
7   Fraser, A. (2007) 'Developing innovation in education: A disciplined undertaking' (this paper is based on a presentation, 'Creativity and innovation in education: Moving beyond best practice' given at the 2007 Australian Council for Educational Leaders conference).

Conclusion

The world of teaching is politically charged; there are so many conflicting ideologies and beliefs that you are almost doomed to offend as soon as you place your head above the parapets. This book was created out of practical experience and solid research and is designed to be used as a handbook by school leaders and classroom teachers to ensure that every classroom in a school or group of schools is an outstanding one that puts the student at the centre.

Hill's 2010 think piece *Chain reactions* picked out the key features of the best school chains. The best chains had (amongst other things):

- clear vision and values, describing the central educational ethos of the chain;

- a distinct Teaching and Learning model;

- a system for training teachers and other staff;

- development of key leaders across the chain;

- strong quality assurance arrangements.

If a high-performing school group can be defined as possessing the above qualities, then a high-performing school and a high-performing classroom should follow the same principles. It is vital to place pedagogy and thinking about teaching at the core of a school's mission. Being a Headteacher means being head of teaching. It is all very well to come up with a snappy new logo and 'Mission Statement' – the rhetoric of launching a new school is the easy part – but if the classroom experience fails to match the quality of the signage then it is a waste of time. Shining the spotlight on the classroom and ensuring that every classroom operates to the same standards and expectations is the only way to be truly outstanding. It is time in this country to move beyond blame and excuses – 'these kids are un-teachable' or 'I taught it they didn't learn it' – and finally create the system our students deserve.

At Ark Academy we had three simple questions we came back to again and again. They helped us create a reflective staff culture – one in which all teachers were learners and the quality of our lessons was on a continuous upwards curve:

- *How do my students feel when they line-up outside my classroom?*

- *Is my lesson worth behaving for?*

- *How could I have taught that lesson better?*

The best schools have a clear and widely shared understanding of what outstanding looks like – an understanding which is co-constructed through training, observation and co-planning lessons. They also have the systems and processes in place to ensure every teacher can reach that standard and that every Line Management conversation revolves around the learner experience. This means gathering robust evidence and staying true to the stories that the evidence tells you; even if it is one you do not want to hear.

In a general sense, we need to shift the conversation in our schools away from management, interventions, data, targets and accountability (the tail wagging the dog) and onto training, development, lesson observation (as a formative process), curriculum design, co-planning, and research (the dog wagging a happy tail). If there is cynicism about CPD in some schools it is because teachers have not seen world class training, and the training is not built on an underlying model of Teaching and Learning. Our rule of thumb is that every hour of CPD should take a day to plan – it is a privilege to have those (tired and overworked) teachers in front of you, so invest time in preparing each training session.

Creating an open, collaborative culture in a school, where teachers view lesson observation and staff training as an entitlement of their professional development and not an imposition from senior management, is not a naive idea only applicable to start-up schools with their highly aligned staff and the space to develop new approaches. It is not an idealized notion based on our experience of opening a new school. Over the last ten years we have worked in fragile, good and great schools – in transitions and start-ups – and seen that teachers in all of these contexts respond to this approach.

Specifically, we need to develop leadership structures in each school which recognize the centrality of classroom practice. As we said at the start of this book, all indicators of school performance – pupil outcomes, standards of behaviour, attendance, school culture and ethos – will flow from six consistently great lessons each day. All management levers should pull in that direction:

The problem is that school leaders often don't have a firm grasp of teaching and learning and are more focused on 'visible strategies' such as behaviour management, as quiet corridors are more instantly gratifying than developing outstanding teachers – which takes longer. They then try to plug the gap with constant interventions. (Knight, O. quoted in Emery 2010)

We offer this simple leadership model to accelerate classroom practice in any school:

New ideas circulated

T&L Model: This is more than just plan / teach / mark. It is a developmental model which guides our planning & teaching. The one outlined in this book is an example. It's not a document to leave on the shelf; it should be with you when you plan lessons & schemes of work. All other policies & systems are there to support the model. It should be consistently reinforced from top to bottom in each school, and any induction of new staff should focus on it. The core business of any school is teaching, and no school can be great without a coherent approach to T&L, which is widely understood and adhered to.

Lesson observation: Not as an imposition from management, but as an entitlement of teachers' professional development. We need a culture shift around lesson observation in our country: no successful education system in the world has the resistance to it that some UK schools do. Observation should be formative and ongoing, open and non-hierarchical, and involve all teachers. People still feel "X isn't strong enough to observe and give feedback". If we think like that then X will never be strong enough. We should train everyone on lesson observation, and when we observe we should be discussing the aspects of our agreed T&L model which we see.

Embedding practice

Observing implementation

Staff Training: High quality, ongoing staff training. Delivered weekly, not just on set piece INSET days each term. The training focuses on the model, bringing it to life through illustrations. Training is delivered in house by expert teachers, so trainees can identify with it and derive confidence from their colleagues. The use of classroom video is key. Partnering with external providers is only appropriate if they can amplify what you are doing at school level.

A leadership model to accelerate classroom practice

Bibliography/ further reading

Alexander, R. (2004) 'Towards dialogic teaching: Rethinking classroom talk': Dialogos UK.

Bruner, J. (1962) *The process of education*: Harvard University Press.

——(1966) *Toward a theory of instruction*: Harvard University Press.

Counsell, C. (2011) 'Disciplinary knowledge for all, the secondary history curriculum and history teachers' achievement', *Curriculum Journal*, 22:2, 201–225.

Dillon, J.T. (1982) 'The effect of questions in education and other enterprises', *Journal of Curriculum Studies*, 14:2, 127–152.

Donovan, M.S. and Bransford, J.D. (2005) *How students learn. History, Mathematics and Science in the classroom*: The National Academies Press.

Dweck, C. (2006) *Mindset, the new psychology of success*: Ballantine.

Gardner, H. (2000) *The disciplined mind*: Penguin.

Geary, D., Wade Boykin, A., Embretson, S., Valerie Reyna, V., Siegler, R., Berch, D.B. and Graban, J., Chapter 4, 'Report of the task group on learning processes', found at http://www2.ed.gov/about/bdscomm/list/mathpanel/report/learning-processes.pdf

Gibbons, P. (2002) *Scaffolding language, scaffolding learning*: Heinemann.

Hattie, J. (2008) *Visible learning*: Routledge.

James, M. (2006) 'Assessment, teaching and theories of learning' in Gardner, J. (ed.) *Assessment, teaching and theories of learning*: Sage.

Lefstein, A. (2003) *Heuristics for designing a community of thinking*.

Lemov, D. (2010) *'Teach like a champion'*: Jossey-Bass.

Lewis, M. and Wray, D. (2000) *Literacy in the secondary school*: David Fulton.

Lucas, B. and Claxton, G. (2010) *New kinds of smart*: OUP.

Mercer, N. (1995) *The guided construction of knowledge*: Multilingual Matters Ltd.

——(2000)*Words and minds: How we use language to think together*: Routledge.

Mourshed, M., Chijioke, C. and Barber, M. (2010) 'How the world's most improved school systems keep getting better' report, 29 November 2010: McKinsey & Co.

Oates, T. (Chair of NC Review) (2010) *Could do better: Using international comparisons to refine the National Curriculum in England*: Cambridge Assessment.

Perkins, D. (2008) *Making Learning Whole*: Jossey-Bass.

Pryor, J. and Crossouard, B. (2007) 'A socio-cultural theorization of formative assessment', *Oxford Review of Education,* 33(5).

Pryor, J. and Torrance, H. (1998) *Investigating formative assessment: Teaching, learning and assessment in the classroom*: OUP.

Sadler, D.R. (1989) 'Formative assessment and the design of instructional systems', *Instructional Science,* 18, 119–144.

Serafini, F. (2001) 'Three paradigms of assessment: Measurement, procedure and enquiry', *The Reading Teacher,* 54, 4, 384–393.

Sfard, A. (1998) 'On two metaphors for learning and the dangers of choosing just one' *Educational Researcher,* 27, 2, 4–13.

Smith, M. and Wilhelm, J. (2006) *Going with the flow. How to engage boys (and girls) in their literacy learning*: Heinemann.

Wolf, M. (2008) *Proust and the squid: The story and science of the reading brain*: Icon Books.

Young, M. (2008) *Bringing knowledge back in*: Routledge.

Index